Nurturing Civilization Builders:

Birthing the Best Schools in the World

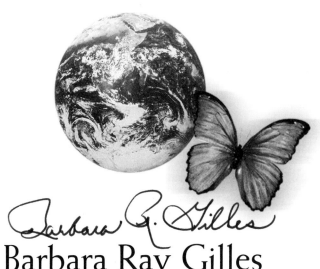

Barbara Ray Gilles

with Dr. Richard S. Kirby

OAK FOREST PRESS & IDEAL PROFIT PUBLICATIONS • IDEALPROFIT, INC. CALIFORNIA, U.S.A.

NURTURING CIVILIZATION BUILDERS:

BIRTHING THE BEST SCHOOLS IN THE WORLD

COPYRIGHT © 2004

BARBARA RAY GILLES AND RICHARD S. KIRBY—- 1ST ED.

ISBN 0-9744708-0-5

1. Education. 2. Political science. 3. Civics. 4. Leadership. 5. Astronomy. 6. International affairs. I. Gilles, Barbara Ray. II. Kirby, Richard S. III. Title.

Published by OAK FOREST PRESS & IDEALPROFIT, INC.

Barbara Gilles
4427 Thackeray Pl. NE
Seattle, WA 98105

Printed in the United States of America
Printed on recycled paper

Dedicated to

Our children and grandchildren

The Children of the World

and for the Children

Seven Generations into the Future

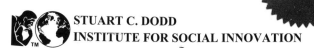

STUART C. DODD
INSTITUTE FOR SOCIAL INNOVATION

Nurturing Civilization Builders. . .Creating a Democratic, Compassionate, and Sustainable Society

Barbara Gilles
Director of Educational Innovation

4426 Second Avenue NE • Seattle, WA 98105-6124
Phone: (206) 634-0420   www.ForumFoundation.org
Fax: (206) 632-1975   www.stuartcdoddinstitute.org

Your beliefs become your thoughts. Your thoughts become your words.
Your words become your actions. Your actions become your habits.
Your habits become your values. Your values become your destiny.

MAHATMA GANDHI

Every quantum leap of man...
has rested on a new picture of the world and the nature of man.

LEWIS MUMFORD & WILLIS HARMAN

Scientific discoveries like going to the moon have forever changed
our thinking and are reframing our sense of world and self.

EDGAR MITCHELL

Love alone is capable of uniting living beings in such a way as to complete
and fulfill them, for it alone takes them and joins
them by what is deepest in themselves.

PIERRE TEILHARD DE CHARDIN

"War is obsolete, you know. Of course the mind can rationalize fighting
back... but the heart, the heart would never understand.
Then you would be divided in yourself, the heart and mind,
and the war would be inside of you."

DALAI LAMA

CONTENTS

1 Seeing The World of Schools in New Ways / 1

Global Mind Shift / 1
Jumping to a New Way of Thinking / 3
Pioneers of Change—the Students of the Future / 4
Creative Children Solving World Problems / 9
Kids Confront World's Problems;
    Propose Some Creative Solutions / 12
World Schools, World Teachers, World Arts / 14

2 Child Honoring and Conscious Parenting / 19

The Patterns of Our Living / 19
Nurturing the Early Years and Conscious Parenting / 20
The Power of Community—A Sense of Belonging / 21
Curiosity, Wonder, and Zest: Many Role Models / 22
Problems Have Solutions / 25
Partnership, Not Dominance / 26
Challenging the Shadow Side / 26
Science and Religion are Not at War / 28
We Can Make a Difference / 30

3 Nature as Home / 33

From Commodity to Community / 33
Nature, Our Best Teacher / 35
Early Experiences / 37
Water as Healer / 38
Pacific Northwest / 41
Nature Changing / 42

4   Conscious Choices & Creativity / 49

   From Status Quo to Embracing Change / 49
   New Ideas at the Dinner Table / 51
   New Ways Seed Change / 52
   The Holy Lands with My Sister / 54
   High School Trip to the Island of Crete / 56
   Growing Up / 56
   Empathy and Action Beyond Ourselves / 59

5   Indigenous Wholeness / 63

   Schools of Wholeness Now / 63
   Connected to Our World / 64
   Deep Connections / 65
   Living Wholeness in Africa / 66
   An American Wedding in the Jungle Bush / 70
   Teaching Sixth Graders / 72
   Kolahun / 72
   East Palo Alto, California / 73
   Recognizing Wholeness / 75
   Living as Nature / 75
   Teaching for Wholeness / 78

6   Partnership for Equality / 83

   From Domination to Partnership / 83
   A Wake-Up Call / 83
   The Domination Model / 86
   Medicine and the Dominator Paradigm / 88
   The Partnership Model / 92
   Partnership in Education / 97
   New Approaches / 98

7   Communications for Trust and Community / 103

   Building Bridges with the USSR / 104
   A Peace Park in Tashkent: Seattle's Soviet Sister City / 109
   Reconsidering the Enemy / 111
   Fear is the Source of Our Separateness / 112
   The Classroom Community / 114

8   Living Democracy / 119

Teaching Earth Democracy / 124
The Road to Teaching Democracy / 125
Democracy in the Classroom / 127
The Children's Dream / 128
Vision and Action: One Student's Experience / 130
Steps Toward Change / 132
Further Steps / 133

9   Awakening Greatness / 139

Small Miracles / 142
Rewards / 145
Light in our Brain / 146
Defining Greatness / 147

10 World Peacebuilder Schools: Problems as Opportunities / 153

September 11, 2001 / 153
A Peacebuilders School / 155
My Interconnected Classroom / 156
Caterpillars—a Metaphor of Hope / 157
Peacebuilders in Action / 158
Poetry from the Heart / 159
We are All Teachers / 160
Citizens of America and the World / 161
Teamwork and Cooperation: We Are All Gifted / 162
Self-Reflection/Evaluation / 163
A Personal Opportunity / 164
The School of the Future / 167
Making meaning of the world is the essence of education / 169

11 Action for a New World / 173

The Great Mixing / 174
The times, they are a-changin' / 174
Education / 178
Business / 181
Economics / 182
Globalization / 184
Science and Technology / 186

Society / 187
Governance / 188
Environment / 190
Health / 192
Values / 194

Afterword / 197

StarSchools: Birthing the Best Schools in the World / 197
Cosmology for People / 199
The Astronomical Outlook / 200
The Star Charter / 206
To the Teachers of the World / 207
The Federation of Galaxy Explorers / 209
Quantum City of the World Youth / 211
Enlightened Science / 212
The Children of the Stars / 213

Appendix / 215

2002 Earth Charter / 215
Examples of Elementary Children's
Communication with Compassion and Concern / 218
Hippocratic Oath for Teachers / 224
Two Leading Theorists of Civilization Building:
Dr. Richard J. Spady and Dr. Stuart Carter Dodd / 225
Endnotes / 236
Bibliography / 239
Contributors / 247
About the Author / 251

INTRODUCTION

From the beginnings of human history, parents and teachers have made alliances to create schools for children and for adult learners. There is a deep instinct in human nature, which recognizes schools as sacred places. They are communities of trust, and all who are involved in designing, building and managing them sense that they deserve the very best that human goodness, intelligence and imagination can offer.

In every continent and in all recorded times, thinkers and visionaries have dreamed of better schools. There is a natural gradient of excellence that leads the human mind from the idea of the good, to the idea of the best, to the idea of the Ideal. In this book we use an essentially autobiographical approach to the question, "What would be the best of all schools for our human need today?" In telling the personal story of Barbara Gilles, we are conveying some images of how a "Teacher of the Year" accepted her calling to become a "Teacher of the World."

We live in a global civilization, connected by the Internet, our human nature, and the shared fruits of science, technology and invention in all lands. All good educational ideas belong to all schools and teachers everywhere.

It is becoming more and more evident to global thinkers that the world as a whole needs a new educational philosophy, one suited to the crises and opportunities unique to our precarious time. It is a way of seeing the whole world as a school, it is a way of seeing what kind of world-schools are needed, and it is a way of searching for the ideals which must guide the best schools in the world. Some communities, such as Business Colleges, call this "The Pursuit of Excellence," and this is a reasonable name for our work. We are inquiring into the best visions of educational excellence that would lead to the creation of the best schools in the world. This does not necessarily mean new schools. It can mean imbuing with fresh ideals, fresh energies of inspiration, existing schools, teachers, students, educational administrators and journalists, educational entrepreneurs, political and social scientists, college principals and the governors of academies everywhere.

Educational ideals! What is their use? Excellent learning; goodness creation; wealth creation; happy students and teachers! Philosophical theology in the last few thousand years discovered a great truth: the best Idea, which is also the 'Ideal idea' or simply the Idea, is of necessity a practical one... otherwise it would not be ideally useful and therefore could not be ideal! This is not a mere abstraction; it tells us that our practical ideals are the ones we need, and this in turn tells us that the educational ideals most needed now are galvanic: they are those ideals which awaken civic energies internationally and result in the immediate change of educational activities towards the perfection of school activities by teacher and learner.

In other words, the best schools in the world are like quantum moments waiting only a heartbeat away from our present time, needing only to be invited to penetrate the present world of teaching. *Every school in the world* is like a great mouth, open, waiting to be nourished with the highest, best and most useful ideals. In our time such issues as planetary survival—enshrined in the *Earth Charter*—and the need for astronomical conceptions of culture, suited to the Space Age, shape our ideals. Still the fundamental ideals for schools remain: to be places of perfect justice, beauty, health, abundance and intelligence; schools which are safe, caring and open centers of learning and love, in harmony with nature. Connected to other schools and places they teach students practical ways to be loving to all that lives. They are little communities of world consciousness, of international harmony and global civilization. This combination of ideals makes a constellation of hopes that we think of as global civilization building. Teachers, from this perspective, are nurturers of civilization builders.

This book, accordingly, is a manual for nurturers of civilization building. It is a textbook for global citizens, a curriculum and a charter for ideal-world schools. And it is a summons to the creators and builders of ideal world-schools. It is for teachers and other educationalists that are imaginative and aware of the global nature of political and biological life. It is for parents who want their children to be world citizens. It is for students who want to be civilization builders.

Nurturing civilization builders is centered on visioning what we call StarSchools (see Afterword): our goal is birthing the best schools in the world. Such schools have many tasks. One is urgent: the prevention of global degradation. Positively, these schools have as their concern the maximum in innovation by the human family, in *caring for children and our earth*.

Nurturing civilization builders could, in some respects, have been entitled, "Child Honoring: 10 Ways to Create a Better World".

All around the world, the importance of the world's children is a central unifying principle. We are moved by children's needs, admiring their genius as children and reveling in their promise as future adults.

To be their best self, the world's children all need some of the necessities of *physical* survival: clean air and water, healthy whole food, and reliable shelter.

To be their best self, the world's children all need, too, some of the necessities of *social* survival. They simply *must* have healthy parental and other human bonding, consistently from birth onwards, otherwise their emotional development and its brain wiring cannot be wholesome. Moral and spiritual human nature cannot develop normally without these social basics. The world's children—each one—deserve the maximum of *respect* which one human being can offer another. They are not slaves or nuisances, chattels, monsters, commodities, economic burdens or simply 'a drag'! They are enchanting islands of cosmic love, comedy, loyalty and genius, each one encapsulating divine nature and here to lead the world to heaven. They deserve, every one, to be honored!

All the world's children deserve to be honored Here we are stating an axiom of world civilization building.

All the world's children deserve to be loved. Here we have a statement, which can set the standard of justice, and summon the highest inspiration of the Spirit, the arts, science, government and society. This is the approach to the absolute good, for all civilizations and their contributing nations. It is a way we can sense the Ideal Life touching society—if and when it happens, as it must, as it shall. To be loved.... every child's hope, every child's entitlement. In the musical *Oliver!* By Lionel Bart, the hapless child Oliver Twist sings plaintively, gut-wrenchingly, *Where is Love?* This is the question of questions for all global citizens.

To honor all the world's children: here is a vision to inspire the whole world to its best international and global art, science, and politics for the near and far future. It is a heavenly, and therefore a spiritual but also a political vision, which summons the best energies of every moral community (e.g. congregation) in the world. For as Dostoevsky pointed out in *The Brothers Karamazov*, it is morally intolerable that even one child should suffer...unless we are misbegotten moral monsters.

To sum up: every child ever born or to-be-born deserves, requires and shall have (when the world-political will is there and universal compassion is awoken) a loving caring environment.

We live and teach now in the USA. It often seems that the USA puts all U.S. citizens' money in problem-fixing/solving, rather than problem-prevention.

America's government has not yet adapted its conceptions of science to the new, holistic, quantum science. This new scientific truth is ignored or sidelined in many political arenas of planning, policymaking and decision making for the people of the nation.

America's government—in many of its departments, or so it feels—won't let us teach we are all interconnected, part of the universe, and like all mammals…it often seems that government policy in such Departments as Education pay only lip service to the crucial fact of newborn life. They disregard in many ways, the crying need which babies and infants and toddlers have: the need for a lot of loving attention in our developmental years. Without this, lives can be ruined from the get-go. For we need this early love and nurture, if we are to be our whole self. It is high stakes game—the highest—for the world today. UNICEF and other international agencies support this viewpoint, as they propagate such distressing facts that 50,000 + children perish *daily* from starvation; and that millions are stunted or warped or morally destroyed as persons, by infantile neglect and abuse.

This book distils Barbara's life story into channels of hope for better schools and ideal parenting of the world's children. It is about my hope of *Nurturing civilization builders*. It is filled with love, both given and received. It shares lessons rich in both joy and pain. It is offered in a humility that has come from feeling deeply about the richness of the world—and its unnecessary human poverty. It is a revolutionary blueprint leading to a transformational community—its purpose: to turn the discarded, unwanted (and all the wanted children too!) children of the world into loved, sane, creative global citizens!

As we reflect on the themes unifying Barbara's life, three things stand out and join together: love of life, passion for children, and a zest for life's unanswered questions. What does it mean to be human, and to truly know myself, to live and die? Why is our oneness and home in nature so vital to me? How am I like others and how am I different? How can we collaborate, how can we humans of all races embrace love? How can people of all faiths share, as we find how to transform hate? What *must* we do to create a world that nourishes all life? Barbara's own words will close this Preface.

"As a public school educator for twenty years, people don't hesitate to ask me hard questions. Why do I stay in public education? Why don't I start a charter school or an alternative school? Why don't I go into private education? My answer is always the same: because these are the schools for all America's children.

I feel my whole nature is fundamentally oriented toward caring about children. I have cared about so many—my three children, my four grandchildren, and the several thousand students I have taught. I care about the world's children, the masses of children born everyday. Many, perhaps most, of these little bundles of wonder are discounted by family and society; and a bewildering number of these young geniuses of love—scores of thousands—are known to be dying daily of neglect, abandonment and abuse.

It is time for a new era for the world's children. We can now awaken our faith and hope by proper beliefs. We can now believe the way to solve our problems is through deeply knowing ourselves, through communication, and through understanding and finding the common ground. Instead of one person making the decisions for everyone, we must work together in a creative process to yield a solution that's amenable to all. Education is about bringing forth the greatness within, building understanding, and finding workable solutions for a peaceful, just and sustainable world.

I want to share with you my truth. I want to empower your thinking. And I want you to have more options in making your own choices and decisions. My thoughtful daughter puts it simply, "Mother, how can we choose when we don't know there are real viable solutions waiting for us?"

This book is about giving you more choices. When people leave public education I believe they are looking for equal partnership and an opportunity to connect their calling with the needs of others. Along with needs for food, clothing and shelter we need connection and the opportunity to make a difference. I have spent my life as a seeker, exploring and questioning our true nature and universal truths. September 11, 2001 was a wake-up call, both globally and for me personally. It shouted the time is here to mature—to reflect and love more deeply—to speak out about our limitless potential, our interconnectedness, and embrace a life-centered world. Humanity's unifying theme, our highest vibrations, comes from love… an unconditional warmth we give off naturally. As Gandhi so beautifully expressed, "Where there is life there is love."

Entering a bookstore, I see hundred of ideas detailing new ways of thinking. These books come in all sizes, shapes, and colors for all professions—except educators. So why my book? Because education is the most important tool we have for change, and yet it is the last to change. I share my experiences with you to illustrate the roadmap I see for the changes needed to create a world that works for all and to show how changes in education can be the seeds for change in life.

This book is about a completely new and simultaneously very old worldview. This book is not about changing parts of the system or adding more to it. It is about completely changing the foundation of our world, beginning with education: education not only for children, but most importantly, education for our parents, community, and leaders. Education needs to be on the cutting edge, not at the bottom, for embracing a life-centered world, for nourishing our inner greatness and for creating a world that works for all.

This bold vision is not new. It comes from the greatest visionaries in fields ranging from philosophy to physics. It has been evolving since the beginning of time and synthesizes the best of science, religion, and spirituality. Out of its magnificence, it moves us from a history of fear to a future of hope, which honors our diversity, while empowering us to live as one world, one humanity in a world that works for all.

This higher vibration and energy is in the air. It is manifesting itself in different forms, touching our souls, waiting to be called on. It provides the foundation for creating and building a learning community worthy of the 21st century. It rejoices in life, celebrating and nurturing this amazing world and universe. Moreover, it is a living legacy on earth, worthy of our children and the world's future generations.

Let us choose to have fun together while seeking to question, to dialogue, to act for creating a world that works for all. Let us grow together as members of a mighty team while nurturing one another to live life fully alive, making friends, tearing down walls that separate us while learning and enjoying all the rich diversity around us. Let us nurture our children with a life-centered foundation, rather than a material and me-centered foundation. The nurturers of civilization building are a global community. It is a community without geographical limitations. It has no political membership conditions. It is one that supports families and extended families, and connects them with compassionate life-long learning communities and sustainable ways of living.

Let's celebrate and share our own special gifts—visible and invisible, inner and outer—while uniting our vision for balance, sustainability, justice and peace. The foundation for this vision is built on an acknowledgement of the value of all life. As we create together a world that works for all, we become worthy models and leaders for our children, our future.

It's up to us, the global citizens.

We are nurturers of civilization building; we already are a global community of goodwill and love and intelligence and creativity.

It is up to us *now.*"

Barbara Ray Gilles and Richard S. Kirby
July 2004
Snohomish County, Washington State, U.S.A.

Butterfly Brother & Sister

By Richard S. Kirby and Barbarba Ray Gilles

July 4th 2004

Butterfly flew by, our teacher and friend.
Having no worries or possessions,
No shopping to do—you are world-healer.
No stress or heaviness in you;
No career to plan.

Butterfly being,
You are a Time-Queen,
No moment but this:
No job but Beauty-bearing
Effortlessly.

We, too, butterfly-bright,
Butterfly-light,
Shed all cares and plans
And roles and rules
And fly free.

For I am light and love:
losing my separateness
with each wing-flap
I find my family, my friends, my folks...
Are my wings.

My own working assumption is that we are here as local Universe information gatherers. We are given access to the divine design principles so that from them we can invent the tools that qualify us as problem solvers in support of the integrity of an eternally regenerative Universe.

BUCKMINSTER FULLER

When you are inspired by some great purpose, some extraordinary project, all your thoughts break their bonds; your mind transcends limitations; your consciousness expands in every direction; and you find yourself in a great, new and wonderful world. Dormant forces, faculties and talents become alive and you discover yourself to be a greater person by far than you ever dreamed yourself to be.

PATANJALI

The splitting of the atom has changed everything but our way of thinking. We need a whole new way of thinking if we are to survive.

ALBERT EINSTEIN

CHAPTER ONE

Seeing The World of Schools in New Ways

Global Mind Shift

Thoreau wrote, in *Walden*, "Old things for old people, new things for new people." New schools for new children! We are in the midst of a global shift in our thinking that is potentially as significant as the Industrial Revolution and with repercussions that will be just as dramatic. This global mind shift is changing how we think about everything. Its impact is beginning to be felt in all realms, but most noticeably in the contemporary sciences, especially physics. If you look closely, you can also see these changes taking place in how we think about the environment and living systems; how technology works and can be designed for benefiting the planet, health care, and healing, and how we learn and understand our world. We understand now the world of schools in new ways; so we can build schools of the world. A new community of teachers is coming to maturity—to give a new birth of freedom to all who work and sing and laugh in the schools of the future.

This global shift may turn out to be a turning point in human history. Because the effects are still largely unreported, and because we as humans often would rather deny the truth, and follow our old ways, this revolution is not yet recognized as such. Historically, it can be shown that we don't immediately recognize this kind of change. For example, the shift from the Middle Ages to the Renaissance was vast, but in many ways the concepts that shifted an entire civilization and society's way of thinking were not that many. If you had been in the midst of it, the effect of these changes might have appeared infinitesimal; that is, until these ideas had reached a critical mass of individuals. At that point, enough people were aware of what these new ideas were and the change was happening quickly. Suddenly, the fact that the Earth is not the center of the universe was common knowledge; our collective worldview had to change to accommodate this new understanding.

Two things happened. First came the acceptance of the new knowledge that we are not the center of the universe. Second were the ramifications of this simple idea; all our notions about our place in the universe had to change because our old ideas no longer fit with the newly learned facts about astronomy.

As with such jumps in our current thinking, the initial simple facts are often ignored, refuted, and simply not believed, not because the facts don't support them, but because the ramifications of accepting them are enormous. If we accept these ideas, we must shift our whole belief system and our entire thought system. Suddenly, our unexamined assumptions aren't valid and we have nothing with which to replace them. We no longer have a way to order our world. This is the nature of worldviews; they are so fundamental that often we do not see that we make these assumptions in our thinking. Imagine waking up one morning and finding that gravity no longer ordered our world. Chaos would reign until we created new ways of living without it. Changing our worldviews is similarly chaotic and disruptive. The new teacher is a bridge over chaos to schools of beauty.

Recognizing a new truth goes through three distinct stages. In stage one the issue goes unnoticed and is ignored. In stage two our response is characterized by vehement denial. In stage three we recognize the truth as being self-evident. It is becoming self-evident that all schools must be global schools of healing love.

Jumping to a New Way of Thinking

The change occurring now is equally as great as the change between the Middle Ages and the Renaissance. Because we are in the middle of it, it is difficult to perceive how the change is happening in our daily lives. It's like the classic story of how to boil a frog. When the frog is in water that slowly warms it becomes numb, so it never senses the need to wake up and jump out of the pot when the water boils. It is asleep, lacking consciousness of the world around it, and it boils to death. But a frog dropped into boiling water is quickly sensitized and fully awake. It is alerted by its survival instincts and quickly leaps out of the water to safety.

Today, millions of us are like numbed, unconscious frogs, living in slowly warming water that is gradually nearing a boil. Our boiling water is the times we're living in, times where we humans are destroying our planet and ourselves. We are living in ways that life on this planet and our own species cannot sustain.

Plenty of facts and information make this clear. For example, in 1992 The Union of Concerned Scientists told us in their Warning to Humanity that we need to make a "great change in our stewardship of the earth" or we're on a collision course with our own extinction.[1] Like the frogs, some awake and conscious people are leaping to radical new ways of thinking in order to survive and care for survival of all life on our planet. The Schools of the Future are Schools of Species-Survival.

With creativity, vision, and determination, people are saying, "Yes" to a world that works for us all. Everywhere people are opening to new possibilities and discovering principles that can help them solve the problems in their own communities. This book examines some of the new principles.

The New Teachers are infinitely far from powerless. We have believed many things that do not help us: we don't have the answers. We are told it will always be this way; that a more sane, beautiful, just, loving, and compassionate world is impossible, that we will never truly be free. Yet these assumptions are just stories; we can certainly write new ones. The

New Teachers tell a New Story of our powerfulness.

We know we can change our thinking by telling new stories. Change is all about storytelling and communication. Most of the world's problems are at heart about communication. Our future depends on how we communicate, tell our stories, and use our technology and communication tools to dream the world we know is possible. Yet to change the earth successfully often requires we dream in groups—it is not a solitary project, but about community building. We need each other to tap into our collective wisdom.[2]

Pioneers of Change—the Students of the Future

We are now learning that we each have the inherent ability to solve problems, to imagine a clear way out of our global and local mess. Anyone who is living new stories, telling new stories to friends, family, and the larger community, is a "prophet of change." We hear stories from people in businesses that can pollute; they have become people who are creating sustainable businesses. We hear stories from people in houses using large amounts of energy: they are now converting to straw bale homes; and people who were habitual drivers of the automobile now riding bicycles to work. People are making conscious choices to transform anger with conflict resolution and communication skills. People with housing problems are becoming empowered with participation in Habitat for Humanity.

Researcher and author Paul Hawken reports that these prophets of change are appearing around the world, developing communities of resistance to the old worldview—communities where creativity, cooperation, compassion, connection, and trust are the guiding principles. The number of these people is growing daily. They are creating changes as big as the Agricultural Revolution that so changed life on this planet some ten thousand years ago. They are the leaders who hold up the mirror of past extinctions and say, "No!" "Basta!" "Enough!" We want to see a different world and we aren't going to wait for someone else to do it. We're not going to wait for our parents, the government, or all the well intentioned nonprofit and charity organizations doing good around the world. It isn't enough to wait. They are taking our collective destiny into their own hands. They are going into our communities, creating communities where there were none, and telling new stories, stories that come from a place of hope, love, and vision— dreaming something beyond our currently lived history.

These prophets of change are saying "No" to the destruction of the Earth's living systems and "Yes" to the possibility of human greatness. They are saying "Yes" to being the change they want to see, and "No" to waiting for the old institutional power centers to shift. They are showing humanity the path to transformation by asking, "If not us, then who? If not now, when?"

Where are these visionaries, these futurists, and why don't we hear more about them? Because our current media doesn't often see change agents as fitting into their programming. Television has become the way people know what is happening in modern society. It's our social brain, but it is not living up to our evolutionary potential. Rather than these stories of human potential and solutions to ecological disaster or vision-ary ecological design, modern society is fed on a media diet of consum-erism, violence, and scarcity. None of this supports the needed global mind change. Just as we are being programmed for ecological failure by T.V., we can reprogram ourselves for regeneration, love, social justice, and future sustainability. The Teachers of the World can make this happen.

How do we reprogram ourselves? By beginning to talk to one another, by educating one another, joining book discussion groups and conversation cafes. By listening deeply to our inner wisdom, going out into nature, ac-knowledging our gifts and trusting ourselves. We need to notice where we are stuck and afraid, feel our fear and open ourselves up to new ideas. We need to be willing to embrace our life long learning capacity and the many means now available to change and facilitate others in the changing processes. The new World-Schools are the homes of these changes.

The messages we receive from the media do not tell us the stories of solutions and positive change. Instead they fill us with the messages of war and convince us that there is nothing else we can do for a dying economy except invest more in the military. This is old thinking; this is the old mind. This is also not true. What is true is that we are made to believe that there are no options. The Teachers of the World show us the new options.

Often we change our minds because we hear something that inspires us, or we learn about something we thought until then was impossible; suddenly, our worldview shifts. The possibility for a global shift in consciousness to happen quickly is growing greater and greater. There are evolutionary accelerators (something that pushes us to change more quickly, like the war in Iraq) and we must use them as tipping point memes (new stories with new choices to replace the old stories with only one way). Our worldview changes and what had once been a flat world becomes a round world in the middle of a beautiful universe.

Our worldview expands, and we learn that mushrooms can clean up oil spills, that we can design buildings comfortable to live in that do not need artificial heating or cooling. Our worldview changes, and we learn that healing can happen with love and hands-on touch. All of a sudden, the world that once seemed plagued by perpetual war, may now be on the brink of a kind of perpetual peace. This is possible.

Why the media does not tell us stories of hope is the subject of another book, but the stories are getting out there anyway. The Internet— with its instant network of mass communications which acts as a kind of checks and balances— is sometimes helping us see ourselves as one world, together, and it is possibly providing a more truthful and hopeful mirror to our global potential and our collective intelligence. Although it is not the sole answer, the Internet is a powerful communication tool. There are many, though, who worry about the Internet. They think it is easier for our children to pull up a violent sadistic video game or porn than to find a wholesome, thought-building site, unless of course you have your kids in Encarta. They are alarmed to see their children logging on and experiencing a kind of cultural pollution. They are bothered by incessant advertising in the form of a 'pop up' on the screen, and they say frankly that those 'pop-ups' aren't civilization building. They are a form of degradation.

The Internet, too, needs the Teachers of the World to bring it healing. The incredible thing happening right now is that millions of people are acting to make a difference. They are becoming the change they want to see, living from love rather than fear. Fear only creates enemies and perpetual war, leaving millions of people hungry every day. We can seek out the solutions that innovative seekers have currently found, and make them known. For if we allow our children and ourselves the space to figure out dynamic solutions to seeming insolvable problems, we will shift to a new world. We will free ourselves from being bound by old minds and old mindsets, from 'leaders' who wish to keep us in a world being destroyed by fear and expressed greed. A world where we can resolve our conflicts by dialogue is the subject of our new schools. The Teachers of the World are spokespersons for a coming world of hope. This will be a world where the environment is cared for, where people are not slaves to their work, where food, water, housing, and health care are rightly regarded as human rights. These happy circumstances are within our current human and technological capacity. They are the foundations of schools for global citizens.

Our hope lies in recognizing our fellow beings everywhere as global companions on this journey. With our recognition of the problems we've created and how our thinking plays a large part in perpetuating these situations, we can participate in what Duane Elgin calls "civilizational awakening". We can become like the caterpillar transformed into the butterfly. As the caterpillar hibernates in its cocoon, the "imaginel cells" of the butterfly waiting to awaken slowly become more and more aware of other imaginel cells in the organism. At a certain point, they start to recognize one another and then the shift to a butterfly happens. It is the cell's recognition that they are all part of the same being that allows the transformative shift to happen.

The same is true for the earth and the people on it, who truly are one organism. As we see the similarities within our species and with other life forms, as we acknowledge that we are all part of the same larger being, our earth, our thinking can shift swiftly. We can recognize that we can have a world that works for all. So even with television being the domain of 'old minds,' more and more people are making these kinds of connections with people across political, social, and linguistic barriers. The walls that have separated us are coming down; we are on the verge of truly becoming a global village. Our schools are, potentially, global schools. The Teachers of the World make the potential actual, in schools old and new.

This is possible now because of the digital communications revolution and the Internet. The Internet is allowing individuals to have their own communication system that bypasses the dominant mass media. With this alternative, we can claim our right to tell our own stories, share our visions with each other, learn how to govern ourselves, and make collective decisions about the things that impact us. In essence, we are creating a kind of secondary government, one with larger, more important implications for the future than nation-state governments. But more important than bypassing the mass media, Internet connection can highlight the work being done for evolutionary change.

There is no doubt that many people would like to see the mass media changed into something that inspires us and tells us stories that are alive and nurturing—a global best practices storytelling program. What if all the organizations, people, and communities in the world who were solving problems, big and small, could share solutions with one another? Not just problems about local situations, but global economic situations. How would we then look at our world?

We would see the hope that is blossoming because of the incredible, creative, and inspiring work that forward thinking people are doing everywhere. These efforts, these people, these projects, these solutions are like those imaginel cells in the caterpillar, awakening to one another's possibilities. It's really quite simple. We are just becoming aware of how many of us there are, how strong we are, how resilient a web we weave across the world, and that we collectively truly are a kind of global brain. The global brain is ready to work with the global heart.

When we look around and try to find these prophets of change, these global mind shifters, we often forget to look to the newest members of the human species. Most of us do not think of children as the designers of solutions to society's problems; but our pregnancy rates for children and the fact that 25,000 children die each day show us that they better be included in this process or they will be in big trouble in the future. What would happen if we allowed them the freedom to explore what concerns them? And what might they do about the problems they see in the world today? As adults we have been taught and continually told to leave the big problems in the hands of the government officials. But how well have they been doing over the course of our country's history, past and present? Perhaps now is the time to change how a government by and for the people works. If the old ways do not work, let's stop doing them and try something new. Let's brainstorm some new possibilities and try for solutions that bring us closer to a living participatory democracy. The Teachers of the World are hosts and hostesses of this festival of creativity.

Creative Children Solving World Problems

What happens when children are allowed to believe in themselves as problem solvers, as creative contributors to their world, and are inspired by a great purpose? What would happen if teachers created a classroom community that let them break out of whatever box they were in. In my wildest dreams I couldn't have imagined how seriously they would take the challenge of creating solutions to our real problems!

From 1988 to 1990, in Steilacoom, Washington, I ran a program for a group of gifted third, fourth, and fifth graders at Saltar's Point Elementary. My intention was to empower these students to develop a conscious awareness of their responsibility as respectful citizens of the world. We focused, as many gifted programs do, on developing the higher-order thinking skills: analysis, synthesis, evaluation, and creativity. I brought to class my training in creative problem solving, to which I had been exposed over two summers at the Creative Problem Solving Institute (CPSI), in Buffalo, New York. I had the opportunity to be exposed to many of the learnings from the program because my partner and several of his associates were paid to go as an innovative team from their lumbering company. For over four decades, hundreds of business leaders have gathered at CPSI every year to collaboratively ignite each other's creative ideas.

CPSI had a profound effect on my perception of learning. It introduced me to brilliant innovative speakers like Willis Harman, former president of the Institute of Noetic Sciences, and George Land, author of the book *Grow Or Die.* The CPS Institute opened up new vistas of possibilities within me for teaching and engaging children. At the heart of the curriculum, developed for leading business executives around the country, was a seven-step creative problem solving process. To adapt it to the classroom, I used a condensed four-step version.

First step: Brainstorm the problem. (We learned that often what we thought was the problem really wasn't the deepest, root problem). Brainstorming, of course, was a very open and creative space without critique or comments.

Second step: Choose the root problem and analyze, synthesize and evaluate it in order to develop greater understanding of related root causes.

Third step: Brainstorm solutions. Each solution suggested was put on a grid rating from 1–4: workability, time, cost, other needed factors. Once all the solutions were rated and described, points were added for each solution and the team considered those with the highest points. A solution was agreed upon.

Fourth step: The solution was put into practice and the needed reflections by the team made. Is it working? Does it need to be adjusted? What would support the solution to make it even better?

Frequently, I have also used this format to address classroom interpersonal and/or learning problems. When a student had a concern, they were to ask two classmates and then an adult to brainstorm solutions with them. If this strategy did not bring a satisfactory solution, then the student wrote down the problem and dropped it into a box for the children to problem solve together at a class meeting. I also used the CPSI approach for class projects where students would explore a problem, like pollution, and then in teams of four or more brainstorm causes and solutions.

I worked with my students to develop their skills in creative problem solving as a conscious choice in the early weeks of my classes. Although students are not normally taught to do this type of creative problem solving at the elementary school level, they are naturally skilled at doing it. Because of the profound impact CPSI had on my students, this class decided that you were not allowed to bring up a problem without a possible solution.

This guideline was transformative. The kids were empowered; they recognized they were participating in something purposeful. For some students, life became like a game, full of problems or challenges, but always with many possible solutions. CPSI opened my mind to the simple reality of the beauty and power in engaging students in teams and working together for solutions. The ways in which we all teach one another all the time also became crystal clear to me. Not only do we learn content, but also the way we approach the lesson teaches so much about what is possible and how to communicate in a way that is respectful of one another.

In Steilacoom, the CPS theory fully became practice in my classroom. My theme for that first year was "Living in Harmony: Humanity, Earth and the Universe." By having such a broad theme, students were able to see themselves as citizens of the world, not just of the United States. Students learned that what they do personally often has an impact on the entire planet as a whole.

During the first part of the school year, the students studied other cultures, trying to understand their own responsibilities as citizens of Earth. A college student from China visited us, sharing a way of life dramatically different from the life of a Steilacoom resident. Students also adopted a sister school in Costa Rica, which led to studying tropical rain forests and planting one hundred Douglas fir trees. To help preserve the Costa Rican rain forest and purchase a short-wave radio so that their Costa Rican sister school could receive broadcasts on ecology from the World Peace University and Radio for Peace, the class raised $394.

Kids Confront World's Problems;
Propose Some Creative Solutions

During the second year, my gifted classes chose to create some memorable projects, which reflected their inclusive democratic pursuits, engaging the larger community in a vital, living and peaceful vision for the future. They wanted to take part in something called the Million Cranes Project for the opening ceremonies of the 1990 Goodwill Games happening in Seattle, Washington. A book we read together inspired their interest in this project, *Sadako and the Thousand Cranes*. This story tells the sad but uplifting tale of a little Japanese girl who, as a baby, acquired radiation sickness from the atomic bomb explosion at the end of World War II. As she grew, the illness slowly took its lethal toll, yet she desired but one thing—world peace. There is a Japanese legend that anyone who folds one thousand origami paper cranes will be granted one wish. It was Sadako's hope to fold a thousand cranes before she died and spend her one wish on world peace. Even though she died before completing the thousand cranes, her friends finished them for her.

The Million Cranes Project called for one thousand Washington state schools to make one thousand peace cranes each. My kids figured that by enlisting community support, they could create three thousand cranes. I was excited by their idea, because they would gain a powerful experience of active citizenship at the same time contributing to their own project. They started by teaching the school community how to make origami cranes; then they worked with Steilacoom's senior citizen community. Finally, in May, they invited the entire community to a "Peace Crane Night." As the kids taught adults how to fold, the spirit of democracy and the wish for peace filled the air. Four of my students were chosen to carry the three thousand peace cranes to the opening ceremonies of the Goodwill Games in Seattle. My students were fast becoming citizens of the world.

Like caring global citizens, we did our best to solve the problems of the world. In fact, the previous year, each student in the class chose a world problem to research and to explore. Then they got to suggest possible solutions for 'their' problem. The culminating activity was a Projects Fair where the students exhibited their work. War and pollution topped this list of problems that concerned the kids; but hunger, nuclear proliferation, water shortages, animal rights, and even biotech issues were also troubling the students that year. Using miniature scenes, games, and drawings, the kids illustrated possible solutions to what they saw as society's most urgent problems. A news story in the *Tacoma Tribune* stated: "Kids Confront World's Problems; Propose Some Creative Solutions." It described third, fourth, and fifth graders coming up with viable solutions to serious world problems. How is this possible when our local, state, and federal governments seem incapable of addressing our deepest human needs and rights? Perhaps children are the closest to a different mind from the one that created the problems in the first place.[3] Perhaps these children were successful because they were not told they couldn't come up with solutions, but were encouraged to believe they could do this. The process was less about a teacher telling them the answers, telling them what to do, and more about them discovering solutions on their own, with a teacher letting them know, "You have this knowledge inside you." As Willis Harman writes in *Global Mind Change*, "perhaps the only limits to the human mind are those we believe in."

Respecting their need for self-determination, I let children work alone (which really meant with their chosen friends and family) or in small groups. When they came up with solutions to the problems they were working on, I encouraged them to evaluate the feasibility of those solutions and wherever possible to put them into practice and report the results. All of this had been inspired by the CPSI trainings I had been involved with. Implementing a methodology designed for top-level business executives in an elementary classroom seems at first glance to be outrageous, but that kind of outrageousness is exactly what we need today. Our kids are more brilliant than most give them credit for. They don't have the kind of limits adults have after years of social conditioning and repression of knowing their true self.

For example, one group studied the depletion of the rain forests. These kids collected funds to be put in trust to buy rain forest property as their creative solution to ensuring that at least part of the rain forests would remain untouched. In the meantime, they educated the school community and their families about the value of rain forests and how their continuing destruction is devastating to the health of the planet.

When young people take on projects like these at eight, nine, and ten years old, the potential of their democratic citizenship is unlimited when they become adults. One student's parent was quoted in our local newspaper, saying, "If these children grow up and follow through on some of these ideas, we'll certainly have a better world."

My life's work has been about empowerment for our children, our youth, and our adults to continually learn to know ourselves more deeply, to become aware of some of the socially imposed limits and to be as creative as possible in creating the learning environment—the world— we choose as a group. From the literature about creativity it is clear we have yet to really explore the limits of human potential. What would happen if we allow the liberated, creative, and intuitive mind of the child free-reign in the classroom? Would we stumble amidst chaos? Or would we discover patterns within ourselves that showed us how to see solutions where there were none before? Or perhaps, in reality, there were no solutions only because we believed there were none? In the classroom, I could put aside the current dominant system of education where discipline, domination and punishment reign and replace it with a model that inspires and encourages each child's unique gifts and contributions to the classroom. This practice unleashes their creativity and showed me how we must change the way we teach children so that we are not hindering evolution, but encouraging it.

World Schools, World Teachers, World Arts

"World Music" has made a place for itself in our culture. WOMAD is a well-respected festival of music drawn from many lands and cultures.

WOMAD stands for *World of Music, Arts and Dance*, expressing the central aim of the WOMAD festival—to bring together and to celebrate many forms of music, arts and dance drawn from countries and cultures all over the world.

WOMAD was originally inspired by Peter Gabriel: "Pure enthusiasm for music from around the world led us to the idea of WOMAD in 1980 and thus to the first WOMAD festival in 1982. The festivals have always been wonderful and unique occasions and have succeeded in introducing an international audience to many talented artists." [www.womad.org]

But World Music is only the tip of the iceberg of new "world arts." World writing, world teaching, and world arts, are part of the movement of global community and global citizenship through new arts into new schools. Delightful, musical, dramatic, educational ideals are arriving in human minds all over the planet. Civilization builders are beginning to design world schools of love. Schools of hope and love, schools for world citizens, are just over the horizon. In this book we are learning to be the teachers, students, architects and administrators of the new world-schools of global love and creativity. For this lovely task, this beautiful destiny, we need to remake our minds: "new wineskins for new wine."

For we are learning to SEE in New Ways the whole WORLD OF SCHOOLS.

We are discovering the blueprints for the schols of the world.

we are constructing the first generation of world-schools.

we are imagining the first generation of Star-schools.

Declarations and Affirmations

We are convening the best schools in the world.

———

We know now the schools we must have.

———

Teachers and Students are honoring their own deepest inner knowing, and our educational principles enshrine the new understandings in all the modern and sub atomic sciences.

———

Science is showing us that everything is energy, and the highest vibrations come from love. Can we open Schools of Love?

———

Together, Yes! We shall find the common global Schools where religion, mystics, poets, spirituality, a healthy earth and science come together at the highest Vibration...LOVE!

———

Schools of our own deepest truths are being born.

———

How do we open our hearts to love in the midst of fear? Through teachers teaching world love.

———

At the crises point of grow or die, we learn to live in balance with life and our home, Earth.

——

In the Schools of Tomorrow we create peace through justice, and we celebrate all of life by honoring its beauty, mystery, and wonder. Our global schools will create a world that works for all.

——

If we are to have real peace, we must begin with the children.

MAHATMA GANDHI

The best and most important things in the world cannot be seen or even touched. They must be felt with the heart.

AUTHOR UNKNOWN

Many say, "Humanity, wake up!" I say, "Do one thing for our children. Nurture their inner knowing, this deep aliveness and creative expression children are born with. Don't put them to sleep."

PAMELA SACKETT

Child Honoring &
Conscious Parenting

The Patterns of Our Living

In childhood, much is determined for us; those around us make the decisions about how we will be raised and live. The patterns of our lives are waiting for us when we arrive, set by parents and society. Some of us are fortunate, others are not. The lucky ones find patterns that fit like a tailored suit. These patterns may grace their lives, leading to happiness, fulfillment, and a healthy effect on the world. The unlucky find patterns that lead to despair, suffering, and the potential for violence.

The patterns of our childhood create the world we live in. Children who go to bed each night surrounded by loved ones, who are told how much they are loved, how wonderful they are, and how much they have to give and honored for their own inherent worth, are children who can grow up to make peace. Children who go to bed each night with no one to hold them and assure them they are loved, wanted, and cared for, children who feel fear and pain and have no one to trust, these children often become adults consumed with fear, self-centeredness, and an insatiable greed and desire for the material, abuse, violence, or even war. They never feel good enough about themselves or have enough self-esteem to feel worthy.

Most of us had childhoods that included both healthy and unhealthy experiences. However, we can change the modes of thinking laid down in our own childhoods, even from the very foundations. We can ask ourselves, what did we accept that we now wish to discard? What paths would have benefited us more? We can take action on the answers.

I was one of the lucky ones. The "golden" lessons I learned in childhood far outweigh the patterns I have had to change. Of course my parents made mistakes, but their love propelled me to believe in myself, to travel the world as a seeker of truth and to grow in my own sense of inherent worth. This is what I want for all of us. A healthy earth, with justice, peace, and equality for all.

I know it all begins with me and choosing to be a loving presence. But I also know I was privileged; my parents gave me a rewarding and rich beginning—a head start. They were committed to the lessons learned before, during, and after birth in these most critical early years. I share my stories and hope you will share yours. We have so much to learn together that we cannot learn alone.

Nurturing the Early Years

My mother, Virginia, held a college degree in Home Economics from DePauw University. After college she spent her twenties as a career woman. During the Depression jobs were hard to come by, but she persisted until she found a good job at Meier and Frank in Portland, OR, although it required her to move halfway across the country by herself. She enjoyed her job as a demonstrator for creative cookery.

After Mom and Dad were married in 1937, Mom, at age 29, took on the job of a dedicated professor's wife and full-time mother. She gave this career even more attention than she had her job with Meier and Frank, working hard with my father to make positive conscious choices for raising their family.

The Power of Community—A Sense of Belonging

Helping others and building a sense of community were my mother's primary values. Her job was to make her husband, children, and community happy. When she became a wife and mother, she did not longer want to work at a job outside the home; instead she volunteered constantly in the community. "What can I do to help?" was always the first question she would ask.

Mother made sure her girls and other children had access to many different opportunities. She orchestrated birthday parties for us and the children of friends. She was the PTA president of the grade school and the high school. We took art classes at the museum on Saturdays. Mother led our Girl Scout troop. She ensured we learned to swim! She supported the YMCA' swimming education program. Lessons from "just learning to swim" to "junior life saving" were available. And most of all, she was a frequent volunteer for the Presbyterian Church, working in many roles, seemingly for most every church program.

At home, Mom worked to teach us life skills. Every evening she helped us with our homework, teaching us responsibility and ensuring we learned our school lessons. Beginning while we were still in grade school, each of us girls was given a monthly clothing allowance. To stretch the ten-dollar allowance, we learned to sew in the Gold's Department Store sewing room because anytime we bought fabric, Dad would cover half of the cost.

Whenever someone new moved into the neighborhood, my mother had a little get-together with all the neighbors to meet the new people. We knew everybody on the street, and everyone knew us.

Mother loved to cook gourmet meals nightly and to entertain. One of my favorite traditions was Sunday nights during school terms: Chili night. Mom would serve her famous chili and Dad's foreign students were always invited. My sisters and I loved talking to those students from all over the world. They taught us games and tricks and told us about the customs of their countries. We loved all the attention they paid us, and, more importantly, it opened our minds to cultures besides our own.

Curiosity, Wonder, and Zest: Many Role Models

We had a dinner table ritual: Mother would serve a beautiful formal dinner each evening at 5:30. Dad sat at the head of the table and served each of us individually after grace. During the meal we had lively conversations that would last through dinner and sometimes for hours afterwards. Television was never considered. Dad would throw out topics of conversation and encourage us to discuss them with him. He loved to explain how things worked so he could share his appreciation and amazement at the complexities of our world. Because he found it all fascinating and his enthusiasm was contagious, we found the world fascinating, too.

Perhaps one of the greatest good fortunes I had in this life was in being exposed to people who believed life was a glorious adventure. First among these was my father, Winfield Ray. He was a man who had a passionate curiosity about anything and everything, forever questioning and seeking. On the alert constantly for wonders, he loved to share his joy in new things with my two sisters and me. He did this constantly. If he saw someone building a house, he'd stop and say, "Well, look how they angled that! What a great idea! And see how he rigged up his ladder so he could take all his tools up with him as he climbed? I wonder how he made that?" He led us to open our eyes and wonder about things other people might pass right by.

My father valued thinking for oneself. He had been expected to follow his father and grandfather's profession and become a doctor, like his brother. But he broke with family tradition to become a professor of botany instead. This decision to make plants, not people, his life's work was not popular with his family. During most of my childhood, we lived in Lincoln, Nebraska. Dad was a Professor of Botany at the University of Nebraska.

Each summer we would vacation at my grandparents' lake cabins in Indiana. We would drive all night in our Plymouth sedan, we children asleep in the back seat until Dad would wake us to cross the Mississippi. Even if it was midnight, he wanted us to be awake to see the Mississippi pass under us. He would usually make jokes as we stared sleepily out the windows into the night.

Dad loved jokes. He read *The New Yorker* routinely when he came home from work, and we could hear him chuckling in the living room as he read the jokes. In my whole life I cannot remember ever hearing Dad's voice raised in anger, and he never touched me except in a loving way. Even in his eighties, as he was dying, his curiosity was alive and well as he laughed and joked with the nurses, and asked them endless questions about new medical procedures and techniques.

Dad was not the only person close to me who was imbued with infectious zest. My mother's father, T.T., was also filled with curiosity. Like my father, he, too, was a scientist, even holding patents from inventions during his years with General Electric. Many of his inventions were related to the first "moving pictures." He loved figuring things out and learning anything new. His love of reading was legendary. My mother said you could always find him by following the trail of books he left in his wake. During our summer vacations with T.T. and Nana, my grandmother, we always spent the afternoons reading together, each of us engrossed in our own book.

My mother learned her community activism from her father. T.T. was always working on community projects such as fixing the canoes or the docks, cleaning the beach area, and in general keeping things organized and neat for the summer families who congregated at the beach.

The summer communities were as much our own as our neighborhood in Lincoln. In the evenings at T.T. and Nana's, we would gather with the rest of the lake families to play cards (hearts or canasta were the favorites) or go square dancing at the community hall. Everyone would dance—children, married couples, old people. Because many families had been coming to the lake for generations, everyone knew each other. Often, their grandparents or even great-grandparents had built their cabins as far back as the 1880s. It wasn't a fancy place, but it had a great sense of history and belonging. You could go up to any house and be given a cookie or hot soup, whatever you needed. People cared for one another.

My other grandparents, my father's parents, were quieter than Mom's, but their community ethic was just as strong. My grandfather was a family doctor who delivered babies almost every day of the week. On the weekends he drove out to the Amish community nearby and worked with them. Accompanying him on his weekend calls gave me a wondrous sense of a very different way of life. When he died, his obituary said that he had delivered more babies than anyone else in Fort Wayne.

Another role model for conscious living was Sidna Hazen. She was a friend of my mother's, and her daughter and I were close friends, too. Sidna believed in elegant but simple living, delicious healthy food, and humble leadership. She was active in our church and through the Junior League of Women Voters, where she was always the master of ceremonies for their yearly drama. But best of all, she was playful, unlike most grown-ups. We lived about a mile away from Sidna, and we kids would often roller skate back and forth between our houses. I remember my delight when one day Sidna strapped on some roller skates and came along.

Sidna drove a red convertible, a car that all the kids regarded with awe. I'll never forget one winter afternoon when Sidna was driving a bunch of us to the YMCA for a swim. It was freezing out, but someone asked if we could put the top down on the convertible. Of course it was a stupid idea, but Sidna just said, "Why not? Let's do it!" And so we rode the couple miles to the YMCA in the winter cold with the top down on her red convertible. It was freezing, yet magical. That was Sidna—a free spirit, full of zest, fun, and daring. She did things that no other mother in Lincoln would ever do.

Mrs. Cabot was my sixth grade teacher, and she too shared a passion and love for life. It was in her class that I decided—all those decades ago—that I, too, would be a teacher. In the classroom Mrs. Cabot was the happiest woman in the world because she loved teaching so much. "We're gonna do this!" she'd say, and you could hear in her voice that she could hardly wait, it was going to be so much fun.

She loved to read stories to the class. She was a heavy set woman, and when she sat at the front of the room her knees would be apart and her bottom would bulge over her chair, but once she began to read you forgot everything else. There was only the story. She read with such expression, such delight!

Mrs. Cabot was fascinated by science. Because she felt that our school curriculum at the time did not contain enough science, she created science experiments for us to do. In social studies she introduced us to class plays. We wrote them ourselves and then acted in them. I remember I had a big part in a play we did on South America. How much fun I had raiding our garage and attic for props we could use.

Everything came alive when Mrs. Cabot was involved. She believed in her students. She brought out their best because she knew the best was there. So you came to know it, too. Mrs. Cabot was the one who taught me that passion is what motivates learning. And her passion was teaching itself. I wanted to be a teacher just like her.

Problems Have Solutions

My mother was as active a problem solver as Dad was curious. She seemed to be a fearless, determined, and tireless worker. That attitude, combined with her absolute belief that everyone was born good, led her to know that every problem had a solution. It was up to you to find it.

Although a great problem solver, she did not make the mistake of solving other people's problems for them. She taught that you don't sit there whining about things that are wrong. You listen to your feelings, you honor them and then you get out and do something to fix it. My mother couldn't stand it when people would say, "Well, what can you do? You can't do anything about it." She would say, "What are you talking about? You can do something about it."

I am reminded of the indigenous thinking that requires that at least three solutions be proposed and considered, before action is taken towards solving a significant problem.

Both my parents saw humanity as good. They didn't like complaints. If you came home from school talking about a situation that was causing you frustration or making you angry, they would always ask you to look for whatever was good in the situation. They didn't want to hear anything else. They interpreted it as whining.

Because we always focused on solutions and the bright side, my sisters and I emerged from childhood exceptionally naïve about the darker sides of the world, with little understanding why people choose manipulative, greedy, hurtful, even violent paths. An understanding of Hitler's behavior and of those that followed his orders has led me to deep questioning and exploration of the roots of such behavior.

Partnership, Not Dominance

From the outside, my parents' marriage seemed an average male/female model for the time and place. My father worked and supported the family financially, while my mother kept house, raised the children, and volunteered at the church. But from within the family, I could see that both my parents were independent individuals who exhibited great respect for one another and functioned as a team. Each took the lead when it was their turn to do so.

Fortunately, I also had models for independence and interdependence outside my family. Sidna Hazen was an independent woman. Although she was married, she did things without her husband, which was different from what most married women of the time did. I had other friends whose mothers were slave-driven and slave drivers. The dishes and the laundry had to be just so; things were very controlled. These women served as unhealthy models for me—I didn't want to run my house like that.

Challenging the Shadow Side

My father, like many men of his time, internalized the cultural norm that dictated men's repression of emotions. In retrospect, he really carried the suppression of emotion too far. Feelings, especially "negative" ones, were not encouraged. We did not talk about them. Instead, we were encouraged to discuss what we thought, or what we did, but seldom or never how we felt. We lived in an intellectual and activist atmosphere. My father especially felt uncomfortable talking about emotional issues. If we were upset, we were not encouraged to vent or cry; feelings of anger or sadness were ignored. We were "cheered up" instead. Because it was harmful to my family to not have all our feelings acknowledged, this is one of the patterns from my childhood I was determined to change when I became an adult. I consciously worked to become more emotionally honest and open and now honor and share all my feelings.

My mother had a quick temper. When her high expectations for her three girls were not met, she could get mad. Recently, when I asked her what is one thing she would change about her past, she responded that she would change how she handled her temper. She explained that in her family it was okay to lose your temper. In fact, losing your temper was taken as a healthy sign that you were determined and committed. It wasn't until her family was grown that she realized she not only could, but should, control her temper and transform that energy into more understanding and compassion.

Because Mom was strong-minded and Dad was easy-going, my sisters and I grew up unaware of the traditional male dominated system. My older sister was the first to encounter it when she wanted to go to medical school. She received no support from either the medical profession or our parents. She was told that the medical profession was not the place for a woman. Then she won a scholarship to Columbia University in philosophy instead. Halfway through the program, she was told again that a woman would never get a position as a university philosophy professor. This was the late 1950s, and unfortunately our family belief system was overpowering; she dropped out.

My younger sister's ignorance of this system was devastating to her as well. Because marriage and family were of primary importance in our family, my little sister married young without a college degree. She put her husband through college, but never did the same for herself. Her marriage eventually ended in divorce sixteen years later. She remarried but died of heartache at the end of her second marriage. Though hundreds of caring people mourned her death and she was dearly loved in her community and work, both of these marriages were with dominating men who smothered her light. Her last words to me were about how it had taken her whole life for her to understand that there is no possibility of full empowerment as long as we have relationships based on domination. This insight was not about blame, but about waking up, becoming conscious, making changes and enlightened choices. She was always sorry she had married so young; she had felt trapped, dependent, and unable to find her own way when the going got rough. Our hearts joined and tears rolled down our faces as we talked about how little education prepares us for life and our own children.

My role in the family was, sometimes, being the peacemaker. Because we were all dynamic people with big personalities, we naturally had conflicts. Finding the solutions to these conflicts was my role. Being a combination of my father's easy-going, happy personality and my mother's absolute belief that you can find a solution to any problem, made me a natural peacemaker. I'm like one of those dolls with sand in their bottom; you can punch them and knock them over, but they always pop right back up again.

Science and Religion are Not at War

Religion always played a big part in my life. My mother was active in the church, and we attended the Presbyterian Church together as a family every Sunday. At home we said grace at every meal.

Today, with many contemporary sciences bringing us new ways of thinking, it is like Science and Religion are both saying the same thing. It seems that they are speaking in two different languages about the really important properties of humanity: 'being,' and 'unity-with-diversity.' And these seem to find a fundamental harmony and identity in love, the human vocation.

The summer cottage of my paternal grandparents was at Winona Lake, a strong religious community where I walked past the home of Billy Graham every Sunday. He often preached there; busloads of Christians came all summer long for worship. My grandparents were devout Baptists; in fact my Grandmother taught Sunday school for fifty years. Each summer morning when we were at Grammy's she gave us coins for the Bible School collection plate. I loved the programs at Bible School, especially the music. My favorite song was "Jesus Loves the Little Children":

> Red and yellow, black and white
> They are precious in his sight
> Jesus loves the little children of the world.

I often went to the afternoon or evening revival meetings for adults, too. Hundreds would go forward as they were called to take Christ as their savior. Warm tears flowed down my cheeks as I watched people open their hearts and walk forward.

Although my grandparents were Baptists and I was being raised Presbyterian, I remember thinking that those details did not matter. Even at age seven or eight I was always looking for the big picture and our wholeness.

In the same way that religion was important, so was science. I come from a scientific family: My father was a scientist, my mother's father was a scientist, my father's father a doctor, and my uncle a doctor. Scientific knowledge was sought, and questioning was encouraged.

My family accepted that both science and religion were true. Not until recently, relatively late in my life, did I realize that many people strictly separate science and religion. When religious fundamentalism became more prominent during the 1990s, it began showing up in my classroom. I then realized not everyone saw these two fields blending easily. My family always saw them as complementary.

We Can Make a Difference

I always think of my mother and T.T. when I hear people express despair at their powerlessness. Neither Mom nor T.T. ever wasted time in despair. Instead of asking, "Oh no, what can we do?" they were out there doing it. Action is the key to change. Doing something is always possible. Broken things can be mended. Nothing is irredeemable. Taking the first step is how it all begins.

The belief behind apathy is that nothing can change. Yet change is not only possible, it is certain. It is only in mechanistic systems that nothing changes. Machines are static. But we are not machines. The earth is not a machine. We are a holistic, organic system, and everything is growing and changing.

Take a deep breath. Believe that you can make a difference. And begin.

Declarations and Affirmations

Brain development in the child depends on so much: the synthesis of nature and nurture, a mother's positive attitude, conscious choices and total health, the chosen birthing environment and most especially the first three years of the child's life. From birth a child needs to experience the body warmth, the heart beat, the eye contact, the tender voice of a loving, nurturing human holding them, meeting their needs and building trust.

———

We *can* find the will to change and put in to practice all we are learning. This is the task of the dedicated 'Teacher of the World,' bearer of the absolute ideal into education.

———

The 'Teacher of the World' is a teacher of the heart. Now can we engage our largest brain—our heart—and our newest brain: the pre-frontal cortex. The heart-brain educates us in our need for love and connection.

———

We *can* connect our lives with the healthy food, exercise, quiet spiritual/reflection time and rest we need for the health of our whole being: mind, body, emotions and spirit. The next generations of schools exist for this curriculum of wise living.

———

We are learning our power: We now can we take all our learning at the beginning of the 21st century and move away from a society of 'reactive' solutions—homes for unwanted children, increasing emotional and cognitive learning problems and special education, drop outs, violence, detentions, greed, increasing prisons populations, war. We move now towards proactive solutions, so our schools form happy, healthy children who feel cherished, nurtured, inherently worthy, children who want to share their gifts in a way that nourishes all life and honors the balance of all live. At last we can educate the masses, via all our media tools.

———

We now see children as our greatest natural resource and our future! We now see education as our greatest tool for change. We now move from a culture of violence to a life affirming culture. We create together a community, a world, where every child feels healthy, whole and worthy. Now we collaborate to better connect for Creative Solutions, for a child denied these may be damaged emotionally, spiritually, mentally, and physically. We have begun to work together to create our hearts' deepest desire, a world that works for all!

———

Nature is our greatest teacher. It reminds us of who we are and what we are connected to and responds to our hunger, our longing for transcendence.

MICHAEL COHEN,
ENVIRONMENTAL EDUCATOR & AUTHOR

Nature and the wilderness provide us with opportunities to listen to our inner voice, learn to trust our own inherent self worth and commune with nature.

DAVID W. ORR,
ENVIRONMENTAL EDUCATOR & AUTHOR

CHAPTER THREE

Nature as Home

From Commodity to Community

Earth is a planet that is the cradle of humanity. It is our first home. But we have reason to believe we have hurt our native, our natal, planet. If we open ourselves to the ecological degradation that pervades our world today, we can see the staggering destruction of our world and ourselves. This destruction is unprecedented, and despite dire warnings from the scientific community (global warming, mass extinction, dwindling re-sources, etc.) our society continues with business as usual. Regrettably, this business has other interests in mind than the health of our world. Indeed, greed has perverted our vision so that nature is perceived as a commodity—to be consumed without consideration of the consequences. How can we as a species be so blind to the level of havoc that we are wreaking upon the planet Earth, our first home in the cosmos?

As Westerners we have been so well trained in the model that we are separate from the world around us, that when we hear scientific statistics they remain abstract and disconnected from what is happening around us. Indeed becoming numb to the ravages of our terrestrial world may be a survival tactic, so that we are unaware of the immediate and obvious deleterious effects. On some level, as human beings, we are connected to all of life and we instinctively sense that something is very wrong. If we are not 'earthed' we are by definition out of touch with reality.

Our culture is suffering from a crisis of conscience, with its disconnect between our conditioning in consumer consumption and lifestyle choices versus their affect upon the broader environment. To truly make a difference, we need to bring about a change in consciousness. We must become more aware of both our dependence upon and the effects of our behavior on the world around us. We must come to understand that what we do to our planet, we also do to ourselves—for we are a part of this larger system. New models are emerging based on sustainability instead of the "extractive economy," but until a more significant shift in values occurs, alternatives to the dominant systems will not take root.

Education can make an impact by cultivating earth-centered values and providing sustainable models that express principles of wholeness. One of the most radical changes we can make towards this change in consciousness is to raise our children in a way that nurtures their "ecological self." * A deeper understanding of ecology and a strong sense of connection to nature from the very beginning can ground the next generation in the understanding that although society and human relations are important, we are also intimately connected to the larger community of all beings. 'Earth schools' will be schools of survival.

The primary way to cultivate a relationship with this larger community is through direct contact with it. In many ways, there is no greater teacher than the living earth and it is every child's birthright to have access to the inherent wisdom exemplified here. Biologist Elisabet Sahtouris describes nature as a viable and democratic community that provides a

---

* Our "ecological self" is the self we identify with when we fully acknowledge our interconnectedness. We then see the world around us as our self, for we are intrinsically connected to and dependent upon our world.

model for us to participate in, where we can learn lessons that can transfer to our human community. Unfortunately, our fast moving culture is based more on artifice than on the natural world. In our time it is no longer a given that children have fundamental contact with nature. We are on the brink of ecological holocaust, largely because we have lost our sense of place in our planetary home. To be 'un-earthed' is perilously close to being non-existent.

Further, Elisabet Sahtouris has said, "advances in physics, biology, and complexity theory, in recent decades, have shifted science toward a worldview where nature is understood to be composed of self organizing energy or information. Biologists call this 'autopoiesis' meaning 'self-creation.' This is now becoming our new definition of life: Anything that continually creates itself is a living entity."[4]

A guiding principle for me as a teacher has always been to give the children in my care an opportunity to explore nature. As a child, a sense of belonging within the natural world was strongly fostered; and I have always tried to impart that to others. I was fortunate to have a myriad of occasions to spend time in the great outdoors, both growing up in the temperate grasslands of the Great Plains, and being exposed to other bioregions as well.

Nature, Our Best Teacher

My father loved plant life and graduated with his doctorate in botany from Cornell. His passion for the physical world and all its inhabitants was passed on to me. When I would visit him at his University of Nebraska office, he would always take me out to see the greenhouses. He loved the greenhouses and knew the names and histories of each of the hundreds of plants living there. Because the plants were individuals to him, they became individuals to me also.

Dad loved the outdoor life, and as children we were encouraged to be physically active. He was a great ice skater, so in the wintertime we went skating together as a family every night after school. On the weekends our parents would take us to the big lakes that had been cleared of snow for skating, and we'd build a campfire by the frozen lake. Dad could do tricks and taught them to his girls. Often Sidna and her kids would come, too, and we'd be a big party. I loved the outdoors like Dad, and still do. I was good at sports, and played baseball, volleyball, and anything else girls were allowed to play. In school, I was the fastest runner and the jump rope champion. I rode my bike everywhere.

In the summers, at my grandparents' cabins, we practically lived outdoors. My maternal grandparents, T.T. and Nana, had a cabin on Lake James, near Angola, Indiana. We spent many summers there without running water, hiking to the outhouse for the bathroom and pumping water into a bucket for cooking and cleaning. At night we would all stand around a big bowl of water and brush our teeth together. To this day camping in the wild is one of my favorite things to do, and my early experiences stood me in good stead for my later adventures in Africa.

T.T. took my sisters, our cousins, and me on hikes through the many forested acres of the Pokagan State Park, which bordered the lakeside cabins. T.T. would cut each of the five grandchildren a walking stick of our very own, which we would use all summer. At least once each summer we would all arise early to climb to the top of the highest hill, past the toboggan slide at Potowatami Inn, to watch the sun rise.

Another mentor, who taught me about the natural world, was Auntie M. Auntie M was another person full of zest and fun. At night she would let us play hide and seek throughout the whole house, even encouraging the adults to join in, too. Auntie M would be laughing just as hard as the kids were. There weren't many limits in her house; you could do or say most anything as long as it wasn't cruel or destructive.

They lived on about ten acres and had lots of animals; chickens and rabbits and cows and I don't know what else. Uncle Fred was a professor of biology, and Auntie M was a naturalist. Her specialty was birds. She was an avid birdwatcher, and taught us how to band birds.

Auntie M and Uncle Fred were different from my family in that they did not attend church. I was puzzled by this difference because church was a big part of my life. I asked my mother, "Why don't they go to church? Don't they believe in God?" My mother said, "Well, they believe in the earth, animals and nature; the outdoors is their church." Even though this was different, I liked thinking about their ideas.

Early Experiences

My earliest memories are of Stillwater, Oklahoma where my parents grew their own food, using a horse drawn plough. When we moved to Lincoln, I played outside in the garden under a huge pine tree that my father cleared to make a place for us. How many tea parties we had under those branches! We grew sunflowers and currants, and each spring the air was filled with the scent of lilacs. My mother kept busy with canning and freezing; our kitchen was filled with the sweetness of the earth's bounty.

When I was ten years old or so, I attended a Presbyterian Church Camp on the Platte River, home to thousands of migratory birds. We were given thirty minutes each day to have "quiet time" outside. This simple practice completely opened my perception to the natural world. We each had our own special place, out of talking distance from other campers, and each of us sat there in silence observing the life around us, connecting with an underlying presence.

I still remember vividly the place I chose. I sat on an old stump and looked out over the muddy water, amazed at how the water was illuminated in different ways each day and how the current's flow would vary, depending on the movement of the wind. I learned the river's hues and watched its surface change from relative stillness to rills and waves in response to the breezes. The trees across the river would mirror this movement in their own calmness or dance. I would listen intently to the sounds of water coursing, the branches swaying and the call of birds. In all the changes, I felt an underlying presence, a unity that I was part of.

These contemplative moments in nature had such a profound effect on me that, first as a camp counselor and then as a teacher, I have offered this same quiet time to my children whenever it was appropriate. In each situation, I have seen their sensitivity unfold as a result of this gift of quiet time. A little quiet time is such an easy thing to create, yet so often overlooked in our busy lives. It turns out that this is a basic exercise used in environmental education to build awareness of nature and sense of place. Respect is not a concept but a living feeling, informed by a sense of wonder. When we take the time to be awe filled by the world around us, we cannot help but respect it.

Water as Healer

Looking back, I see the theme of water flowing through my relationship with the living earth. All the special places in my formative years were never far from the flow of water. From the murky backwater of the Platte River, to the clear ripples of the lakes where I spent my summers, I was deeply influenced by the quality of water—flowing from one place to another, bringing life.

One vivid and joyous memory I have is being twelve years old and accompanying my father as he attended a botany conference at Cornell University in upstate New York. There were gorges with high rock walls, many with streams running through them and freely cascading waterfalls. I had never been in such a lush place before, dense with foliage and soft with moss. While the botanists moved slowly with their magnifying glasses, examining and collecting new specimens, my sisters and I danced and played in the creeks. In great delight, we jumped from stone to stone while the sunlight sparkled on the leaves, reflecting off the water. We slipped into the gurgling streams to cool off and then lay on the warm rocks, laughing with joy. In the vibrant green, the adults huddled around their special finds from the plant world. We heard the Latin names float around us from time to time, but we were far more interested in their beauty than in what they were called.

My love for the water had a practical ramification as well. From an early age I took swimming lessons at the local YWCA. With my mother's encouragement, by the time I was twelve I had earned my Junior Life Saving Badge and was a Red Cross Safety Instructor. In addition, I participated in a water ballet class where we performed our own choreography to music. We even made our own swimsuits! Besides the pleasure they gave me, all these skills would come in handy. Indeed they opened the door for more opportunities just as I was getting old enough to leave my family.

The first occasion came when we were living in Turkey. I had just finished my sophomore year of high school in Ankara and got my first summer job, working at an international camp on the Bosphorus, the strait that runs through Istanbul. There is no color in the world like the sparkling turquoise blue of the Bosphorus. I found it breathtakingly beautiful and loved to look out on the vastness, knowing that the expanse of waters before me would eventually join the Atlantic Ocean. I had a sense of geological time—that these waters that were part of the great cycle of life, had been here since the beginning of the Earth

The land was majestic and dramatic, lush with short, green plant life. I taught swimming and was also responsible for a cabin of ten to twelve-year-old girls. To my great joy, I was able to return and work there again the following summer.

My mother knew how happy I was while doing this work, and when we came back to the States, she helped me find other interesting, well paying jobs as a camp counselor. I worked in various locations for four more years.

Being in the rustic cabins of summer camps was a natural progression from the lake cabins of my grandparents. I was still spending my summer in the way I had grown to love—living in the wild, sharing companionship with others, waking with the sun, and sleeping soundly after physically active days. Each camp became a community in the true sense of the word, a fellowship forged through a common experience. The word "wholesome" is often used to describe a season in the outdoors. It is a good choice of words, articulating the quality of wholeness. I especially felt this at campfires. This ritual took place in so many different settings, yet always had the sense of the human community, circling the primal flame, surrounded by the grandeur of forests and the stillness of a starry night.

One of my favorite camp activities was to take the girls hiking. I would watch a transformation from the early days, when they would arrive fresh from the city, to the end of summer, when they had grown accustomed to living outdoors. Our first hikes were tentative, and they'd all get blisters. But in the weeks that followed they shed their urban skins and a new buoyancy emerged. I, too, went through a transformation, from the pallor at the end of my school year to a vibrant renewal. My mother always used to remark, "You come home from school, and you look dead. You come home from camp, you look alive."

After the two summers in Turkey, I worked at a camp outside Omaha. Here I got to lead all kinds of activities aimed at heightening children's awareness of nature. We'd explore a berry for instance: its shape and color, its scent, texture, and taste. We never ceased to find that the more we focused on one thing, the more connected we felt to everything.

Camp Greylock on New York's Racquette Lake in the Adirondacks the following summer was one of my most memorable summers. The director of the camp was a talented and compassionate Manhattan lawyer who did this each summer for a change of pace. This was 1961, and she was a strong role model in a time when there were precious few.

Another counselor and I led a canoe trip through the Finger Lakes with a group of young teenage girls who had done most of the planning. We spent a week gliding through the peaceful waters, sleeping in island lean-tos, and feeling utterly at home.

My last summer before college graduation was spent at Camp Beaupre, a wonderful arts center in the Berkshires of western Massachusetts, where I taught water ballet. I spent hours a day in the crystal clear water of a turquoise pool, accompanied by "The Nutcracker Suite". Being out of doors with music combined with movement in water was an ecstatic experience. I loved providing a means of relaxation for the girls who were involved in strenuous artistic pursuits for the rest of the day. We benefited from being in proximity to the lovely grounds of Tanglewood—summer home of the Boston Symphony Orchestra —and Jacob's Pillow, a dance performance center. We attended weekly shows at both places; a favorite dancer at Jacob's Pillow was Maria Talchief.

Pacific Northwest

After these summer forays to the East Coast, I went in the opposite direction from Nebraska for my last two years of college, transferring to the University of Oregon. I was introduced to rolling hills and the countless conifers of Northwest forests and the magnificent ocean! I compensated for my landlocked years by spending vacation time at the rocky coast, delighting in the tide pools, which seemed to always be revealing new forms of life. I learned to ski and also enjoyed going to the Cascade Mountains—Three Sisters near Bend, and the daunting majesty of Mount Hood further north near Portland.

It was in this gentle Northwest landscape I made the transition to adulthood by graduating; and seven years later my husband and I returned to raise our family here. We put down roots on two acres alongside the South Umpqua River in Southern Oregon. We chose to live in this idyllic rural setting so that our children could be raised close to nature. Besides caring for our three small children, I taught a class for local parents and children called *Art in the Outdoors*. This provided a natural setting for participants to explore their creativity. In many ways this was simply another version of the Quiet Time I had learned years ago. I have found that sometimes people just need a reason to pay attention to the natural world around them.

As time passed, it was a shock to find that our natural surroundings had not only changed; they were not as perfect as they once had been. The waters that flowed by our home were no longer pristine. Parents in the neighborhood were divided over who would or wouldn't allow their children to swim in the river, and that created a rift. This was in the early seventies, and people had just begun to wake up to the effects of industrial pollution that had come to public attention through the work of Rachel Carson. The South Umpqua was a case in point: it was downstream from a pulp mill and a mining company. The great forests of the Northwest surrounded this region. It was a stronghold of the timber industry, and I came into my first contact with clear cutting. I witnessed the rampant destruction of forests that had stood for generations. It seemed they were being stripped down for human need and greed. My soul ached to see the land razed so entirely.

Nature Changing

Within a few decades I had seen a massive change take place. No longer could I depend on wild lands being protected or take for granted the purity of unspoiled nature. I began to comprehend the different attitudes we humans have toward nature, and the impact of those attitudes. Isolating ourselves in our human culture leads to viewing nature as a commodity rather than a source of community. I realized that there were many children who might not have spent enough time in nature to know it as their home. In response to this, I was determined my teaching would always promote the cultivation of an awareness of nature and a love for the outdoors. I believe that children have an innate rapport with the natural world, and it is this connection that will ultimately make a difference in the way the Earth is treated.

In the decades since I became aware of the precariousness of our earth, the ecological situation has grown steadily worse. It seems to have approached a crisis point. According to the Union of Concerned Scientists:

> Human beings and the natural world are on a collision course ... If not checked, many of our current practices may so alter the living world that it will be unable to sustain life in the manner that we know. Fundamental changes are urgent if we are to avoid the collision our present course will bring about. Our massive tampering with the world's interdependent web of life—coupled with the environmental damage inflicted by deforestation, species loss, and climate change could trigger widespread adverse effects, including unpredictable collapses of critical biological systems whose interac-

tions and dynamics we only imperfectly understand. No more than one or a few decades remain before the chance to avert the threats we now confront will be lost and the prospects for humanity immeasurably diminished... (We) senior members of the world's scientific community hereby warn all humanity of what lies ahead. A great change in our stewardship of the earth and the life on it is required if vast human misery is to be avoided and our global home on this planet is not irretrievably mutilated.

We can find an inspiring blueprint for a way forward in the objectives of the Earth Charter, an international document that serves as a manifesto of ecological ethics. Through an extensive collaborative effort involving many nations over a number of years (first initiated by Mikhail Gorbachev's "Green Cross"), a final version was produced in March 2000. It is waiting to be ratified by the United Nations. The charter outlines fundamental principles to guide humanity into a more promising future. As we face the perils of the twenty first century, it declares, "We must join together to bring forth a sustainable global society founded on respect for nature, universal human rights, economic justice, and a culture of peace. Towards this end, it is imperative that we, the peoples of Earth declare our responsibility to one another, to the greater community of life and to future generations."[5] Worldwide, the values of The Earth Charter are being implemented on many fronts.

Education is a vital component for "developing understanding of the critical choices facing humanity and the urgent need to commitment to a sustainable way of life."[6] A sustainable way of life is paramount to a positive future. Sustainability literally means the ability to keep in existence, as well as to maintain and nurture. According to Webster's Dictionary the word "sustain" also means strengthen; to provide comfort and encouragement. What could be needed more?

In order to be truly life sustaining, we need to engage a wholeness that exists beyond the confines and constructs of the human-centered world. We need to expand our boundaries of self to become truly ecological, identifying with where we dwell on the planet and in the cosmos.

Then we can act on behalf of the whole community, truly honoring the interdependence of all life forms. Because when we see that we depend on our surroundings, we see ourselves in them and them in ourselves.

When we are open to this perspective, we are naturally willing to make adaptations on behalf of the whole. Our role of using nature for our own ends changes to one of stewardship, one of watching out for, and caring for, all living things. This responsibility demands nothing short of a revolution that takes into account the implementation of sustainable lifestyle. We are challenged in this regard, as described by William Ruckelshaus:

> Can we move nations and people in the direction of sustainability? Such a move would be a modification of society comparable in scale to only two other changes: the Agricultural Revolution of the late Neolithic and the Industrial Revolution of the past two centuries. These revolutions were gradual, spontaneous, and largely unconscious. This one will have to be a fully conscious operation, guided by the best foresight that science can provide. If we actually do it, the undertaking will be absolutely unique in humanity's stay on earth.[7]

The schools needed to bring about this kind of transformation are truly radical, it requires engaging a change of heart that melds feeling with knowledge. As David Orr, a leading voice in environmental education points out, we need better scientific models and theories that are "calibrated to our inner loyalties—ones that create less dissonance between what we do for a living, how we think, and what we feel as creatures who are the product of several millions of years of evolution."[8] Simply presenting empirical facts leaves little room for wonder and the resultant care that comes hand in hand with a sense of awe and engagement. The Teachers of the World, the Teachers of Tomorrow, have learned how to bring a caring dimension to the cold facts.

For an excellent example of bridging the divide between cognition and emotion I recommend an inspiring work begun by eco-theologian Thomas Berry and cosmologist Brian Swimme to renegotiate our understanding of the origins of the universe. Referred to as "The New Story,"[9] this narrative version of the creation and evolution of the universe and our own planet presents raw data enfolded in a story. It integrates the head with the heart, giving a sense of wholeness, sustaining a sense of connection, which is crucial to our planetary future. People will only protect what they care for and feel connected to, but before they can even do that they must experience being cared for themselves.

By fostering a personally caring environment, ecological values are awakened, thus supporting the next generation to experience and genuinely care for themselves, each other and the earth as their home. I recommend we read *The Universe Story* by Berry and Swimme.

Declarations and Affirmations

Parents, family, caregivers, friends and our media are life long models. They are our teachers as they bond with children through love amid Nature, our home. It is a basic human responsibility that we care for the earth and its ability to sustain life. Our children, grandchildren, and generations to come have a right to be nourished by a healthy sustainable earth.

——

Now is our time to act decisively. Now we *can* work together in our family, communities and world, to create a healthy Earth. In our new schools we will use the Earth Charter 2002, a grass roots document created by people around the world as a place to begin We see our schools, communities, counties, states, and countries all around the world choosing to come together in groups. There they join together, to learn the Earth Charter principles. They find ways to embrace lifestyles that begin to endorse and practice the 16 Earth Charter principles.* It is fair to describe the Earth Charter as the people's desire. Following its spirit, today and tomorrow we will care more for our home, planet Earth. Here on Earth we learn how to care for *all* the planets we may inhabit and even build.

——

---

* Please see appendix for sixteen principles from the Earth Charter

"Earthiness" is a way of learning! In our "new schools," we learn even more earthily.

———

Together with many others we are learning how to walk more lightly upon, and give more respect to, our beautiful home, Earth, in its place in the solar system, at home among the starry, friendly heavens.

———

*The transition to a higher order is universally accompanied
by turbulence, "perturbation".*

ILYA PRIGOGINE

Choice follows awareness. In the absence of awareness habits run my life.

JOEL AND MICHELLE LEVY

*The creative process had more impact, power, influence, and success
than any other process in history.*

ROBERT FRITZ

*The 'Creative Human' challenges assumptions, recognizes patterns,
sees in new ways, makes connections, takes risks, takes advantage
of the unexpected, constructs networks.*

SEATTLE SCIENCE CENTER, SEATTLE, WASHINGTON

The only constant in nature is change.

PLAQUE NEAR MT. ST. HELENS, WASHINGTON

*Listen to your inner voice ...
and become the change you wish to see.*

MAHATMA GANDHI

CHAPTER FOUR

Conscious Choices & Creativity

From Status Quo to Embracing Change

Along with our genes, our cultural mind maps, imprints, and habits control our lives. Every new awareness brings the possibility of change in our habits and life patterns; but it is our choices in consciousness that make the difference. Change happens most naturally when we have a new awareness, new models, or new experiences, and we change by choice. The less coercion and the higher our sense of personal empowerment, the greater is our ability to embrace change. Schools of personal empowerment are now appearing.

Modern scientists tell us that the one constant in nature is change. Yet, history shows us that the human customary response to change is fear. The easiest path is to follow the herd, stay with the pack, maintain the status quo—be a follower. The expression of fear, with patterns and habits of hate, fundamentalism, and resistance to change in response to fear, leads people to be closed, attached to old habits, and resistant to anything new. Fear has kept us locked in patterns of power and control. This habit historically can be traced back by anthropologists to the Agricultural Revolution. Since we are "what we know," no change can happen unless we gain an awareness of a new way of being, of new possibilities.

In the 1600s these ideas of separation, fragmentation, and patterns of looking at only the parts, were developed by the mechanistic thinking of the Newtonian Age. A major belief of this era is that we are all separate; everything can be understood by looking at its individual parts. Today we often are told we are in the midst of the biggest changes in history, even greater than the Agricultural Revolution. New technology, communications, the population explosion, resource depletion, and earth's destruction are forcing us to change. We now know that one really cannot get an accurate understanding of the whole by merely examining the parts.

As people are becoming more aware, we can begin to see the biggest shifts occurring in the world are from people changing their minds. New understandings that lead to change come in many ways; but unless we see other possibilities and understand that making this change improves our lives we won't change. Today, with a new worldview emerging, we have the possibility to change not only incrementally but also in quantum leaps. For this new worldview, we are training world teachers for world students in world schools.

Choosing to change our thinking today comes from many influences. Consider Martin Luther King's approach to equality or Gandhi's approach to freedom. Their invitation called on us to open our minds and hearts to new ways of thinking, and some say, to a higher consciousness. The call reverberated with greater knowledge of what it means to be human. Indigenous peoples and traditions of wisdom from ancient cultures are now proving to align with today's new scientific understandings. The new sciences support traditions of wisdom that emphasize we are all connected, rather than separate, beings. This clarity of vision of our interconnectedness to the web of life is possible for all humanity; but awareness, education, communications, and our inner knowing must be tapped for true change and transformation to occur. It's much like Galileo saying the sun, not the earth, is the center of the solar system. It took more than four hundred years for some to shift their thinking, including the Catholic Church. Only within the last century has the Pope acknowledged this truth.

Today, we are experiencing worldwide examples of people breaking out of their old ways of thinking, the habit patterns that have led to pollution, hunger, poverty, and war. People are seeing they have the power to create their own world by changing how they think. Our system has always relied on the visible and measurable. From patriarchal family patterns to schools and national test scores, this narrow mindset has continued to separate the rich from the poor, the old from the young, and the dominator from the victim. This deference to authority is beginning to break, as new awareness travels and people realize their power within. Their sense of inherent worth comes from seeing our interconnectedness and honoring a living system that benefits all. If we are intimately interdependent, caring for those around us is one way of truly caring for ourselves.

New Ideas at the Dinner Table

The day in 1955 that Dad arrived home and announced he had turned down a job offer in Turkey, the dinner table was abuzz with shocked teenage girls' screams. Why, we asked, would he not want to take that opportunity? Dad told us he had regularly turned down opportunities to work overseas because he did not expect that any of us would be interested in being uprooted. Both sets of my grandparents had lived in one place their whole lives; he hadn't thought to question that his family might think or do differently.

For the next week, dinner table discussions lasted far into the night as we talked about the pros and cons of such a drastic move. No matter how much we talked, analyzed, and tried to prioritize, it was clear that we all wanted to go. One week later (at the dinner table, of course) Dad shared the news he had accepted the position to live and teach in Ankara, while helping to establish a new university in eastern Turkey. We had six months to prepare, rent out our house for two years, and pack up what we'd need, and say tearful goodbyes to friends and family.

Departing on that airplane was the beginning of my lifetime journey of exploring the world. On our way to Turkey we made a two-week tour through Europe. My parents were as thrilled as my sisters and I to see what we had only read about. For Dad, the massive rebuilding of entire cities bombed during World War II was amazing. For Mom, it was the artistry, antiques, and culinary specialties that enthralled her. For me, the real fascination was the people and our similarities and unique differences.

Then it was on to Istanbul, Turkey—the only city in the world that sits on two continents. We headed on to Ankara, the capital, and found a home just across from the tomb of Ataturk, the founder of modern Turkey.

Our senses were immediately overwhelmed with the richness of the culture. The smells of the spices, the coffees and chai (Turkish tea), the sounds coming from the minarets calling all to worship Allah five times a day, and the deep colors and textures of the goods in the marketplace, all blanketed us with a sense of history and hope.

New Ways Seed Change

And so the seeds of a new story were sown. Unconsciously I was developing taproots that traveled deeply, connecting me to a culture so different from mine, yet resonating with a universal self that spoke to our oneness. I could not have imagined how it would set the course for the rest of my life. Moving from a small, homogeneous community to a global community, filled with the richness of diversity, only reinforced the inherent worth growing within my teenage spirit. As we settled into our new home, life just outside our door bustled with the energy of a city at work and play. A man walking down the street with a refrigerator on his back followed a woman herding sheep past our house. The bread baked just one block away arrived at our doorstep still hot, delivered by the baker himself. Small children in brightly colored clothes appeared around every corner, and we soon realized our family was part of the dynamic curiosity alive in all of us. The neighbors peered out their windows, absorbing the comings and goings of the white family with three teenage daughters.

Long after our belongings were moved in, the curious Turks still kept us in view and we kept them interested in our busy American family abroad. It wasn't long before the neighbors reached out, bringing gifts, sharing chai and Turkish coffee, including us in their community and their lives. Mother hired a woman to help with the household and marveled at the technique she used to wash our terrazzo floor: just dump buckets of water and stand ready with brooms to sweep the flood out the front door! Preparing food with a local flair included shish kebobs and wrapping rice spiced with cumin and garlic in grape leaves to make dolmas, a local specialty. Another favorite was phyllo dough filled with spinach, cheese or sugary syrups and nuts.

My sisters and I attended the local American school where we joined other teens in exploring the new world around us. Our classmates included military families, often of very high rank, the children of embassy officials and others, like ourselves, from the University of Nebraska. The faculty changed as the school changed from an American school to a United States military school, adding diversity to an already eclectic learning environment. My first year was filled with weekend outings to the historical places that brought Turkey's past to life for us all. Intermingled with the history were our sports nights of basketball and soccer followed by dances at our house, which happened to be nearby. While fifties rock music blared from the record player, parents took turns chaperoning the festivities that included the American staples of homemade Coke (with an excelsior bottle), vegetables, chips and dip.

A favorite family outing was traveling into the villages, where life was quieter and more traditional. The ancient rhythms of the land filled the countryside. From thatched-roof cottages to shepherds escorting livestock down country roads, these places spoke of another time in history. Arriving in our red sedan generated both curiosity and the generosity of spirit we became familiar with. The villagers, dressed in colorful scarves— the men in baggy pants and the women in modest veils covering their lower faces—would surround us even before we could exit the car. Known for their hospitality, the Turkish peasants would often invite us into their homes to share their traditional foods from the local area.

As we left the house each morning, we were greeted by the monument across the street, Kemal Ataturk's Tomb. The history of the nation we now lived in, dating back to 6000 BC, reminded us we were living in what once was considered the center of the world. Ataturk was determined to win Turkey's independence after the fall of the Ottoman Empire. To achieve this end, he instilled great pride in his countrymen and respect for Turkey's unique history. In 1923, he became the first president of the Republic of Turkey. During his fifteen-year tenure, Ataturk made massive changes in the way Turks were governed and educated. For the first time he separated the laws of Turkish government from the rules of Islam. Ataturk wanted religion to be separate from the state. His innovative thinking created laws allowing women equal rights, including the right to vote and limiting husbands to one wife, rather than a harem. Primary education was made free for all children. For the people of Turkey, Ataturk's Tomb symbolized their hero who brought them independence. For three teenage girls from America it symbolized a visionary able to manifest great change and benefit his people.

The Holy Lands with My Sister

My horizons continued to expand when my sister and I had the opportunity to travel to the Holy Lands—Egypt, Jordan, Jerusalem, and Lebanon—with an international group from our expatriate community. We landed in Cairo and as we walked through the airport I was taken aback with a sight I could not have anticipated: Russian people. Here we were in 1957, the cold war era in full swing, faced with individuals from the "evil empire." I was shocked when I realized they were just like us! My head began circling with questions. Why were we so afraid? What did evil really mean? What sense was there in this label given to an entire group of people? The qualities of kindness, peacefulness, and gentility filled the air around them. The juxtaposition of the dogma I had been indoctrinated with as a young American with what I could see and feel first hand clashed loudly.

We were in tourist heaven in Egypt, visiting the ancient tombs of great kings and leaders. The pyramids and the sphinx spoke to feats of architecture, design, and building that were difficult to imagine, especially in a hot, desert climate. Some now claim that the sphinx is a model of modern man's brain.

In Jerusalem, walking in the footsteps of Jesus was transformational. Steep streets paved with softly colored pink and beige stone gave rise to magnificent hilltop views, making Jerusalem one of the loveliest cities on earth, radiating the love of the Wise Ones. So many call Jerusalem home—Christians, Jews, and Muslims. It was the cradle of the three major monotheistic religions that saw God as Creator of the cosmos and humanity. In addition, it was the birthplace of unitheism, where God and man are viewed as one: the Jewish Kabala, the Christian Celtics, and the Islamic Sufis. While there are many shared beliefs and hopes, this holy city of three diverse faiths echoed with weighty divisions. Yet it also sang with power, beauty, and wonder.

The seeds of our interconnectedness had been continuously planted in me since our plane left Lincoln, Nebraska. Sitting silently on the Mediterranean with the sun on my face, my deepest inner knowing came into my awareness and flowed forth. Although I was only fifteen, I unconsciously sought the common ground, the threads which tie us all together. As my heart filled with love and compassion, my mind connected with our rich wealth of diversity, our greatness, our oneness, and our unity.

Back in Turkey, a land of the Muslim faith, the call to worship came from the minarets high atop the mosques five times a day. This repeated reminder to connect to the sacred place within further opened my heart to the human need for transformation and connection. I began to see religion as a river flowing to the great ocean of spirit that is universal. Although I could understand how countries could separate church and state to function and honor all ways, I could not understand how we could separate the sacred from the universe itself and maintain any meaningful life. Today science, spirituality and some religions are recognizing the sacred in all life.[10] The Teachers of the World are the teachers of the sacred in all things.

High School Trip to the Island of Crete

During our second year in Turkey, our school became accredited as an American school financed by the military for its overseas staff. This association provided a bountiful culmination for my youthful experiences abroad. Our new principal had connections with a military base commander on the island of Crete in Greece. If our student body was able to raise funds to travel there, the base commander said they would provide the room and board for our stay. Could our junior class possibly meet this challenge? The principal believed we could, and his show of faith proved to us we certainly could. I was class president and also a student council leader. We started brainstorming ways to generate the money. One idea led to another, from selling popcorn at the weekly movies to creating a school carnival that brought in a thousand dollars. The cooperation and team spirit bonded us together long before we set off for that magical island.

Located at the southern edge of the Aegean Sea connecting with the Mediterranean, Crete is the largest of all the Greek islands. It is also home to Knossos, center of the Minoan civilization, dating to 14,000 BC. The Knossos Palace is one of Europe's largest ancient palaces with five floors and thirteen hundred rooms. Coming from a male god tradition, I was startled by the endless statues of goddesses filling the museum halls and stacked to the ceilings in storerooms. They came in many different forms: the snake goddess, the sea goddess, and the cave goddess, often dressed in similar fashion. A flounced skirt draped their lower half, while most were bare breasted in their beauty. Shrines were built and offerings of sweet honey, oils, and wines were left in tribute. The gods played only a secondary role. My mind was flooded with more questions: What happened to the goddess? What happened to that reverence for women?

Growing Up

During those two years in Turkey, I experienced fundamental changes in who I was and how I saw the world around me. Many influences supported my ability to change: my genetic makeup, my parent and family modeling, my friends and environment, and the opportunity to reflect on my experiences. I was beginning to make conscious choices, while strengthening my own inner sense of self. My family seemed to blend into the Turkish way of life easily. We blossomed with the enrichment of all the new experiences and prospered from the exposure to new cultures. Furthermore, because so many parents had meaningful careers in Turkey, many of our friends reflected a sense of positive well-being as well. My junior year in Turkey nourished both my ability to lead from a partnership model—treating one another as equals—and my faith in myself that I could happily adapt in many new surroundings.

Soon the time arrived for our return home. Externally we had all grown into young women. New hairstyles, clothes, and makeup transformed our outer selves. Internally, the change registered in more dramatic ways. We had each realized the inner power we held. For my older sister, her vision of becoming a medical doctor was stronger than ever. My younger sister, exposed at a youthful age to many men, grew up too fast. I was determined to be a peacemaker in the world, one who was able to celebrate diversity and unify the oneness of our hearts. Entering my senior year at Southeast High School back in Lincoln, Nebraska, I began to sense how my recent life experiences impacted my teenage world.

Home for just a few weeks, my best friends invited me out for a Saturday night. Three guys and three girls piled into one car. We had not been driving long when the police pulled us over, found an open beer bottle in the car and placed us under arrest. Shortly after that experience, a friend in my carpool was pronounced dead after drinking and drag racing on the outskirts of town. I was devastated at the loss of someone so close to me, someone who had been a good student and on the National Honor Society with me. I was further shocked as I realized how differently my teenage friends in Turkey expressed their need for independence and individuality. In Turkey our social activities were more supervised and purposeful. We were too busy planning activities, trips, and events with adults to consider the thoughtless and unsupervised pastimes that greeted us at home. While abroad, we had created the world in which we lived; in

Lincoln, the teenagers followed traditional drinking and driving scenarios without always considering the potential consequences. My exposure to such different worlds strengthened my direction; I would listen to my inner wisdom and follow my heart.

College brought me to the University of Nebraska, where my father taught. It was easy to choose an education major since my passion was teaching children. While I joined a sorority early on, the selection/exclusion process gnawed at me from the beginning. When my wonderful Turkish friend wanted to join the group, the women of my sorority stood behind her completely. Unfortunately, it took only one dissenting alumni member whose fears of difference took control of the decision, eliminating my friend from pledging there. However, eventually there was a positive outcome. The following year, one of the top sororities pledged her, and the entire university campus voted her Homecoming Queen.

After deep discussions with my mother, I felt it was time to take a stand and move to a place where I found more common ground with those around me. I started at the University of Oregon my junior year. Because I was a transfer student, housing was limited, and I moved into dilapidated housing formerly designated for families. Four women shared each space, with one student counselor overseeing fifty or more units like ours. The counselor, Sharon Gearhart, and I became great friends and recognized the leadership potential in one another. She suggested I get behind her bid to be president of our sorority. In exchange, she thought I had the potential to be vice president of the University Women's Association. We were both elected in the spring.

The Dean of Women, Golda Wickham, was advisor for the women's association and modeled a new way of leading for me; I saw the success of a partnership approach in an academic context. As vice president I was charged with leading a board accountable for facilitating the growth of responsibility in all university women. It was a collaborative environment, where the concerns for each person were based on the good of the whole.

This relationship of equality that manifests in partnership continued a familiar pattern for me, one that resonated with my dream of cooperation and peace. In 1961 John F. Kennedy established the Peace Corps. Two years later my best friend and I decided to spend the next period of our lives in service.

As I entered my senior year I knew this was my heart's desire, and I spent countless hours in discussion with my parents about it. They were very vocal in their disagreement with my choice. My father's medical knowledge had him greatly concerned with all the tropical diseases that I might contract. Since he had helped pay for most of my college, he was incredulous that I could think of going out and working without an income. My mother visualized her three daughters marrying delightful young men who would provide well for their future families. While I understood their concerns, nothing could stop me from pursuing something I felt called to do. While parents were filling out Peace Corps character references and neighbors were verifying I had the right characteristics for the job, my friend and I took off for a graduation gift to ourselves—skiing and enjoying the good life in Sun Valley, Idaho. When we returned to campus, we learned where we would volunteer—she in the Philippines, I in West Africa.

Once I was accepted, my parents did a complete turnaround and supported me in every way imaginable. The first step was to endure an intensive ten-week training course; Liberia's was held at Syracuse University in New York. One out of ten applicants was accepted into the training program; fifty percent of those were dropped by the program's conclusion, before we had even left the country.

Empathy and Action Beyond Ourselves

In *The Great Turning*[14] scholar and author Rennie Davis and speaker author Joanna Macy theorize there is a vast revolution taking place because our way of life cannot be sustained. They identify three dimensions to this shift: *sustainability; shift in consciousness, so we can go to the deep roots;* and *to see all life as sacred.* Seeing the world as sacred rescues us from loneliness. I don't have to go to Chartres Cathedral to be in the presence of the Divine. It's right here. This means our sorrow is sacred too. Rather than going into denial of the pain and suffering in the world, which locks us into the status quo, we can accept the suffering with compassion and empathy.

People protesting the WTO (World Trade Organization), and in peace marches around the world, are taking a stand for our oneness, interconnectedness, and need to connect with our hearts. They are standing up with their fellow citizens, taking risks for the sake of something greater than their separate, individual lives.

When we act on something greater than ourselves, we begin to feel it surging through us with a power that is greater than our own. We feel a sense of empowerment or grace and perceive it coming from the divine. We need to practice and know we are sustained by each other in the web of life. People at war with each other are truly in bondage to our real enemy of ego: greed, hatred, and ignorance—the delusion that we are separate, that we are immune to what we do to other people.

People are tired of being pitted against each other, says Joanna Macy, who is reflecting so many voices today. As we intuitively know, or are learning, we are ready for the walls to come down between us and reconnect and honor the life we share. Divinely inspired Teachers of the World empower world-students learning in a divinely inspired world of grace.

Declarations and Affirmations

Two earlier great revolutions, the Agricultural Revolution and the Industrial Revolution possibly happened without humanity's conscious choice, understanding or awareness of what they were creating. In the 21st century, we are moving to a new place of understanding ourselves as we stand on the shoulders of history's greats. We know our minds create our world, and we are learning how we might co-create with the universe/life force (or add your word that flows from your chosen belief system). With technology, we are connecting with the peoples of the world and their rich diversity. We can make life giving conscious choices.

Today is the first time in our history when we can have enough understanding and awareness, along with the tools of technology, to realize we have 'Conscious Choice' and 'Creativity'. We can choose to grow as human beings with compassionate hearts or die possibly by blowing ourselves up or polluting ourselves to death.

———

We now know what kind of world we want. We no longer want to continue to be separate, to hate, to blame, to develop our highest weapons of mass destruction. We do not want to consume the earth's resources while watching the starving masses. We do not want to be controlled by our lower brain of fight and flight, greed and control. We want teachers to connect students with our new higher brain, our heart, our higher self and help us *feel* our compassion, our connection, our hearts deepest desire to make a difference in a world that works for all. We choose to grow not to die.

———

As we choose life we begin making Schools of the World. Where do we find the will? In our universal love! How can we work together? In Schools of the World! The Heart of the World is beating strongly, calling us to create a more nourishing and fulfilling life for all, especially our youth and the elderly. Schools of global sharing are being conceived. They are places where we share ourselves on many levels of our social and cosmic being. We are learning that sharing leads to power, not to weakness. Our sharing with each other creates wealth. It enables us to empower another person, another group with less than us. Our talents and skills are what we have to enjoy, teach and share with another. Schools of the World are where we support dialogue for change, for the new, for the different from us. They celebrate the world as a whole, seeing its racial and ethnic diversity as like a vast treasury of talent for global prosperity, creativity and happiness. The Heart of the World is calling us to open our hearts and minds. The Teachers of the World show us how we might interconnect. They encourage global thinking, they facilitate planetary planning, they teach us to bring forth the best in all we meet The Teachers of the World inspire us to make conscious choices for the betterment of humanity and all life on our home, Planet Earth, Third Planet from the Sun.

*My deepest longing is to live in a world that respects life in every form,
a world whose people have a fierce love of, and loyalty to, the earth
and their particular place thereon. The world we live in is not that
world but it could be. To get there from here, we need to recognize
that our own well-being is intimately connected
to the well-being of the land and of other creatures.*

LORRAINE ANDERSON

*I am certain that after the dust of centuries has passed over our cities,
we, too, will be remembered not for victories or defeats in battle or in
politics, but for our contribution to the human spirit.*

**JOHN F. KENNEDY, PEACE CORPS
BEGAN UNDER HIS LEADERSHIP 1961**

CHAPTER FIVE

Indigenous Wholeness

Schools of Wholeness Now

In the western world, we come from a mechanistic worldview, one that sees everything as separate, fragmented and disconnected. Unknowingly, this world view often leads us to put humanity's survival at risk with thoughts and actions disconnected from the larger picture, the greater whole. Our wisdom traditions, great prophets and modern sciences all are bringing us to a worldview that honors life and wholeness. We are just beginning to learn, understand, recognize and appreciate all life, and its inherent worth, interconnectedness and wholeness. In a life centered world, sustainability, democracy, connectedness and wholeness are valued. Such a world simultaneously solves many problems. Why? It revitalizes and values the many connections we currently don't see. The World Teachers of the Future are appearing, ready to raise new generations of students who see the world alive.

Many of us have not lived or experienced a culture of wholeness. Because we have lived for so long in our fragmented world, we no longer know what living holistically feels like or how it might function. Like fish that don't recognize the water they swim in, we don't recognize the fragmentation in our lives. As a Peace Corps volunteer teaching the sixth grade in Kolahun, Liberia from 1963 to 1965, I had the unique opportunity to experience the Bandi tribe's holistic manner of living. I felt immediately at home in Africa, alive and healthy in an unfamiliar way. Clearly dependent on the surrounding forest—lush, green, vibrant—I experienced a new awareness of my connection to the environment. In my personal relationships I also felt a deep connection and sense of purpose. Intuitively, I recognized a sense of self and well-being—a wholeness, in which my deepest senses came alive.

Since that time I have carried the memory of living holistically. Comparing life in the U.S. to my life in Kolahun draws attention to the fragmentation in our lives here. Considering this experience more closely highlights why a sense of wholeness in our lives is important and what we can do to create it. Our new Schools of Love are the places where we create this wholeness—with the new organic norm of global education: teachers and students working together. We are conceiving Schools of Wholeness now.

Connected to Our World

The surroundings in which we place ourselves and our relationships to those surroundings, impact us in ways we cannot easily identify. We are complex living systems. Taking in energy and material from the world around us, we use these inputs to function and then transform them. Every interaction in which we engage, involves taking in the world in some way, and thereby changes us.

Realizing we engage with the world through our own changes is a radical notion. This means the world we create is of the utmost significance to our well-being, personally, for our society, and for the natural world. We can create many different worlds through the choices we make. By paying attention to how the world affects us, we can choose to make changes that better support our well-being.

Simply put, we are the embodiment of our interactions. Everything we do, think, say, feel, or perceive (whether we are consciously aware of it or not) affects us because it is through changes within us that we are able to do these things.

Taking this process one step further, we see that each past interaction sets us up for the future. The changes that occur for us to engage with the world are not temporary, rather they become a permanent part of us, shaping us for the next moment. Smelling the coffee this morning altered my brain biochemistry. I am not the same getting out of bed having smelled the coffee, as I would have been if I had not smelled the coffee. While this is a trivial example, it clearly makes the point that not only do we change through our interactions, we carry these changes into the future.

Equally important as the idea that we are affected by every interaction is the notion that at the same time we are affecting the world around us. This process is symmetrical. Much of the world around us is also made up of complex systems—plants, animals, weather, social systems, and ecosystems—all of which we depend on in one way or another. These systems, too, are interacting through changes within themselves. By engaging in a conversation with my neighbor, not only am I being changed, but also so is she. How we interact becomes important not only for my well-being, but also for hers. Hence, because we each carry these changes with us into the future, our conversation is also affecting the larger social system in which we live.

Because everything we do not only affects us, but we also affect that with which we interact, our actions reverberate throughout the web of life. Bringing together these ideas, we are affected by our interactions, we are affecting the world around us through our interactions, and both we and other living systems carry these effects into future interactions. We see that our actions have effects that ripple throughout the web of life. If we are to consider fundamentally changing our society, all aspects of how we live and interact become vitally important.

Deep Connections

Wholeness and health are closely related. Both words come from the same root, as do the words: 'heal', 'hale,' 'hearty,' and 'holy.' In the correlation of health and wholeness, health is more than our immediate physical well-being. A deeper health includes not only our physical health, but also mental, emotional, and spiritual well-being. Creating a world that is healthy for ourselves, our society, and the world around us is the same as creating a world that is based on wholeness. We saw above that it is important how we create our world because we are so closely connected to it. If we are to be healthy and happy, so must the world around us—both our social and natural environment. Likewise, if we want to create a world that is healthy, we must also support individual well-being.

Living Wholeness in Africa

I am comparing my life in this particular African town, Kolahun, to life in the affluent western world. My experience in Liberia was limited to living in an individual town and its outlying villages, not in Liberia as a country. Many aspects of the country and life there would benefit from western ideas and practices. Likewise, Liberia has had its share of political difficulties. Nonetheless, the day-to-day life in the bush was steeped in holism.

Kolahun was the last town on the road that heads northwest from Monrovia, Liberia's capital; it served as the region's market place and center for many of the small surrounding villages. To get to outlying villages, one traveled to Kolahun by money bus—an overcrowded Land Rover that ran from Monrovia to Kolahun and stopped at all points in between—then continued on foot. The Bandi tribe inhabited this region.

My experience of wholeness living in Africa did not come from one easily identifiable characteristic; rather, as is inherent in wholeness, a number of factors worked together to generate this pervading sense. Living in Kolahun was characterized by a sense of total acceptance and respect. This respect was extended to life with a willingness to embrace whatever happened, including the pain and sorrow inherent in life. Not only did the Bandi know they relied on nature to meet their needs, they lived accordingly. Simple, yet wholesome, fresh food contributed to my physical well-being. Ceremonies and celebrations, with much singing and dancing, played a central role in Bandi village life. It was clear throughout everything the Bandi did that they understood their connection to, interdependence with, and consequent responsibility for both other people and the natural environment around them.

When I arrived in Kolahun, I was welcomed with a respectful curiosity. From the start, I was taken by the effervescent personalities, the charming and indigenous ways, and the sense of tribal and family responsibility of the local villagers. Immediately my neighbors asked what I needed and how they could help me settle in and my requests were enthusiastically and quickly filled. Over time I came to love the simplicity of life in Kolahun.

The indigenous people understood and accepted that I came from a very different place. They understood I had different needs and customs because of my background. In our Peace Corps training we were warned repeatedly not to go into the water for fear of schistosomiasis. Most of the Africans had long since been infected with this parasite, and therefore had little reason to avoid the water. So, when traveling together our African friends would carry us across the water. Although they did not understand our reasons in the same way we did, they accepted that our bodies were different because we came from a dissimilar environment and that going into the water would make us sick.

Mealtime traditions provide another example. It is the Bandi tradition to eat in silence. When other Peace Corps volunteers and I were guests in an African home, we recognized this tradition and joined them in silence. However, when we had African guests in our home for a meal, we followed the American tradition of lively conversation over dinner.

Just as they respected differences among people, the Bandi willingly embraced all of life, including grief and sadness. This acceptance added to the sense of wholeness. Instead of trying to run or hide from life, they eagerly took it all in, understanding that the good and bad come intertwined. They loved life, were always curious, and took joy in all they did.

They lived a very simple life and accepted whatever happened as normal. No one ever called them bad, evil, stupid, or sinful. Without a sense of excessive stress or fear, they were able to live in the moment, with no excessive concern for tomorrow. The only fear I noticed was of snakes; several highly poisonous species inhabited the region. When one of these dangerous reptiles was seen near a village a drumbeat was sounded to let others know to be watchful. Because life was fully embraced and all members of society fully accepted, there was little sense of exclusion, otherness, or labels. For example, one young boy in our school couldn't walk. Because he used his arms to drag his limp lower body behind him, other boys carried his books. There was no sense of him being different, of being labeled "disabled." This example also illustrates the Bandi sense of responsibility and understanding of the interconnectedness of life. Recognizing their integration with each other and the world around them, they understood that they were responsible for each other and to nature.

Although we often think human society is separate from nature, we are as much a part of nature as the rest of the Earth. Recognizing this and living accordingly is an essential aspect of living holistically. Again, this concept is clearly illustrated by my experience in Africa. The Bandi recognized their connection to the earth around them; they understood their dependence on the rest of the living world. Much of their time was spent outside, where the world was alive with wonderful tropical sounds, brilliantly-colored butterflies, and rainbows of wildflowers set off by the vivid red of the wild poinsettias. They retreated to their huts only to sleep at night—even the cooking was done outdoors in communal kitchens shaded by thatched roofs. Although there was no plumbing, a designated spot at the edge of the village served as a bathroom. Families had their own garden plots and orchards, but individuals did not own property— the land belonged to no one—the notion of land ownership was unknown to them.

My physical well-being, another important aspect of my experience of wholeness in Kolahun, was supported by wholesome indigenous foods. Just as the Bandi did, I ate a simple diet, produced locally. The main meal of the day consisted of country rice—brown rice, topped with greens freshly harvested from the surrounding forest, peppers, and occasionally chicken or fish, all in lush red palm oil. Fruit and nuts filled in as snacks. These were either harvested from the surrounding forest or grown in orchards nearby.

Like most people around the world, the Bandi enjoyed celebrating with singing and dancing late into the night. On weekends, our students often invited me and another Peace Corps volunteer to visit their village families and homes. Frequently the invitation coincided with a ceremony of some sort. If not, our visit was cause enough for a festive meal followed by singing and dancing.

A runner would go ahead to let the village know we were coming. When we arrived everyone would stop working and smile as we entered the village. After we rested, we'd meet the chief in a ceremony with our students acting as translators. Exchanging gifts was always part of the ceremony, where we typically gave baked bread or canned goods and they offered their country cloth, the narrow, hand-woven cloth traditionally used to make garments. We would share our binoculars and use our camera to take pictures, which we later sent back with students. The entire village would come together and share a meal with us. Because it was a special occasion, the meal often included chicken or fish. Afterwards, the women would line up to examine us more closely, meticulously feeling our hair. Many had never seen a white woman before. These gatherings were always fun, light, and filled with much laughter.

At some point they would show us where to wash up and go to the bathroom. Our accommodations consisted of a hut with a wood slab several inches off the ground, the typical bed. In the morning someone would bring us water to wash up. During the day we watched what the villagers were doing as they went about their work, whether in the rice fields or preparing food. Generally, we stayed one or two nights, leaving in time to have Sunday to prepare for the following week's classes.

I was fortunate to observe many rituals and ceremonies during my visits. Rituals played an important role in recognizing the connections in life by preserving knowledge, marking life transitions, and creating community. Most ceremonies incorporated specific protocols; some required secrecy. I can recall being ushered into a hut and instructed to stay there until my host fetched me, for if I witnessed this portion of the ceremony it would be necessary to take my life.

Sometime between the ages of seven and nine, children attended village tribal schools to learn traditional customs, rituals, and skills. Tribal school, "Poro" for boys and "Sandi" for the girls, lasted about six weeks and took place far away from the village. The celebration of a child's return was the one occasion when children were the center of attention. In addition to educating the children in the ways of the tribe and in the skills needed for survival, going off to tribal school and the celebration upon return served as an initiation into adulthood.

Another important ceremony, the Monkey Bridge ceremony, was a secret ritual that took place at night. This vine bridge crossed the Kaihi River at Kolahun. Just crossing this bridge took skill, let alone maintaining it. During the ceremony, the men and boys of Kolahun would rebuild the bridge over the river as needed. Because there were not many rivers to cross, this bridge was unusual. Incorporating the repairs into a secret ceremony ensured the knowledge was retained through generations.

An American Wedding in the Jungle Bush

At the end of the school year I organized a treasure hunt for my students. This game was new to them and they had fun following the clues. The treasure at the end was the announcement that I would be marrying a fellow Peace Corps volunteer, who was stationed in Monrovia. While they were happy for me, many of the students (one girl and twenty-seven boys) cried because I would be leaving as their teacher. Afterwards, I realized this had not been an appropriate way to tell them I'd be getting married and leaving Kolahun. My students' honest reaction to the news that I would be leaving again illustrates their emotional openness and honesty.

Nonetheless, our wedding became a community event. Using local resources we threw a typical American wedding in the nearby Swedish Pentecostal mission church. Sharing the wedding with our Liberian friends was a chance to introduce them to one of our ceremonies, just as I had been included in many of theirs. My students climbed trees to pick frangipanis, a local tropical flower, for the bouquets. Peace Corps friends from around the country came to help us celebrate and prepare the food and reception. We decorated the church and reception area with local greenery and wild poinsettias. One student had borrowed ten dollars from me. As repayment he brought many huge gunnysacks of fruit, which we hand squeezed to make wedding punch.

Making my dress and the bridesmaids' dresses became another teaching tool. My sister mailed me a pattern for my wedding dress and the bridesmaids' dresses. On one of my occasional supply trips to Monrovia I went to the fabric store and bought material for all of the dresses. I had no concern that our dresses might not turn out beautifully. While growing up I had learned to sew in the classroom at Gold's Department Store in downtown Lincoln, Nebraska and had come to enjoy the craft. Three fellow Peace Corps volunteers and three Liberian friends were my bridesmaids. In addition, my roommate sang in the ceremony. I taught all three African bridesmaids how to sew as we made the dresses on one of the few treadle sewing machines in town.

The wedding turned out imperfectly beautiful. A friend took photos of the ceremony; however, we later found out that the camera had malfunctioned. Fortunately, we had taken more formal, posed wedding pictures at an engagement party in Monrovia. As there was no electricity in Kolahun, we didn't have a standard electric iron. Using a charcoal iron, my roommate accidentally burnt a whole in the back of her beautiful new green dress, the day before the wedding. Because there was no way to repair the dress before the ceremony, she wore her dress in the wedding, hole, scorch mark, and all.

Teaching Sixth Graders

Although observing indigenous ceremonies and being a guest in many villages were once-in-a-lifetime opportunities and gave me a good understanding of the sense of wholeness of the Bandi's lifestyle, it was in my day-to-day teaching that I most clearly saw the effects of this wholeness. Comparing my students in Kolahun with my students the following year (in East Palo Alto, California) clearly illustrates the effects of two widely differing ways of living.

Kolahun

It was unusual for schools in Liberia to be started by the local people; typically town schools were started by outside agencies, such as USAID or a mission. However, because the local chief realized the young people needed to learn, the school had been built through a unique tribal community effort about eight years before my arrival. While I was there the school consisted of sixteen staff teaching close to five hundred students. The upper grades (six through eight) were taught by Peace Corps volunteers and the lower grades by local graduates of our school.

Students in my sixth grade class were eager to learn and grateful to have my guidance as their teacher. They ranged in age from twelve to twenty years old. Because schooling had not been available when they were younger, many of the students had started later than typical school age. Also, many children waited until after completing Poro or Sandi before beginning a western-style education.

The children were thankful to be in school. Each student paid twenty five cents in school fees, and most had to take the initiative to earn this money on their own. Because being in school meant leaving their family short-handed in work, many children were not encouraged to go to school. In a society that does not use money, finding a way to earn their school fees required dedication not seen in American students. In addition, many of the students came from outlying villages for the school week and stayed with relatives or in the CARE-supported dormitory in Kolahun.

My students' classroom behavior was exemplary; there were no discipline problems. I could trust these students implicitly—they showed a natural sense of responsibility, putting books away at the end of a lesson and cleaning up after themselves without being asked or reminded. In my teaching I emphasized research skills so the students could continue to learn on their own. So eager were they to learn, they would help us at home with our chores in exchange for extra tutoring and instruction. Their natural sense of responsibility and understanding of their interconnect-edness with the larger community, also was illustrated when they scored close to the highest of any class nationwide on the sixth grade exam. Rather than thinking about how smart they were and what they might do for themselves, these students wanted to help students in the lower grades and others in their villages to learn. The extraordinary interest in learning shown by these students is especially clear when compared to the class I taught immediately upon my return to the U.S.

East Palo Alto, California

My husband and I returned to the United States in 1965 after a motorcycle tour of Europe. On the way home we visited family in Germany, Boston, Illinois, and Nebraska, arriving in Palo Alto, California in October. Although the school year had already begun, I was offered a position as a teacher at Ravenswood Elementary in East Palo Alto.

The difference between these American students and my African students from the previous year was immense. In East Palo Alto I was hired to teach a sixth grade class that had already seen two teachers quit in frustration. During my first week one student threw a pair of scissors across the room; they landed in another student's cheek. The students exhibited a general sense of disrespect—lots of noise, talking, and destructiveness in the classroom. When asked to be quiet, the students would make more noise; when my back was turned, they would talk and call me names.

I attribute the difference between the two classes to the different worlds in which the children lived. In the U.S. the students had been told in many ways that they were not any good. Full of hyper-energy, junk food, and pollution—and lacking self worth—they simply could not calm their bodies down. They saw no reason not to act out. It was one of the few ways of getting attention.

Fortunately, I had the support of my principal and the rest of the school staff to do whatever I needed to get these kids to a place where they could learn with enjoyment and respect for one another. From my Peace Corps experience I returned with a sense that I could do anything. Seeking help and ideas from others, I worked to create a classroom environment in which these students could learn and grow. During the first few weeks I held a class meeting every afternoon with the students. Through this process the kids made a plan for what they wanted to learn and the type of classroom they wanted. Our classroom mascot, Murphy Monkey, became the rule enforcer. This meant that I was not the one being heavy handed; the students decided what they wanted and Murphy Monkey enforced it. For the first two weeks, up to fifteen students had to stay after school each day. This was because they had not been accountable for their behavior, according to the classroom standards they had set for themselves. After that things started to turn around. By the end of the year there was a big change in the students. They started seeing successes, which meant more trust and pride in themselves and others. As the only sixth grade in the school, the students began to see themselves as role models and were looked up to and respected by the younger students. Even the atmosphere on the playground changed noticeably.

These American children needed someone to believe in them, to support them, and to draw firm boundaries for them. Their parents were grateful that someone had expectations for their children and believed their children had the ability to succeed. In contrast, the integrated home, work, and community life in Africa—which worked with, rather than against interconnectedness—created a social structure that provided appropriate support and boundaries.

Recognizing Wholeness

Wholeness can be difficult to understand because we are only a part of the world, and a part cannot know all of the whole. While we are whole individuals, we are also part of many larger wholes: our family, our communities, and the world. Likewise, wholeness is not something we can test for, measure, or calculate. Nor is wholeness easy to articulate.

We do, however, recognize wholeness through our sense of love and beauty—through our aesthetic intuition. These senses indicate to us what is healthy in a very fundamental, holistic manner. This aesthetic sense recognizes a deep and foundational beauty, one not based on surface appearances.

Living as Nature

Organizing ourselves according to the laws of nature is possible. Janine Benyus writes about the emerging field of biomimicry:

> 1. Nature as model. Biomimicry is a new science that studies nature's models and then imitates or takes inspiration from these designs and processes to solve human problems, e.g., a solar cell inspired by a leaf.
>
> 2. Nature as measure. Biomimicry uses an ecological standard to judge the 'rightness" of our innovations. After 3.8 billion years of evolution, Nature has learned what works. What is appropriate? What lasts?
>
> 3. Nature as mentor. Biomimicry is a new way of viewing and valuing nature. It introduces an era based not on what we can extract from the natural world, but on what we can learn from it.[12]

Not only is biomimicry applicable to our physical production technologies, we should mimic nature throughout society—including in our economic,[13] social, and educational systems. With biomimicry in mind, Benyus identifies many strategies for living that recognize the inherent connections in life.

Use waste as a resource.

Diversify and cooperate to fully use the habitat.

Gather and use energy efficiently.

Optimize rather than maximize.

Use materials sparingly.

Don't draw down resources.

Remain in balance with the biosphere.

Run on information.

Shop locally.[14]

Another set of principles for living as part of nature comes from the field of ecological design. While at first ecological design seems most applicable to physical design, such as buildings, and consumer goods, the principles are equally applicable, just as biomimicry is, to other aspects of life. Stuart Cowan and Sim van der Ryn, authors of *Ecological Design*, list five principles of ecological design.

Solutions Grow from Place: Ecological design begins with the intimate knowledge of a particular place. Therefore, it is small-scale and direct, responsive to both local conditions and local people. If we are sensitive to the nuances of places, we can inhabit without destroying.[15]

Ecological Accounting Informs Design: Trace the environmental impacts of existing or proposed designs. Use this information to determine the most ecologically sound design possibility.[16]

Design with Nature: By working with living processes, we respect the needs of all species while meeting our own. Engaging in processes that regenerate rather than deplete, we become more alive.[17]

Everyone is a Designer: Listen to every voice in the design process. No one is participant only or designer only: Everyone is a participant-designer. Honor the special knowledge that each person brings. As people work together to heal their places, they also heal themselves.[18]

Make Nature Visible: De-natured environments ignore our need and our potential for learning. Making natural cycles and processes visible brings the designed environment back to life. Effective design helps inform us of our place within nature.[19]

These lists and definitions are a few examples of the many ideas available to use as guidelines for living with and in nature. Some additional qualities of wholeness include:

a balance of the masculine and feminine;

a balance of compassion and insight;

an awareness and use of ritual and symbol;

a sense of acting beautifully, acting from the heart;

an awareness of the difference between truth and factuality—ours is the only society to equate truth with factuality;

a recognition of the power of intention and its role in what manifests;

mindfulness;

incorporating our individual wisdom to create collective wisdom;

a wisdom that recognizes the importance of love and beauty, the aesthetic;

a recognition of the interconnectedness of life;

an appreciation of the patterns expressed and recognized in the sacred;

and a pace dictated by the needs of life.

Upon hearing the need for such change, most people seem to be struck with a sense of fear—fear that they will lose all of the good in their lives and fear that such change will mean struggle and hardship. Yes, it would be difficult making these changes within our current manner of living; however, we have the option of creating a different way of living, of altering the systems we live in. Doing the right thing should not be a struggle, should not be difficult, and should make our lives better not worse. Doing the right thing for oneself should be what is best for the world.

We must live as a whole and as a part of a greater whole. Separating ourselves from the rest of the planet is not viable. We cannot live as though we are not a part of the Earth—the Earth depends on us just as we depend on the Earth.

Teaching for Wholeness

If we are to create a world based on wholeness we must teach one another how. Our educational system has enormous potential, but it must be redirected.

Our brains are wired for greatness; we just need to re-learn how to tap into it. Much of our ability to do this has been blocked by our models of domination. When we see we are all connected, we see that caring for ourselves is caring for the world, and caring for the world is caring for ourselves.

Declarations and Affirmations

Where the Eastern World has historically honored the inner life of humankind, the Western world has honored the external life. In America, this is evident most recently in our emphasis on the material values that flourished with the Newtonian, Cartesian mind-set of a mechanistic world view. From the 1600s to recent times, we learned to value our world and ideas for being changeless, broken into parts, reduced to its smallest elements and fragmented. Children in school were treated like little machines in a factory, all lined up in assembly line fashion. Doctors and clients came from a place of one pill will fix it. The world was seen as 'winner takes all,' and Empire Building and competition were dominant patterns. Answers were seen in absolutes.

———

Education today is an example. Sixteen states in America are currently locked into lawsuits designed to adjudicate whether creationism or evolution should be taught in the schools. "Life" regarded as a machine is black or white, right or wrong, rather than creative and open like real organic life is. Problems are swept under the rug and kept secret, just as a broken plate is carefully glued and a cookie placed on top to cover the break. This worldview is not right or wrong, but part of our history and us. In the circle of life, we are all hospice workers and midwives, preparing for life, death and rebirth.

———

The beginning of the 20th century brought many new, great scientific thinkers like Max Plank, Albert Einstein and Fritjof Capra. Sub-atomic physics, quantum understanding, seeing the invisible that we had never seen before, began to change every-thing—everything but our mind, that is. Just as Einstein said in his famous quote, "The splitting of the atom has changed everything but our way of thinking. We need a whole new way of thinking if we're to survive."

———

This new-scientific thinking is here now, ready for us to use. Our new schools should be, can be, and shall be, the "living whole systems" some are talking about. The Teachers of the World help us to design schools large and small, where we can learn what it means to be *a life centered whole system* world rather than a *machine centered world*. We are now learning about this from our govern-ment, businesses, schools, and media. Life-centered whole systems, quantum thinking has been around for nearly 100 years. The Teachers of the World are now preparing to help the vitally necessary few teachers and educationalists who seem to know about centered, grounded, earthed *whole systems, quantum thinking*, who are ready, to become The Teachers of the Future, the Teachers of Tomorrow. The world teachers teach us that change is not so hard, we need not be threatened by new ideas! The Schools of Tomorrow are centered on what the great mystics and prophets were talking about: schools of love. Love, which is life, calls out from the World Heart, today, Schools of Love. These are New Schools designed to be bringing change and transformation to the world of education, to the global civilization, to the family of humanity. Its teachers are banding together, and learning together to gain more understanding of the educational needs of our world culture. Our educational culture is becoming whole life centered through their work and love and faith and harmony.

———

When we are not balanced and nourished, we are fragmented. When we are fragmented, we are diminished. We are reduced from being whole to being only a part of ourselves. A reaction is bound to set in, for our wholeness insists on being recognized and expressed! Being thus wounded, we experience what seem to be rebellious forces within us. Our inner life-force (some say human spirit, or your choice) may rise up. For some, who do not realize they have kindly choices, this may find expression in destructive or hurtful deeds. We may develop some kind of illness; or violence may occur.

———

When we listen to our body we begin to recognize it is trying to tell us something! What is it trying to tell us? Perhaps this: we yearn for schools to learn that true wholeness comes with the balance and nourishment of one's body, mind, emotions, and spirit. The Teachers of the Future lead us to insight, to *know* that wholeness brings inner peace, connectedness, and honors the mysterious unity among all! Now we can build schools where we become more whole! Who wants to join me in this life quest? For we can make a difference as we share our gifts in a world that works for all The answer to these questions is now clear: We become more whole in schools of wholeness. The New Teachers of the World are finding each other, organizing and finding the students of the world wellness, in schools of world harmony, glowing jewels of wisdom in the good Earth.

———

In the beginning is relationship.

MARTIN BUBER

Their minds have been mismanaged with great skill.

BOB DYLAN

*What distinguishes us as a species is not our fear, cruelty and violence,
but our enormous capacity for compassion, caring and creativity.
The primary human relationships—between parents and children,
and women and men—are key to whether a society is inequitable
and warlike or peaceful and equitable.*

**RIANE EISLER,
*THE CHALICE & THE BLADE***

CHAPTER SIX

Partnership for Equality

From Domination to Partnership

Though science and spirituality now agree that interconnectedness is the nature of all things at the heart, our culture has yet to catch up with that knowledge. Materialism, win/lose competition, fear-driven organizational hierarchies, ethnic conflict, and the destructive judgments we level at ourselves and others are all manifestations of the way we disconnect from ourselves and from each other. This disconnection is quite literally contrary to nature. Becoming aware of our systems of controlling rather than connecting, of dominating rather than partnering, is the first step toward becoming whole—healing ourselves, and eventually, healing the planet. *Healing the world* is central to the curriculum of the Teachers of the World.

A Wake-Up Call

The walls of the jail cell were painted pink. I remember thinking, through a thick fog, that the color was meant to be calming; but calm didn't come near to describing the state I was in. Incarcerated for the first (and only!) time in my life, I had nothing to do but think. Thinking came with great difficulty. A creeping mind fuzz had led to my arrest, and was making it exceedingly difficult to understand the chain of events whose final link was this barren holding cell.

Gradually, beginning in that pink barred cubicle and continuing to this day, my life evolved from crisis mode to an inclusive understanding of my relationships—with myself, my family, the medical/healing community, and ultimately the universe. Out of that clarity emerged both an intuitive and an intellectual grasp of two very different ways humans relate. I was beginning to see that my early relationships with family, friends, and community had shown me the healthy way: call it connectedness, wholeness, or partnership. But some of my recent experiences, in which I'd felt devalued, disrespected, and ignored, had shown me a darker side, a joyless, power-driven way: call it separateness, control, dehumanization, or domination. This second way, I came to realize with infinite sadness, is the only model of relationship many people have ever experienced. It still rules human thinking and human endeavors. I have now dedicated my life toward expanding awareness of the first way.

If you knew me, you'd laugh at the notion that I could ever find myself on the foul side of the law. Friends say I'm the kindest, most trusting person they know; but here I was, locked up, a threat to society! However, it was physical illness, not crime, which landed me in jail that night, though I couldn't convince the police of that at the time. It was illness, my mystery illness, clouding my brain so severely the officers who caught me driving out of control were certain I was stoned, on booze, crack, or who knows what. It was April 1986 and I was working as regional vice-president of a small securities firm. I had just finished conducting a training-in program and I was headed home late, about 10 p.m. As I drove away the man I worked with noticed me running a red light. In fact, my body was literally beginning to break down, only I was not aware of it.

I headed home, but I hadn't gotten very far when I started to lose consciousness. It was a bizarre level of unconsciousness, one in which my physical instincts seemed to take over. My mind could still function but it seemed incapable of directing my actions. My body needed food, but it never found it. Instead, the police found me—weaving up and down curbs on a major boulevard at about five miles per hour. The officer thought I was drunk or wasted. She was certain of it. When she phoned my husband to come pick up his "inebriated" wife, he laughed at the thought. He tried to tell her how sick I'd been—physically sick—and how for the last several years I'd been suffering from a debilitating but undiagnosed illness. He tried to tell her how I'd become allergic to just about everything, including most foods, even alcohol, and how I'd have violent physical reactions to walking into a copy-machine store, getting a whiff of cigarette smoke, or turning on the microwave. He explained that these allergies affected not just my body but also my mind.

This isn't as strange as it may sound. Science is showing more and more conclusively that our traditional distinction between body and mind is an illusion, that what affects one always affects the other. They are inextricably interconnected. My mystery illness caused bizarre symptoms! Eggs would make me angry, wheat would make me sleepy, and milk could make my ears ache and my mind foggy. At other times my mind would be perfectly clear. At the jail the attending officer wouldn't test me for drugs and alcohol, even though I insisted. He simply would not abandon his certainty that I was just another DUI.

His mindset, and that of my arresting officer, was the default approach of the criminal justice system (I must say my experience was more "criminal" than "justice"). I would be charged with driving under the influence, and faced having my license revoked for life.

I know my illness presented a challenge to the police and the courts (to say nothing of the doctors—but I'll get to that). My illness, later diagnosed as Epstein-Barr Virus and an insulinoma pancreatic tumor, was hardly common. DUIs were the system's regular clientele.

Still, as my saga unfolded, I couldn't help wondering why the people responsible for determining my fate had such trouble thinking outside the box.

What I slowly came to realize was that the need to be certain—to think inside a carefully protected box—is natural when you're brought up to think that whoever has the most right answers wins; that winning is power; and power is everything. If something mystifies or confuses you, if it doesn't fit in the box, like my husband's description of my illness to the police officer that evening, better to ignore or mistrust it—to make it wrong—than to surrender the power that comes with being certain. The truth is, that outlook describes the culture we all grew up in.

My reflections that evening, in my little cage, led me to some astonishing conclusions: at first, immensely sad conclusions about the state of our world; but ultimately, hopeful conclusions about the potential for our world. The sadness is big, but the hope is even bigger. It's a hope for a world transformed, one human at a time. It's a hope for a world in which our old patterns of domination, ingrained from birth, give way to a flowering of connectedness. It's a hope for a world where humans live as true partners with all of life. Synchronistically 1987 was both the year I finally resolved my court case and found the critical clues to my mystery illness; it was also the year Riane Eisler published her groundbreaking book, *The Chalice & The Blade*. Eisler, a cultural historian and systems theorist, considered by some to be one of the most important thinkers of our time, put clear language and an inspiring big-picture context to what I was just beginning to consciously understand.

Going back to our earliest experiences, we are flooded with influences from what she termed our "domination" culture. This is the way of thinking and interacting that has characterized human societies for the past five thousand years; but it's not the only way, and certainly not a healthy way.

The Domination Model

Our domination culture teaches us to see life as a win/lose battle, a battle for things and for control—more things than the next person, more money, more status, more power, and more certainty. "He who dies with the most toys wins" is not merely a joke on males: it's the core message our culture sends us (note that it's a message embodying male values). If we don't have enough things, enough control, we are losers;

or worse, we are controlled by others, those who have the power. In this worldview, the only alternative to dominating is being dominated.

We absorb this cultural mindset, this way of looking at and acting in the world, more powerfully and thoroughly because it is unconscious. We soak it up in schools and in churches, from the media, from our parents and friends. It comes to us through our economic system, in the games we play and, of course, in our workplaces. Why aren't we more aware of it, and of how it affects our lives? It's everywhere; and the more pervasive something is, the harder it is to gain perspective. We are immersed in our domination culture, minute-by-minute, day-by-day.

Combine that with the length of time this mindset has held sway over humanity—roughly five thousand years—and it is easy to imagine that it's just human nature. In this vision humans are seen as naturally violent, controlling, judgmental, greedy, fear-driven, and power-hungry.

Eisler's *The Chalice & The Blade* paints a different picture, a beautiful, creative picture of what humans have been and can be. She notes that five thousand years, while a long time in the context of a single human life, is a drop in the bucket of human existence. For most of the one hundred thousand plus years we've been here, Eisler argues convincingly, humans have lived in societies oriented toward partnership values: equity, nurturing, compassion, cooperation, and acceptance of diversity. Power was seen as the ability to nourish and sustain life.

War, for example, was almost unheard of until five thousand years ago. Surely, there were conflicts, but they tended to be resolved peacefully, despite the erroneous images we've gotten about the violent nature of early humans. Yes, there were leaders, but for the most part they didn't amass fortunes, leaving the rest of the society poor and hungry. They didn't attain their positions through violence or domination.

"But then came the great change," Eisler writes, "a change so great that nothing else in all of human evolution is comparable in magnitude."[20] So what happened? The shift began with warring, nomadic tribes from northern Europe and Asia repeatedly invading the peaceful civilizations of the south, beginning about 4,500 BCE. It is still unclear how these tribes developed their violent ways. Perhaps climactic changes in the northern European regions from which they invaded made existence a struggle, thus turning them against one other in a fight for survival. What is clear is that values like social harmony, gender equity, respect for nature, artistic sensitivity, and sustenance—which characterized the early human societies—were gradually supplanted by male dominance, authoritarianism, violence, and technologies of destruction.

Another influence pushing these peaceful people towards domination was the development of agriculture, which began a few thousand years before the barbarian invasions. This is most commonly cited as the beginning of territoriality in human affairs, and consequently the beginning of rampant violence to support those territories. Agricultural technologies for the first time gave humans the power to control nature; and early dominators felt the need to safeguard and expand this newfound control with violence.

We're only now discovering, about ten thousand years later, the truth in the old saying, "It's not nice to fool Mother Nature." In fact, doing so always comes back to haunt us. Try as we might, it is impossible for humans to escape natural laws. We are all one. We are all interconnected.

Virtually all of the problems we face as humans result from this domination orientation. Consider this list:

It's a pretty comprehensive list of the ills that trouble us. If you look at each item, I think you'll see how it results from a domination approach. In order to dominate, we must learn to control ourselves, others, and nature; and in order to control, we must disconnect our selves from what we're trying to control, again, ourselves, others, and nature. Since interconnectedness is the natural state of all life, this disconnect from self and others is the root of personal and social dysfunction.

Medicine and the Dominator Paradigm

Forty years ago, I had a life altering experience as a young Peace Corps volunteer teaching school in Africa. I was one of those lucky ones who'd practically never been sick a day in her life—measles, mumps, chicken pox, that was it. All that changed one fateful day in 1965. My students and I were hiking, exploring the glories of nature on the last day of the school year. On a steep river bank, we came across a row of large, black driver ants traveling in a horde like a military formation—fifteen or twenty across, and so thick that it looked like an undulating leather belt.

We found ourselves between the marching ant colony and the water. Peace Corps volunteers had been told two things about being in the wild: first, don't go near the driver ants; second, never get in the river water. (They teamed with alligators and insidious microorganisms). But there was no other option—jump in the river or get stung. The students saw the ants as the greater danger, and they leapt into the water. I froze. Have you ever been in an automobile accident where you knew, a split second ahead, that the crash was coming—but you were powerless to prevent it? That's how I felt. Within seconds the ants had swarmed over my lower body up to my waist. The students grabbed me, pulled me into the water and began furiously to pick ants off me.

As you might imagine, it was more traumatic than I can express in words. Still, I had no idea, even as I was recovering over the next few weeks from the hundreds of stings I'd received, how this incident would change my life. I assumed this episode would have a finite conclusion, as the chicken pox did, and I'd get on with my life fundamentally unchanged. How wrong I was!

The driver ant stings triggered a series of seemingly unrelated health problems that have plagued my immune system to this day. I had a case of malaria that went improperly diagnosed. I had a case of optical herpes. Then I had a lingering and debilitating flu, leading to an allergic reaction to penicillin from which I almost died. There was an ever-growing list of substances that would make me violently ill.

Thanks to a doctor who was able to transcend the domination mindset: "I'm the doctor. I have all the answers." It's now clear to me the driver ant stings initially compromised my immune system in a profound way.

For years I met with doctors who viewed their confusion about my case with denial and even anger. They couldn't handle not being able to find the solution to my mystery illness. In order to remain in control, they had to be the expert; and experts must know the answers. So they made one up; they decided it was all in my head.

I see now how strong and creative these doctors would have had to be to transcend the cultural limitations that framed their values. In addition to the value of being right, they were steeped in the value of objectivity and conversely, the denial of subjective experience—thoughts, feelings, and intuition. The doctors I consulted weren't interested in my experience, only in my test results. And the test results showed nothing. Their conclusion: I was a hypochondriac.

By and large, these doctors weren't interested in me. They were interested in being right. Therefore, they needed to put me in a diagnostic box. When I didn't fit in that box, they got angry, and they wanted to get rid of me as fast as possible. For example, my malaria went undiagnosed because it didn't show up on their tests. I knew I had it. I'd just come back from Africa, where nearly all my students contracted malaria. Meanwhile, the doctors were taking huge amounts of money, and I was getting no help.

Over these years, the middle years of my life, I spent countless hours in doctors' waiting rooms. Much of that time was spent thinking and talking with other patients. It was out of those conversations that insights began to take root, insights that were later given credence and language through Riane Eisler's work on partnership and domination.

I found to my great anxiety that this domination mindset was not limited to physicians, although the Western medical approach seems especially prone to it. Even some of my family and friends seemed threatened by my increasingly severe and inexplicable symptoms. The cognitive dissonance was too great. They, too, had been influenced by the culture of objectivism, to believe if it didn't show up in the tests, it didn't exist. They couldn't trust that I knew my body better than the doctors did. They couldn't trust their own strong connection with me. My mother later said, "We wanted to love you, but we didn't know how."

My mother could not accept my new inability to tolerate cigarette smoke, all her wonderful homemade cooking, and the many smells that come in our air: car fumes, copy machines, new paint, or carpeting. She couldn't accept that I had become allergic to so many foods. I couldn't eat everything she had prepared for Thanksgiving dinner. Along with being brought up to enjoy her surroundings, home economics was her field and her passion. My reactions, however, could be severe. I vomited after being around cigarette smoke. I got big red welts and often clouded thinking from food sensitivities, and at times I would nearly pass out in a copy store.

In looking back on my teaching career, I have most often been blessed with partnership situations, situations in which I've felt respected and honored by my colleagues, loved by my students and their parents. Parents in one disadvantaged neighborhood school came to tell me, "You're the first teacher who truly cares about my children." Although I appreciated the compliment, it was tragic because of what it said about our education system. We teach what we know, and control and domination are what we know. Districts in which the school board doesn't trust the administrators are districts in which the administrators don't trust the teachers, the teachers don't trust the students. And what about the parents, where do they fit in this dynamic? Often, they constitute some of the most ardent proponents of the traditional competition-dominator model. Keep in mind that it is parents who control most school boards.

Trust is the key that unlocks the door to partnership. Most of my teaching situations, as I previously mentioned, have been alive with partnering and that's the reason I've remained in the classroom all these years. I described it before as an opportunity to express my interconnectedness with other life, especially children, and I can also place it firmly under the umbrella of partnership.

In these partner-oriented schools I felt valued, believed in, respected, and heard. There was a heartfelt connection with students and colleagues, and my creativity was honored, just as I honored that of my students. These successful partnership outcomes are dependent upon an ethic of proactive, supportive leadership.

The Partnership Model

As if to underscore the understanding that began to sprout in doctors' waiting rooms and blossomed in the Seattle jail, I had two partnership epiphanies several months after my "run-in with the law." The first was in a courtroom as I attempted to have my DUI overturned and my criminal record expunged. While everyone else in the criminal justice system had assumed me guilty until proven innocent, one empathic judge heard my story. He looked at me and said, "You seem to have all the symptoms my wife has. She has Epstein-Barr Virus. If you could get this diagnosis, we could dismiss your DUI."

When I identify with someone else's truth, I get chills. My body just sings to me, and I feel like crying. That's how I felt when the judge said these words to me. He had heard me, he had empathy for me, and he believed me. He wanted to help me find a solution. He wanted to free me from the myth of the illicit substance allegation. Sitting high up on his bench, he chose not to dominate me, but to connect with me. In one moment (that he might well have forgotten a month later) we formed a partnership that changed my life.

I did get diagnosed with Epstein-Barr Virus. It is an insidious, complicated autoimmune disease that was little known in 1987. My securities job required a lot of traveling by car, but I couldn't drive! After what had happened to me, driving was too risky.

Out of my husband's generosity and phenomenal support came a brilliant idea. I'd go to Los Angeles where I could live with my sister-in-law while gaining access to one of the few experts in Epstein-Barr Virus.

Access to the top doctors would be provided by my husband's brother, a neuropathologist who had been head of his department at Harvard University. I'd teach, if my illness would let me, and hopefully I could get well. Then I would go back to Washington State and get on with my life.

My second life-changing partnership experience involved a job I got at the last minute. It was the end of August, and the district told me all hiring was closed except for one position, a fourth grade class at the 97th Street School. This site was near the infamous Watts neighborhood in Los Angeles where race riots had destroyed millions of dollars worth of property and taken many lives.

The school—students, teachers, administrators, and families—was of mixed cultures, mostly Hispanic and African-American. There were very few European-Americans, and fewer European-American teachers. This was no great challenge to me. I had taught in Africa and in East Palo Alto. I knew I could teach any children, anywhere. And I was desperate for a job in Los Angeles, where I would be close to family and hopefully find a doctor who thought outside the box.

I remember, as if it were yesterday, walking into the principal's office. Charles Barrett was a tall, strong, youthful African-American with a vision. He radiated a sense of power to empower, a palpable air of compassion. We almost didn't have to say a word; we connected instantly. He saw that I would fit and hired me on the spot.

I loved it. The school was truly a partnership, focused on trust and abiding compassion for the small souls in our care. Every Monday morning, the entire school—all one thousand students—would gather and sing Whitney Houston's "The Greatest Love of All," which starts with the words:

> I believe the children are our future
> teach them well and let them lead the way
> Show them all the beauty they possess inside
> give them a sense of pride to make it easier
> Let the children's laughter
> Remind us how we used to be...

To transform the world we must take seriously the understanding that our children are our future. They are so open to the world. We must choose carefully how we treat them.

Social scientists such as Michael Gurian and neuroscientist Joseph Chilton Pearce tell us that our choices of partnership or domination patterns have two origins: first our genetic wiring; second, our experiences in earliest childhood and in our family environment. The neural pathways forged as a result of these two influences have a profound effect on our attitudes and behavior for the rest of our lives. It takes significant effort to change these patterns. As Daniel Goleman wrote in his landmark 1994 work, *Emotional Intelligence*, the brain remains pliable throughout life. In childhood, he says, the brain's adaptability is "spectacular."

> Experience, particularly in childhood, sculpts the brain ... This makes childhood a crucial window of opportunity for shaping life-long propensities; habits acquired in childhood become set in the basic synaptic wiring of neural architecture...[21]

Thus, if you feel trusted as a child, you have a better chance of growing up trusting. If you feel loved, you're more likely to be loving.

In my genetic wiring and early childhood experiences, I was one of the lucky ones. I grew up in a family that nurtured me with trust and respect and responsibility. They listened to me. My mother was always there for me. My father never raised his voice; he knew how to resolve conflict peacefully. As I grew, I reflected this back into my surroundings. This is what I knew, and therefore brought into the world. What I saw in my family, I saw everywhere I went. I felt love and I felt loved. What I felt in myself, I gave to my relationships. This happened totally organically and unconsciously.

This orientation toward love, trust, and collaboration also characterized my experience as a schoolchild. I had a different learning style, yet I always felt honored and respected. I was challenged in math, but my friends helped me so well that I ended up achieving one of the highest scores on a national standardized math exam. My fellow students, after caring about me and working with me, were astounded. I now see that moment of pride as a demonstration of the power of a partnership approach toward learning.

Perhaps these early experiences explain why it took so long for me to begin to recognize patterns of domination in my life, like the prejudice I had witnessed from the sorority alumnae at the University of Nebraska. There were partnership elements to that experience as well: the sorority itself was a strongly democratic institution—once you were selected.

Furthermore, my experience with the sorority helped me to clarify and then act on my own principles. Once I did, I found satisfying partnership experiences at my next school, the University of Oregon. There, the dean of women taught me how empowering a school administrator can be. When female students broke rules, it was the students themselves, she insisted, who should work together to solve problems the violation had caused. This fostering of individual responsibility for the common good is key to the healthy and healing approach called partnership.

My village in Africa had been not only an example of wholeness, but also of partnership. I felt incredibly fortunate to live in a community in which the good of the individual did not seem in conflict with the good of the whole community—where one person's gain was not another person's loss. From students to families and villagers, people seemed aware that helping others, even strangers, was in their own interest. Mutual aid and cooperation, rather than competition, seemed to shape their lives. At the time, I just knew it felt right. I didn't have the perspective that I have now and I didn't have the word: 'partnership.' My husband, too, embodied partnership. He had great compassion for me; he encouraged me; he grew along with me. Even after I got sick and remained inexplicably ill for a long time, my husband was unconditionally supportive. An accomplished and natural musician, Lee would play guitar for me often when I wasn't feeling well. He would come home from work, get out his guitar, and sing to me.

When the traditional doctors (like his brother) and much of my family were telling me my "invisible illness" must be in my head, Lee continued to think for himself. He stuck by me, through eight years and twenty-five doctors, until I found alternative healers I could consult—just as he later generously supported me in my quest for the best traditional doctors in Los Angeles.

When I found Charles Barrett at the 97th Street School, in a sense I felt like I was coming home—home to partnership, where I had lived most of my early life, before getting sick. Charles was always there for the teachers and the students. The teachers were always there for each other. And my students were always there for me: one day when a troubled student became violent, my students intervened to protect me.

Nevertheless, I was fated not to be able to finish out the school year. I became even sicker. The diagnosis of Epstein-Barr Virus had at long last identified the mysterious set of physical challenges I'd been facing for twenty years, but it hadn't begun to identify the solutions. How to effectively treat Epstein-Barr Virus was as mysterious as the disease itself.

My disease did gradually seem to get better, but something else was growing in my body—a pancreatic tumor. It was diagnosed in February of that year, and removed in June. The combination of the tumor and the Epstein-Barr Virus took me out of school frequently during those months, until eventually Charles had to hire a full-time teacher to replace me. Still, I felt total support from staff, students and parents. Not once was I given a hard time about my absences or my symptoms, which must have seemed very strange to them.

What a contrast this was to the treatment I'd received from the health care system. By the time of my surgery, I had seen twenty-five doctors. Only the last one—a specialist who insisted on collaborating, and partnering, with me and with other specialists—truly supported me.

I have a friend who says the opportunity for learning is directly proportional to the quality of the trauma. In that sense, I see my lengthy illness as an opportunity in disguise—an opportunity for me to grow in understanding, of myself and the world. I did so by reading voraciously about healing, by consulting health care specialists of every stripe, by going to a healing and meditation retreat, an alternative clinic in Mexico, and by taking classes in the evolution of consciousness.

It became clear to me that I must take responsibility for my own health, for strengthening my partnership with myself and with the universe. My illness has been part of a creative process in which I become a more whole human being. That was the path to healing for me. I also believe that is how the world heals. Here we can see the cardinal elements of the curriculum of the Teachers of the World. In the Schools of the Future, students learn by becoming more whole, by forging partnership at every level, in every heart, in every institution, in every niche in society and every corner of the globe. Global education is healing education.

Partnership in Education

Once again we come to education, the venue in which I've spent my career, expressed my passion and my compassion. How does our 5,000-year-old domination worldview color education? Let me count the ways.

Our educational culture is focused on cognition alone—training the mind. We tend to ignore the heart, at least in the standards that drive today's educational practices. If we equate healing with becoming a more whole human being, how can schools truly care for our children by targeting the mind alone? How can such a narrow approach possibly educate people to solve our world's complex problems?

In so many classrooms, in so many areas of the world, there is a core of compassion that one day will expand to envelop all of education. For now, however, the culture of education is notoriously domination-oriented. We focus on controlling students, instead of trusting them—because we are asked to make them learn many things they're not interested in, and many things they'll never use. We accomplish this control with grades, rewards, and tracking systems that separate winners from losers. We must do this because, as teachers, we are near the bottom of the authoritarian education hierarchy: the legislature dictates to the school boards, the school boards dictate to the administration, and the administrators dictate to the teachers. Can we help but dictate to our students, when being dictated to is all we know?

We also teach a curriculum that reflects domination principles and the dominator power structure. Traditionally, only half of humanity has been in power—the male half. Men and the characteristics we call masculine are given vastly more space in our textbooks and credence in our worldview. The same is true for Western culture, with short shrift given to the richness and diversity that characterizes our world and that has contributed infinitely to what it means to be human in the 21st Century.

Furthermore, because a domination-oriented system fosters separation rather than connection, the educational system that reflects it tends to teach in parts, in fragments, with isolated packages of information. It evokes a thought-provoking image from Alfie Kohn's landmark book, *Punished by Rewards*:

> We give students a brick of information, followed by another brick, followed by another brick, until they graduate, at which point we assume they have a house. What they have is a pile of bricks, and they don't have it for long.

> We divide education into subjects, but how often in life do we do math alone, or biology alone, or music? Life occurs in context. Life only has meaning in context: the context of relationships, family, work, and place. Yet in our schools there is little context. School itself is isolated from the community. The sixth graders are isolated from the first graders. The teachers are isolated from each other, parts rather than wholes, bricks without shapes or mortar.

New Approaches

What does partnership look like in education? It's about trust and connection, rather than control and separation. In a partnership school mutually supportive relationships abound. We can't partner unless we truly include one another. Partnership classrooms embrace all cultures, rather than allowing the dominant culture to dictate what's taught.

That means a partnership curriculum gives equal time and equal consideration to the two halves of humanity: male and female. A partnership curriculum also emphasizes our rich diversity, while still honoring the unity that is all energy and all life.

Rather than compare students through grades and other rankings, partnership education assesses students cooperatively—students, teachers, and parents, setting goals and charting progress toward those goals. In a partnership paradigm, the child's natural pace is honored, while she receives adult guidance to stay on track.

Such an approach to education values all learning styles, all interests, all talents, however large or small. This inclusive consideration for the needs and interests of the individual learner is placed firmly within the context of the health of the community: the classroom community, the school community, the larger community, and the global community. Schools characterized by partnership relationships are democratic; they teach responsibility not by rote conformity and obedience to rules, but by cooperative participation in the democratic process. What exciting places are schools that function as democratic communities!

The monumental promise of a partnership approach to education is the healing of a profoundly troubled and separated world. Two inspiring visions of partnership can be found in Riane Eisler's work, *The Chalice and the Blade;* and, for education, *Tomorrow's Children.* I urge you to pick up one of these if they are new to you and see if it doesn't change your vision of what partnership can be.

Declarations and Affirmations

Partnerships are about mutually enhancing relationships, not just with humans but also with all life. Activities based on equal acknowledgement for one another give us a sense of a larger significance and meaning. Dominator relationships don't feed anyone. Both the dominator and dominated lose, like victim, victimizer. A life centered world consists of cooperative relationships that enhance the quality of life for all.

In our Star-Schools we create equality and respect in relationships. There, the Teachers of the World move educational philosophy in our dominator society towards the central idea of partnerships. We have a new model of *education as collaboration!* We are learning that in Hunter Gatherer times partnership was perhaps a predominant way of being together. If this is true what happened during the Agricultural Revolution that supported this domination way of relating? Is it true a change in climate and commerce and movement of people may have reinforced men's hunter instinct to protect so they began to kill their own kind to gain food for their family? What would it have been like to be alive 3,000 years ago? Our life is different today. Still, we can we take men's instinct to protect and women's instinct to nurture (since the Hunter-Gatherer days!), and move forward on the shoulders of the giants of wisdom and knowledge who lived before us. The Teachers of the World believe in wholeness and a life centered world, versus one that is broken and material. This means a revolution in our educational philosophy and educational science. It transforms all our educational relationships, our pedagogical institutions, our teaching 'businesses,' our educational media. It offers a new paradigm for our medical system. Our education system is being transformed for the Space Age, transformed into a world of love. The Teachers of the World show us how we must relate differently to our children if we are models and guides rather than dominators who know it all! StarSchools of business and global schools of global government will now be built on partnerships where men, women and children are all valued and respected! New kinds of educational systems are ready to be created. They will create blueprints for schools where all are valued equally. The world-education think tanks of tomorrow are ready to do this.

———

What gives us the will, the motivation to make changes is ...*love.* Americans, model for the free world, are working to set free world-teachers to create an educational world that works for all. Our new schools teach us how we can make friends instead of enemies; this is the curriculum in Schools of Love. We nurture the land rather than destroy the land, for we learn to love the land in Schools of Love. We work in the flow of nature, with the Tao of Nature, the Tao of education, rather than create more landfills and centers of pollution. All over the world, prophets—the moral leaders of the world of education—will help us find strategies for the new world of educational excellence, the world of love.

———

Educational leaders everywhere are on the move to co-create a wonderful new educational science. Educational futurists and social innovators, cultural creatives and spiritual dynamos from all continents and races are connecting with each other. They are forming a teaching community. They are teaching us how to make a difference in the world of schools. They are the Stars of the World of Education.

———

A human being is a part of the whole,
called by us the "Universe." He experiences himself,
his thoughts and feelings as something separate from the rest—
a kind of optical illusion of his consciousness.
Our task must be to free ourselves from the prison
by widening our circle of compassion
to embrace all living creatures
and the whole of nature in its beauty.

ALBERT EINSTEIN

CHAPTER SEVEN

Communication for Trust and Community

In 1983 I attended a presentation at Antioch University Seattle by futurist, Barbara Marx Hubbard. I was so impressed with her words, her vision for the world's future, and our role in it, that she made an indelible impact on me. She said the world was at an evolutionary crossroads and that she saw a growing awareness of our human connectedness. Since I understood how important it is to see that we are interrelated with all others, I resonated strongly with her words.

Hubbard's model for a peaceful world in which people evolve beyond belligerence and hatred was such a vital vision. I had sensed our need to make drastic changes in the way we operated and how we viewed other people across the globe. As a country we had lost our sense of connection to all life. Her model for change and educating people to transform the world was a powerful inspiration for me.

I knew that creating harmonious relationships with one another and our environment is absolutely essential for the sustenance of our planet. I was consciously doing what I could to make a difference—in my classroom, in the workplace, and in my family life.

It concerned me that many in our country seemed to focus on differences between groups of people, based on their religion, culture, gender, class, race, sexual preference, age, and other characteristics. Our similarities and common humanity with others in our world were often unrecognized by many people. The theme of our country, our workplaces, our government, and our communities, seemed to be one of attack and overcome, or at the very least, try to prove we were better than others.

I was often disturbed by the arrogance of Americans who seemed to believe that our culture was superior to others, and that we had a blank check over the world's resources. The attitude of self-entitlement and the excess consumerism many Americans exhibited were creating resentment and alienation from people in countries around the world.

Experiencing my teenage years in Turkey, traveling to other countries, and living four years in Africa gave me a bigger picture, in which I saw us as a single planet, a single living system. I wondered how Earth could continue to survive while some parts of the world had so much and others were deprived of basic needs. Most of all, I was disheartened by the centuries of war, hatred, and suffering. How could human beings be so cruel to one another? This was in the midst of the Cold War. Most Americans were afraid of nuclear annihilation—and of the "evil" people in the USSR. Peace seemed so far away!

Building Bridges with the USSR

When Barbara Marx Hubbard came back to Washington State I was excited by the opportunity to hear her again. This time, Barbara passionately described a project she was planning—one hundred people would travel together to the USSR as citizen diplomats. The Cold War was keeping people in fear of one another. Her response was to build understanding and create a common bond of humanity by having ordinary American citizens visit that distant country. The theme of the trip was "The Search for a Positive Future."

Barbara believed that we could evolve as individual human beings, and her mission was to help bring about a process that she called, "The Formation of the New Human." She claimed that becoming an integrated and fully evolved person was necessary for fulfillment of the dream of both communism and democracy. According to her, we need leaders who operate from this high level of consciousness.

As I listened to her words, I felt a deep stirring within me. Someone in the audience asked, "Who should go? Who will the people be?" Barbara answered by saying that those who were called to join her would know it in their hearts. As I felt my own enthusiasm welling up in me, the friend who accompanied me spontaneously turned to me and said, "Barb! That's you! This is your calling. You have to respond." I knew her words were true as I felt my heart open to this new humanitarian adventure.

I was further convinced that this was my calling when I received a check for mutual funds I had sold only a few days earlier equaling the exact amount of the trip—$2,400. It was a sign to me that I would commit to this peace-building project, to bridge understanding between two alienated countries.

A journey to the USSR would be a way for people, one by one, to meet others and experience our similarities, not only our differences. Change would only come through people connecting with and understanding one another. I believed in the words of Robert Muller, Former Assistant Secretary General of the United Nations when he proclaimed:

> Affirm to others the vision
> Of the world you want.
> Network through thought.
> Network through love.
> Network through the spirit.
> You are the center of the network.
> You are the center of the world.
> You are a free, immensely powerful source
> Of life and goodness.

Affirm it, spread it, radiate it.

Think day and night about it.

And you will see a miracle happen:

Not in a world of big powers,

Media and monopolies,

But of five and a half billion individuals.

Networking is the new freedom,

The new democracy, a new form of happiness.[22]

Within a month, we began our preparation. Barbara gave us audiotapes to listen to each day. Repeatedly hearing these messages prepared our minds and also helped build a sense of unity in our group. These tapes contained principles that expanded our awareness, and readied ourselves for the journey we were about to take.

This preparation was extremely important; Barbara understood the need for our group to be completely united. She also recognized the underlying and unlimited intelligence that resides within all of us—in our heart and souls. The groundwork of listening to those tapes aligned us as a team that operated from a unified awareness and intention.

Finally, we departed on our journey, flying first to Helsinki, Finland. For three days we stayed at a beautiful resort and spa to prepare for our next step. Here we relaxed, adjusted to the time zone, and became peaceful for our journey. Barbara knew the importance of being relaxed and energized before embarking on this mission—a cohesive group focused on peace and learning would help us to experience the best in the people we met in the Soviet Union.

The goal in Finland was to focus on our group's cohesion, our oneness. Each morning we meditated together, forming a strong common bond. Barbara was admittedly a strong Christian and often used Christian references. Several people raised the point that they believed the group should represent all religions. This led to a long discussion, and many different opinions appeared. Barbara wisely insisted that the conversation should continue until we had reached consensus. She knew we had to reconcile our ideas so that we would speak with one voice when we went to the Soviet Union. In the end everyone agreed this was not about any one religion—*we all felt the same on the inside.*

Next, we took a train to Leningrad (now St. Petersburg). What surprised me on the train was that, in addition to ourselves, there were several other peace groups making trips to the USSR for similar reasons. I thought we were an isolated group desiring an opportunity to create peaceful relationships, but here were others doing the same thing. Some groups had been sent by organizations that raised money specifically to send peace ambassadors to the Soviet Union. Other groups were on their own peace-building missions to create understanding and show faith in humanity. I was gratified to know that others were as concerned as we were about the state of affairs in our world.

Prior to our arrival Barbara's team had set up meetings with various groups: hospitals, schools, government, businesses, and museums. We each visited the organizations that related to our passions. I went to schools and museums, where I learned how they educated their children. People in health care visited hospitals and clinics. Those in politics visited people in government positions.

During our entire time in the Soviet Union, Barbara had us maintain our daily ritual of gathering in the morning for group meditation. This was a wonderful tool for sustaining our energy for our work in the Soviet Union. By beginning each day with peace in our heart we could extend this feeling to those we met. Thus we spent our days in open-mindedness and acceptance. Each evening we gathered together in support and to share stories of the day. The support of the group and our daily rituals gave me the sense that I had a bubble of protection around me during the entire trip, literally an indescribable sensation. We were a strong and unified family—a community with the purpose of building new relationships with our brothers and sisters in this foreign country.

Although temperatures were far below zero, everything was so well organized we all were able to carry out our visits with little difficulty.

Wherever we went, people expected us, and greeted us with great enthusiasm. Leningrad was a beautiful, historic city with gorgeous architecture, wonderful museums, and an amazing affinity for the arts. It brought back loving childhood memories of Istanbul.

My most significant and surprising impression of the people in the Soviet Union was their very strong desire for peace. They often mentioned the travesty and devastation of World War II. Its lasting effects were far more evident in their minds than in the minds of the American people. The impact of the war seemed to have left permanent scars in their hearts and they wanted to prevent any possibility of a war occurring again. The most important goal to work toward, they felt, was worldwide peace.

They asked me what Americans were doing to create peace. I had a difficult time answering. Back home, most Americans saw the Soviet Union as the evil empire—the giant enemy. Americans were very much in fear of a nuclear war and had built up huge military armaments in the name of national security. I often questioned myself, how could people believe that more military power and greater threats to other countries would bring about peace or even peace of mind?

After our week in Leningrad we departed for Moscow, a truly remarkable city. I was especially impressed with the schools, and even more amazed by the after school programs. These programs were provided because the mothers were usually working. The women's movement meant more, not less, work for women. Now, in addition to household obligations and child-raising responsibilities, they had to work to bring in an income.

After school the children went to large, once-beautiful apartment buildings with vast courtyards. In these large apartments, the children were able to choose among different educational activities with a strong emphasis on the arts, such as: cooking, dancing, sewing, music, writing, and drama. These youngsters could work on their separate activities and then also join with other children for socializing in the courtyard. They were given loving guidance, much support and attention. The children seemed very happy in these environments. I do realize we were shown their best programs and sometimes wonder how extensive these wonderful programs were. Did all Soviet children have access to such care? Or was it just a lucky few?

Two of the many things I learned in Moscow were especially interesting: first, their forward thinking work on birthing; second, their interest in healing and human energy. In both areas, they were experimenting with very progressive concepts and practices. For example, they were doing experiments with mothers delivering their babies underwater to allow the child to enter the world without the trauma of a conventional birth. These newborns were even fed bottles in the water. The transition from the womb to the water was a more gentle, natural approach to birthing. It was quite amazing to watch.

The Soviets were also working with new ways of using and understanding healing energy. They recognized the power of our interconnectedness, and that we all are comprised of energy—atoms, molecules, and electrical currents. As an example of this connection they cited the following story: A tiny, baby mouse was taken hundreds of miles away from its mother and dropped into the ocean. At the exact moment the baby was dropped, the mother went into a spasm of trauma. They believed the connection was this great for all of life. Not only had they shown these connections are not affected by distance, but they also believed that healing energy travels, regardless of space or distance. In their experiments with transmitting healing energy to other humans, some healers reported dramatic results. These were very advanced concepts for that time. Even today these ideas are not widely accepted by our medical community.

Returning to the U.S. and my hometown with a renewed hope for the future, I gave twenty-five presentations to schools and community groups, sharing the unique experience we had in the Soviet Union. My life was forever changed by the trip.

A Peace Park in Tashkent: Seattle's Soviet Sister City

My husband was so moved by the stories I told him that his own sense of desire to visit and to make a difference in the Soviet Union grew. In 1988, Lee gathered with friends in Seattle to discuss a new humanitarian project in the Soviet Union.

The group was comprised of members of Ploughshares, an organization of former Peace Corps members. We reformed as Peace Corps Volunteers Working for Peace. This new group was led by Fred Noland, a Seattle attorney who took a three-year sabbatical from his practice for the project. We planned and eventually completed the construction of a Peace Park in Seattle's Sister City, Tashkent, in the Soviet Union.

The Seattle Sister City Committee, the Seattle Chapter of Architects/Designers/Planners for Social Responsibility, and the Washington Chapter of The American Society of Landscape Architects all participated. To build the park seven teams, each approximately thirty people, went to Tashkent in various phases. Many more community members in Washington State took part in preparing each of the component projects.

In the Ten Thousand Tiles Project, 8″ by 8″ tiles were given to teachers who responded to an open request for schools to participate. Every student in these classrooms was given a tile on which they painted their own design. A number of other citizens, even the governor of Washington, painted tiles as well. Once all ten thousand tiles were hand-painted, they were fired to make them long lasting for outdoor use.

A second project designed colorful flags with symbols representing the Pacific Northwest: mountains, starfish, sea patterns, and evergreens. Lee led another group that made wood carvings for the flagpoles. The flags were later placed around the Peace Park Café along a trellis so people sitting outside could enjoy their colorful beauty.

As another part of the park Seattle artist Richard Beyer designed an aluminum sculpture called, "Life, Love, Time, and Game." It depicted the four stages of life, from infancy through old age and was designed for children to climb on as well as for visitors to the park to admire.

The fourth project was a spectacular mosaic of the world made from broken pieces of colored glass and tile. It turned out to be an enduring symbol of one planet united for peace.

Lee and I were part of the group whose job it was to finish the park. We were under a deadline and worked day and night, often on our hands and knees in 100–120 degree weather. Not being used to their unpurified water, we had to filter it, otherwise Americans easily got sick from it. In the end, despite sickness, extremely hot weather, and various upsets, the project was completed with great enthusiasm and success. The Soviet people worked side by side with the Americans. It was hard work, but we had a compelling vision.

Reconsidering the Enemy

My visits to the Soviet Union expanded my awareness of the importance of understanding people from other nations—especially ones considered an enemy. We repeatedly saw that human beings are so similar and that we all want peace. We share common desires for love, joy, satisfying relationships, and happy lives. Most of all, we saw that the enemy is not faceless. When we met the people of the Soviet Union, our fellow souls on this planet, we saw them as our brothers and sisters who are loving and caring human beings.

One of the most important things I witnessed in both trips was the incredible dedication and importance the people in the Soviet Union place on family life. Their families are strong communities that support each other over the generations. They care for one another, and extended families often live under one roof. This same hospitality was extended to neighbors and others in their community.

Russia is no longer our enemy; but, according to our government's position, we have new enemies. What changed? Why does the face of the enemy change? Why do we have to create enemies when we are really a single family? Where does the hatred, mistrust, and attack on other human beings come from? And most importantly, is there a way out of this "attack and overcome" mentality?

Fear is the Source of Our Separateness

As Einstein said, it is an optical illusion of consciousness that we are separate. Yet we seem to continue believing we are separate. Individuals, as well as larger groups and even nations, are very protective and defensive of what we deem our territory, what we consider to be our self. This notion of separateness seems to underlie many of our problems, particularly when combined with the dominator model. Why do we hold so staunchly to this idea of a separate self?

In her book, *Tragedy in the Workplace,* Danna Beal examines the phenomenon of ego. She says the ego is a self-created identity.[23] Joseph Chilton Pearce says it comes from our older mammalian brain.[24] Both agree we create the ego to help us navigate through the world and keep ourselves feeling safe. The ego's number one strategy for self-preservation is to blame the other; and this requires an enemy. Once the ego has created an enemy, it must protect itself from that enemy.

The ego builds walls of defense and wears a mask. Human beings have built walls, fences, drawbridges, guard towers, moats, and other barriers to protect themselves, to keep people in or out. The most dramatic example in recent history was the Berlin Wall separating East Berlin from West Berlin. Entire families were divided by concrete and barbed wire from 1961 until 1989 when the Wall came down after a peaceful revolution within East Germany.

Fear is the source of all wars. It is also the source of artificial power. Beal makes a distinction between authentic power and artificial power. Artificial power stems from the ego that requires external validation to substantiate its existence. These "props" are money, material possessions, power over others, property, anything that proves the ego is powerful. However, what looks like power is often false power.

Qualities of authentic power include compassion, humility, integrity, and a vision benefiting all people, not just a chosen few. Authentically powerful people operate from internal strength and guidance instead of relying on external validations to prove they are powerful. Truly great leaders throughout history possess these traits of authentic power: Maya Angelou, Gandhi, Abraham Lincoln, Queen Elizabeth I of the Shakespearean era, Mother Teresa, Martin Luther King, Margaret Thatcher and Nelson Mandela.

Seeing others as only separate and different is the path of the ego. Since the ego isn't real, it is very fearful of exposure. We can all identify with that mode of thinking and sense our own fears of being discovered as a fraud. If we understood that looking behind our fears is the way out, we could stop casting others as the enemy. All battles are really with the self, but we project them onto others. When we face our inner fears of inadequacy and weakness, we actually empower ourselves from an internal source. Scientists Michael Gurian, Daniel Amen, and Joseph Chilton Pearce all show we have a more highly evolved brain than we typically use. Our newer prefrontal neocortex and heart-mind reveal humanity's connection with the universe—what Pearce calls our "ultimate intelligence."

Giving up the barriers to peace with one another is the path to rebuilding relationships at all levels. We must look in the mirror at our own inadequacies and learn to give up our defenses and attacks. When we project our fears onto others individually, we have personal conflicts; when we do it as a nation, we have wars.

James P. Carse, in his book, *Finite and Infinite Games*, said that, "Evil is never intended as evil. Indeed, the contradiction inherent in all evil is that it originates in the desire to eliminate evil."[25] Has this not proven true throughout history?

When we form divisions and draw lines, forcing people to choose sides, we alienate ourselves from our fellow brothers and sisters. When we see others as different, we can then objectify them, leaving ourselves immune to their suffering. This alienation allows us to disguise our guilt and diminish our compassion or caring for others. This tragic game goes on and on, as we look the other way when there is suffering in our community and around the world.

If we are to have a world of peace, social justice, and ecological balance, we must begin to recognize it is fear, not power that starts wars and makes enemies. We must start to build harmonious relationships by giving up our own fears. As a country, it is time we looked at ourselves. For all the good we do, we must ask ourselves, what have we done to alienate so many countries?

So we can have a world honoring the spirit in others and ourselves, we must replace fear with trust and compassion. We need to be concerned for all of life, to stop seeing others as the enemy—be it in the family, workplace, community, or world; and we must guide a new generation of children to understand the sanctity of all life and the interrelationship of all people.

The Classroom Community

An important path to peace is building community and connections right where we are, at every opportunity. My mother provided a natural family community for us. She offered the same caring to everyone we met. Peace comes from knowing others, understanding others, and seeing our common humanity. It occurs when we reach out to those around us.

The classroom is also a community; for some children it is their first opportunity to interact and learn how to relate to others. Children need a community for learning to share, cooperate, trust, and have opportunities to build their self-esteem, in addition to studying the regular curriculum.

Communities provide support and possibilities for cooperation in many different ways. Through community we create synergism and an unlimited power. When you combine the individual wills of each person in a group focused on a unified goal, a "group will" occurs that is greater than any individual. This collaboration is necessary to bring about a massive transformation in consciousness. Leaders who suppress or act superior to those they lead squelch the full potential of the group will and power.

Teamwork can occur only when there is trust within the group. As long as we have alienation or power struggles, we cannot work as a team. Barbara Marx Hubbard understood this when she insisted we resolve any differences before we went out to the communities in the Soviet Union.

School classrooms encompass the largest community that young people experience. It is time to expand the opportunities for preparing our children to be the next generation of leaders. When we limit education to basic skills, such as some of our political leaders are advocating, we are missing many important aspects of education. When administrators operate from their fearful ego, they succumb to political pressure and fail to take a stand for the best quality of education for children. The ego drama in schools has never been greater, and the energy wasted can never be recovered.

The creativity of teachers and their passion for positive learning environments has been greatly diminished by politics in education. Many teachers agonize over their exhaustion and discouragement in the current educational environment. We will continue to lose some of our most creative and forward thinking teachers dedicated to educating the whole child, if we do not recognize and change the path we are on.

Declarations and Affirmations

Building trust and community is essential to people's need for connection, purpose, and sense of contribution to the enhancement of life. At birth our deepest roots and our first models are community. As we grow, open compassionate communication enhances the flow and building of self, family, school, city, country, and a global community.

———

Moving from accumulation and competition to simplicity, trust, cooperation and community nurtures us in life-giving ways and allows us to create something greater together than we could apart.

———

Strong communities and deep relationships are the roots for building harmony and balance in a life-centered world. Opening the heart is what changes hurtful communications to compassionate communications and a sense of connectedness. Honoring the land as our home is the foundation on which we build.

———

I begin with myself to nurture love for myself, for my deepest pain and suffering along with my times of joy and gladness. I can communicate with myself, when nothing is working, to gently nourish myself with compassionate self-talk. As I move to communicating with my family, community and the world how I can listen with an open mind and heart and truly see the loving life force in the other person. Schools of Love are aborning, to help me to love myself so I can love the world. There, I can remind myself that as I see the world, so I see myself. Schools of Love are where we work together to strengthen our listening skills, our communication skills, our openness to new ideas and to being loving partners from the heart.

———

We can truly believe greatness lives within all of us. As we contemplate the roots of our belief system. We can let it change into something better, something more loving and kind and good. The models that empower me and build my skills are ones I can see in local community in Africa, New Zealand, Iceland…. everywhere humble people live simply together in harmony and love. So many networks, organizations, communities are already laying the groundwork for global civilization. In Schools of Love we are nurturing global civilization builders. I need to let go of that kind of educational outlook that is not working? I facilitate my own growth by daily meditating on the Ideal School, and I nurture the best kind of studiousness, scholarship, and passion for teaching and learning in all the folks I meet. In little groups designing and forming Schools of Love, we work together: manifesting conscious choice and compassionate communication skills. We *play* together to build networks of communities modeling social and economic justice. We *sing* together to create instantly the seeds of schools for a sustainable way of living. We *dance and tell stories* together to plan the blossoming and flowering of schools where all life is flourishing.

———

We honor this time in the history of humankind, for we know we are being called to educational GREATNESS! For this great purpose, this Magnum Opus—the Ideal World school—we can let go of our egos and our need to compete; we *can* find that place of compassion in our hearts where cooperation and the win/win lives. Together, we nurture our greatness through our innovative, loving, magical, artistic communications. As a team of the Teachers of Tomorrow, we form educational communities of the Teachers of the World, so together we can create classrooms of love and peace—classrooms and curricula that engender a world that works for all!

———

I have a voice
I have been silent,
I keep it in a box
When I open the box
People hear it,
and it makes peace

JOEL, THIRD GRADER

To develop our capacity for self-governance,
education must be the means by which we learn to be free.

FRANCES MOORE LAPPÉ

We teach reading, writing and math
by [having students do] them,
but we teach democracy by lecture.

SHELLY BERMAN, FORMER PRESIDENT,
EDUCATORS FOR SOCIAL RESPONSIBILITY

CHAPTER EIGHT

Living Democracy

What comes to mind when you hear the
term democracy? Perhaps 'freedom' or 'a system of government.'
Maybe you associate positive feelings with this term, or consider it as
a topic in social studies classes. Democracy isn't only what we teach or
a system of govern-ment; democracy is deeply connected to every
aspect of life. True democracy nourishes the inherent possibilities of
human development. We learn democracy not just by studying it, but
also primarily through how we are taught, by enacting it.

An Indian creation myth goes straight to the heart of *democracy*. The
world began as a smooth sea of milk, and then a small wavelet formed.
Forever after, that wavelet was torn between loving its own identity and
wanting to rejoin the whole from which it came.

If you talk to a biologist, a philosopher, and an Indian mythologist,
you may get three very different perspectives on life; but on this point
they'll agree: all living things possess that little wavelet's two basic drives—
the drive for self-determination and the drive for connection. In other words,
all living things are driven to survive and thrive as individuals, as well as

to connect with their environment, community, and family—with something greater than the self.

These two drives may seem conflicting. The first focuses on *me*, the second on *we*. When we harmonize these two needs—when we support them simultaneously so that synergy happens—we can be fully human. That is the definition of true democracy: our two basic drives, self-determination and connection, are nurtured together. They are two sides of the same coin: rights *and* responsibilities. With responsibilities come participation, and participation means action and being engaged. With this balance, freedom is placed securely in the context of collaboration with all of life. In this sense democracy is not a mere concept in civics but an expression of the natural state of all living things. True democracy requires not only that we integrate our individual needs with the needs of other people and society, but also that we integrate human needs with the rest of life.

To highlight the inherent democratic quality in all living things, the term "Earth Democracy" was coined, extending our traditional sense of the word to encompass the entire planet. We humans have been disconnected from nature for centuries, with the tragic results becoming increasingly obvious: global warming; ozone layer depletion; deforestation; pollution of air, water and earth; the extinction of thousands of species every year. Seen from a biological perspective, democracy acquires a deeper meaning. We are a part of Nature and because of this, to be true to our own nature, we must participate in, connect to, and have respect for nature. This acknowledges a core scientific truth—we are not separate from our world.

Scientists and sages now know it is important not only to include all living things in the definition of democracy, but also to expand our definition of living things. You, of course, are a living thing. You take in resources and information. You self-regulate. You maintain a delicate balance of various forces and impulses. And you must co-exist with your environment, or die. All living things, all living systems, do these things. On a smaller scale, your heart and lungs are living things as well. They take in resources, maintain biochemical balances within themselves, and must interact cooperatively with other organs. On a larger scale, our culture is a living thing. It uses resources, maintains itself (for example, through norms, laws, customs, language, and stories), balances competing interests, and, if it doesn't co-exist with its environment, it will be destroyed. From the macro to the micro, the dynamics are the same. From the smallest bit of energy to the great expansiveness of the universe, these are all living systems and they are all connected.

By these criteria, the Earth itself is a living thing. If one "organ" of the earth (say, a developed country) drains resources from another (say, an underdeveloped country), then competing interests are out of balance, and the whole is not healthy. Even worse, when resources everyone needs are destroyed (say, the rainforests, the "lungs" of the planet), then the whole "body" is threatened. This is true on every level, every scale—when one part, a single competing interest, sacrifices the health of the whole to its own greed, the result is catastrophic. On the cellular level, cancer destroys itself by devouring everything around it until it destroys the host that sustains it. On the bodily level, as Elisabet Sahtouris asks, "What if some of your body's organs drained resources from other bodily organs?" Would the whole of you survive? On a cultural level, think of Hitler; his megalomania was the seed of his own demise. And on the planetary level, we humans are in the process of devouring our host, our ecosystem, our planet, and thus are dangerously close to writing our own obituary as a species. When we pollute our air, our water, and our soil, we pollute ourselves.

In short, no living thing can satisfy its need for self-determination by denying its need for connection. Nor can we do the opposite—be truly connected to the rest of life by denying our selfhood. If we don't develop as individuals, we can't contribute fully to the community. This is why diversity is so important. The community draws its strength not just from healthy connections, but also from nurturing the full potential of every individual's unique gifts. A democratic society is only healthy if both individual potential (self-determination) and responsibility to others (connection) are honored and nurtured.

Sadly, the notion of democracy that inspired our country's founders has become polluted like our air and water. For one thing, the competitive, win/lose nature of the economic system that drives our brand of democracy makes collaboration with others difficult and makes disconnection a universal pattern in our society. As long as we focus on competition, we narrow the possibilities because we can't build on each other's strengths. Instead, we fear each other's strengths, believing they may defeat us. Courage and will (necessary for self-determination) have always been important to democracy, but compassion (the road to connection) is what moves us to a place where we all become greater by working together, greater than we can ever imagine working separately.

Thus, if a healthy society is one that simultaneously supports its citizens' needs for self-determination and for connection, then the measure of a healthy society would be an active citizenship—citizens developing their full potential to contribute to the common good.

In his book, *Schools That Work,* George Wood notes that "in recent times democracy has been stripped of its participatory basis, as voting and representation has come to replace the active involvement of citizens in making public policy and community decisions."[26] Even in voting, the most basic activity of participatory democracy, the average turnout in our country is telling. Not even the most popular elections elicit more than 50 *percent* of eligible voters showing up at the polls. Frances Moore Lappé and Paul Martin Du Bois write:

> A cycle of disaffection has begun, feeding on itself...The more citizens withdraw from public participation, the more politicians ignore them. The more irresponsible the politicians act, the more citizens withdraw in anger and hopelessness.

> Democracy needs to be viewed as a way of life, a civic culture in which people creatively participate in public life...We call this vision of democracy 'living democracy.' We believe that without such living democracy, without the active participation of citizens, the unprecedented challenges of the 21st Century cannot be met.[27]

A huge part of the problem is the disproportionate amount of power that corporations wield in our society. This power imbalance greatly diminishes our potential as individuals to contribute to our democracy. Considered persons under the law (but *not* under the Constitution), corporations have all the rights that we do as individuals, but with vastly greater power. They have more power and rights than persons but without any of the necessary responsibilities to society so that we can then hold them accountable. When corporations were first established back in the mid 1800s, it was possible to revoke their corporate charters. These charters were held by states and required that for corporations to do business in that state, they must uphold the public interest. In this way they could be held accountable to the local community. By the 1880s, that all changed when corporations were granted the status of persons in the U.S. court system. Anyone with an ounce of common sense can recognize the absurdity of such a legal decision. It is at this point in our legal history that corporations began to gain their uncontrollable, rampant, and monopolistic power. One need only think of Enron to get a picture of what happens when corporations get out of control. Fortunately, there is a movement to revoke corporate charters in this country, which may provide more balance to corporate monopolies and this system of rights without responsibilities. As movement leaders have articulated, it is people who confer the rights onto corporations. We give the corporations their rights; we can also take them away.

Balanced power relationships are crucial to enlightened social progress. If some of us (say, corporations or wealthy interest groups) have vastly greater power or influence than others, then the uniquely valuable contributions of those disenfranchised "others" cannot move forward. Someone once said, "All of us are smarter than any of us." A truly democratic group or society "finds ways to utilize (and even enhance) the knowledge, perspectives and aptitudes of all its members," according to Tom Atlee, founder of the Co-Intelligence Institute.*

This leads us to equity as another measure of the health of a democracy.

---

* Atlee defines "co-intelligence" in part as the "capacity to … integrate the diverse gifts of all for the benefit of all."

If we are truly expressing our drive for connection, expressed by compassion, how could we tolerate vast disparities in wealth? By this measure, neither the United States nor the world as a whole is healthy. There are savage inequities here in America: between classes, cultures, and the genders. Filmmaker Michael Moore quotes a finding that seven percent of the power that white males have in our culture is due to their character and abilities; the other 93 percent is due to the status in society their gender and race alone convey.[28]

If democracy is the natural state of all living things, and our democracy is unhealthy, then we as global citizens must ask ourselves, how can we contribute to its healing?

Teaching Earth Democracy

To what extent are our students' basic needs for community and self being met in school? How much do we allow them to be self-determining, let alone encourage them? How much do we support them in contributing to the democracy with which they will soon be entrusted?

Wood's words are powerful:

Most of [our ideas about citizenship] are reserved for the social studies or history courses. But when citizenship is just social studies, when politics and community are reduced to test-taking skills, schools produce spectators, not citizens. We are trained to watch ... and to seek private satisfaction while shunning the public world.

What students learn in school is not what shows up on the standardized tests. More important is what they learn from the daily treatment they receive in school; this is what tells them who they are, what they can be ...

Thus, students don't really learn about democracy by being pummeled with endless lists of dates, facts and great names. It is in the daily lives children lead in schools that the characteristics of schools that work are found.[29]

Democracy needs education, and education needs democracy. If we want a healthy democracy, we need citizen involvement; and to get it we need to start with our children. According to our earlier description, a classroom community falls under our expanded definition of "living things." Such a community certainly uses resources, organizes and regulates itself, maintains balances among competing interests, and must co-exist with the rest of the school. If democracy is the natural state of all living things, then democracy in the classroom—not unrestricted freedom, but freedom *with* responsibility—is the only healthy way to educate.

The Road to Teaching Democracy

My interest in seeding democracy in the classroom, in nurturing a healthy living organism within the four walls, took root during my Peace Corps years. Teaching in Liberia, I saw African students easily connecting with each other and with nature. I saw what empowering students to be self-directed can do for honoring and developing their inherent worth, and what that could do in turn for their ability to connect with others and the world around them. These qualities seemed to come more naturally to African children than to American children. I am convinced that if a healthy democracy can be created in an African classroom, it can be done in America as well, despite cultural and political obstacles. That conviction came to fruition for me as a teacher in the early 1990s, thanks to some other experiences along the way that fueled it.

In the early 1970s, my young children attended a cooperative play school in Roseburg, Oregon. I became a full-time coordinator for the school and learned the value and satisfaction of working in partnership with parents—a sort of mini-democracy for the sake of our children. We worked as a group to plan and carry out the activities for our children. By its physical situation, the school offered numerous opportunities for the children to interact with the life around them. The school was located in a building on the county fairgrounds near the banks of the South

Umpqua River. Favorite activities included exploring the river and nearby forest, gathering pinecones and acorns, and seeing the horses stabled at the fairgrounds. Because our family lived nearby, the school and surrounding areas felt like an extension of our home. We enjoyed living with the outdoors as a part of our everyday life.

The value of parent cooperation, in a democratic mode, also characterized my work with the Head Start program years later in Olympia, Washington. Teaching the parents how to support their children as they grow and develop is an integral part of this remarkable program. When we visited the homes of our students, we brought materials to support and encourage the parents' active engagement in their child's development and learning.

In both of these early childhood education situations we practiced giving the children choices whenever possible. If we were doing table time, children might be able to choose between various puzzles and games. At snack time they could choose whether they wanted to help set the table, serve, or clear the table. As with other choices in life, these options came with associated responsibilities. Choosing to play with the blocks meant that when it was time to clean up, you were responsible for putting the blocks away. Combining choices and responsibilities in this way helped the children to understand that they indeed have choices in life, but each choice comes with associated responsibilities.

My two trips to the Soviet Union in the late 1980s were also formative experiences—they showed me how unhealthy a culture can look when self-determination is stifled. By contrast, the soil of American culture, despite some challenging metaphorical rocks and toxins, is a far richer mix for planting seeds of true democracy.

Out of these varied experiences I became excited about the prospect of creating, in an American public school, a healthy classroom democracy where every child is a fully empowered participant, and where all students contribute to leadership and decision-making. In short, I envisioned a class where children are actively involved in creating the world *they* choose.

I quickly found that in education, as in American society at large, the notion of democracy was given much lip service but not fully offered to its stakeholders. To what extent would you describe your school years, or your children's, as experiences in democracy? If you're a teacher, to what extent do your school and your district constitute democracies?

Democracy in the Classroom

For many valid reasons, most teachers find it nearly impossible to run their classrooms as democracies. Our educational system's philosophy doesn't value a student's basic need for self-determination, especially if the way students express their unique potential doesn't fit the pre-scribed curriculum. Neither do our schools foster kids' natural desire for connection, except to the extent it helps them achieve purely academic goals. I also found our educational model inhibits self-determination by attempting to treat everyone the same. Equal opportunity is crucial to a democracy. Yet equal opportunity does not mean expecting every child to learn the same material, at the same time, in the same way.

The way we educate children today is substantially the same as it was in the 1890s, when we embarked on a national mission to train children to become factory workers to fuel the Industrial Revolution. Like the assembly line, we moved all children through the same books at the same pace; we moved them from grade level to grade level whether or not they were ready. Anyone who didn't fit the mold was like a defective part, something of no value, to be cast aside. We treated children like machines: resources in, product out.

Despite the tremendous compassion the vast majority of teachers have for their students, we still generally apply this factory model in education. As we move from an industrial model to a communication and technology-based model, education is one of the last fields to change. As evidenced by modern discoveries in the sciences and brain research, in religion and spirituality, we are denying our students the greatness of who they truly are, and the richness and diversity of ideas that make America great. Ironically, my greatest successes in fostering a democratic classroom community took place in programs for the academically gifted, which I would not have described as a democratic approach. After all, I consider all children gifted, and to isolate just the academically gifted from their peers, singling them out for special treatment, seemed to me inequitable. It certainly wouldn't meet their need for connection with the larger community. It seemed to violate in some ways the democratic principle of equal opportunity.

I quickly saw another side to this issue: gifted children often feel isolated and alone in the regular classroom; they need to find each other, to support each other, to synergistically empower each others' gifts. I saw how the principle of honoring diversity supports meeting these needs. I still hold this debate as a question in my mind and heart, a question about fairness and justice that I have yet to resolve. Nonetheless, my experiences in gifted classrooms have opened a door to the possibilities for all children to become active citizens of the world.

The Children's Dream

In the early 1990s, I taught a self-contained gifted program for third graders at Sunnydale Elementary School in Seattle. It was a dream situation: I had eighteen highly talented children, phenomenal parent support, and freedom to develop a democratic student-centered program.

The theme in the classroom that year, 1992–93, was "Choices and Connections," two fundamental drives of all living things. Within that framework the students chose to try to understand child abuse and to make good choices for solutions. They knew a student (not from our class) who had been the victim of child abuse. This one incident engaged the children's attention and concern enough to determine the theme for the school year. In their breathtaking innocence, they simply couldn't understand: how it was possible? How can child abuse be tolerated in America? They named their quest, "The Children's Dream."

This same year Bill Clinton was elected to the presidency. Certainly our new president, who spoke so well and seemed to care so deeply, wouldn't allow child abuse to continue. So the children decided we needed to meet with him!

They worked hard toward that goal. Each student wrote two letters to the President a couple of months apart. (See appendix) In a letter to him from the whole class they wrote, "We talked about Martin Luther King, Jr. and Harriet Tubman in our class and how they had a dream of freedom. We have a dream similar to theirs and hope all children can be free of child abuse." The letter went on to propose a couple of potential solutions: classes on child abuse, and "improving the government so parents don't get so stressed they abuse their children, because we should look at the scar in the mind just as much as we look at the scar on the skin." In a postscript, the kids added, "Can we please have a picture of Socks? Please write back!" Socks, you'll remember, was the Clintons' cat.

In the last week of school, the class finally did get a response from the new president. He thanked them for their letters and apologized that he wouldn't be able to meet with them. "However," he wrote, "I will take your suggestions into consideration and will try to address these issues as I talk to people and give speeches around the country. I hope you will be listening and will continue to work toward your goals."

While they waited for the president to respond, these committed young citizens from Sunnydale Elementary School were not sitting on their hands. Writing letters to public officials was just the beginning. "Democracy is an action; it is something we do with love," wrote one third-grader.

Early in the school year they decided early they needed to know more about what, as citizens, they could do about child abuse. After talking with their parents, the parents agreed—in true democratic process— to join their children in this heartfelt quest. Students and parents decided to meet once a week in the evening to explore what was possible within that one school year to create a society free of child abuse. Each meeting was co-facilitated by a third grader and her or his parent. For six months, every week, we had nearly perfect attendance.

These meetings produced two goals. First, the students found sources of information. Experts were invited to speak to the class, and the children arranged to observe child abuse prevention and treatment programs. Second, they decided they needed to raise money. Either they would use the money to go to Washington, D.C., if the president would see them; or, if not, they would donate the money to help local child abuse prevention programs.

These third-graders and their parents set up five businesses for the purpose of raising funds. Inspired by the book *Sadako and the Thousand Cranes*, the students designed and sold T-shirts with a peace crane logo. They carried the peace crane theme over to stationery and jewelry they made and sold as well. They wrote and published a book of poetry on the subject of democracy (from which the quote atop this chapter is excerpted). And rounding out their enterprises, they made and sold pizzas.

In the end, they raised two thousand dollars for their cause and drew media and public attention. During a ceremony in Seattle's City Hall Park at the end of the school year, these eight and nine year-olds presented checks to two community organizations: one that ran a day treatment program for abused and neglected children; another that worked with incarcerated fathers to reduce the likelihood they would abuse children after parole. The ceremony took place on a day proclaimed by Seattle's Mayor Norm Rice as "End Child Abuse Day," in the middle of a week proclaimed by Washington State Governor Mike Lowry as "Sunnydale Elementary Dream Team Week."

Vision and Action: One Student's Experience

If you asked those kids today what they remember about third grade, it wouldn't be the proclamations and the commendations from public officials that would come to mind first. I am sure many of these kids would remember their mission to make a difference in the world and the pride and joy they took in carrying it out. They took seriously the motto: Vision without action is merely a dream. Action without vision just passes time. Vision and action can change the world.

On November 24, 2001, one of my students from this third grade class wrote me a letter. He was now a senior in high school. "You probably don't remember me," wrote Long Phan, but remember him I do. I remember every child in that class. Long's letter went on:

> The last few years have shaped my character, helped me to define my life's goals, and made me into the person I am today.... But it was the lessons I learned in your class that are still with me even now.
>
> When I first entered [your class], everyone close to me didn't believe I could keep up with a group of talented and gifted students. Nine years later, I am the Student Body President of my high school and at the top of my class with a solid 4.0 GPA.
>
> "Try to imagine yourself in the other person's moccasins." You always used to say this when our class would get out of hand, and this is something I have tried to apply to my own life.

Long went on to share with me some of his many accomplishments and commendations, from receiving a national Disney award to being a Washington state delegate to the National Association of Student Councils conference in North Carolina.

> As part of the trip, we stopped in our nation's capital where I said to myself, "I made it." ... The "Children's Dream" of getting to Washington was finally realized. Even though I didn't get to meet the President, at least I made it to his doorstep.
>
> I thank you for always believing in me. You have taught me more about life and "living" than I could ever imagine and I will always be grateful to you.

That precious year with the third graders, along with those unforgettable experiences in democratic citizenship, was its own reward, like eating dessert all year long. The letter from Long, eight years later, was icing on the cake.

Steps Toward Change

We've come a long way since the days of caning children to keep them submissive—a totalitarian exercise of the dominator model. Still, our traditional educational model has remained substantially unchanged in over one hundred years and has a long way to go before it can be said to support democracy and the partnership model.

Mahatma Gandhi said, "Be the change you want to see in the world." If we want to see democracy, we must *be* democracy—in the classroom and in the school's administration. But democracy is not the standard there. In general, the legislature dictates to the school boards, the school boards to the administrators, the administrators to the teachers, and the teachers to the students. Although, as I have said, most educators try with phenomenal compassion and dedication, their hands are tied. Curriculum, legal, testing, and program mandates all constrain teachers, making it quite difficult to do anything other than control children.

Research clearly shows that allowing children and teachers to be self-determining, within the limits of their responsibility to community, enhances academic achievement in the long term. Our educational system, indeed our entire culture, today is ripe with potential. Educational theorists, administrators, and teachers at every level are waking up to the possibilities of democracy, both within schools and between school and community, and implementing wonderful ways to practice it. Some of these approaches have found their way into the mainstream: participatory or interactive learning, cooperative learning, respecting diverse learning styles. More and more teachers are successfully adopting methods that haven't yet but may soon become the norm: service learning, peer teaching, project learning (driven by students interests), and student-centered classrooms.

In many ways, seeds of democracy are striving to take root in educational soil. For example, in the 1970s, the Free Schools movement created opportunities for children and teachers to exercise great creativity and self-determination. But the American public got nervous about the erosion of academic standards and the tendency of some programs to mistake anarchy for democracy.

Another example of a democratic ideal trickling down to schools took place in the 1980s and 1990s as decentralization and site-based decision-making became popular. Unfortunately, the decisions entrusted to individual school communities were relatively insignificant. The bigger questions, the ones that count—*What is education for? How should we structure school? What should we teach? How should we teach it?*—were not entrusted to a democratic process. Students were generally excluded from the process, and teachers weren't given release time to take part. Not surprisingly, the movement waned.

It's not only within the school but also in the larger society that experiences in democratic citizenship are withheld from our children. Though movements such as service learning and environmental education hold great promise for connecting students with the larger world, they form but a tiny slice of the educational pie at present. If an entire school or an entire classroom was oriented toward these endeavors, democracy could flourish—and achievement would follow kids' natural excitement. Test scores would soar.

These understandings are not limited to public education. Exciting democratic experiments have been taking place in private schools for decades. Even so, studies of private schools show that the vast majority is no more democratic than public schools. In fact, some would say, most private schools merely do the 'old stuff' better.

Further Steps

Philosophers and scientists say we are on the verge of a great transformation. Cosmologist Brian Swimme calls it a "macro-phase transition"—a change so monumental that it has only happened a few times in the history of the universe. Elisabet Sahtouris says it will transform the human race from "an immature, competitive species" to "a mature, cooperative" one. We must recognize that we are only one part of this living planet and that we need to make the transition to an Earth democracy before we destroy ourselves.

Where better to nurture this transformation than in public education? It is the one institution in our society that can still provide equal opportunity for all—a prerequisite for a living democracy. In the future we will take equal opportunity seriously. When we pave paths to self-determination and connection for poor people, people of color, and those with special challenges, just as we do for the rich and privileged, only then will we democratically co-create a future that uses everyone's gifts to make the world a better place.

Everyone who is committed to these principles can take small steps to create a democratic community as an inspirational model for what our society could be. Any caring teacher can do it. I did it. It involves listening to children—their needs, their wants, their concerns, their passions, their talents, and their styles. It involves encouraging children—to find their voice and express it, to make choices within the parameters that constrain us, and to exercise their rights and responsibilities to contribute to the greater good. It involves gently guiding children from the perspective of our experience and wisdom, while allowing them to discover answers for themselves. It ends, as it begins, with trusting children—trusting them to learn from their mistakes, to find the path that's right for them and their community, and to be fully who they are, as long as they don't harm themselves or others.

Classrooms of the future will be democratic mini-societies. In these classrooms, children's self-esteem and potential can evolve organically, not from their scores on standardized tests, but from joyful explorations and connections with their community.

These connections form the glue that binds together a healthy democracy. To forge them, we must dismantle the walls that separate us in the educational community: bricks of control and competition kept in place by the mortar of fear. These are the walls that separate administrators from teachers, teachers from students, and students from each other. They are the same walls that separate the school from the community that has created it and that it is supposed to serve. These walls divide children's minds from their hearts and souls. As long as we continue to define education as an exclusively cognitive endeavor, we do not nurture the full potential of the child and thus of our democratic society.

As we learn to trust our true nature and natural laws, we will learn to trust democratic processes in schools that allow each child, each adult, and each learning community to nurture its *independence* for the greater good of *interdependence*. We will be living the true meaning of democracy. Our schools can become a beacon to the global community.

Declarations and Affirmations

Living Participatory Democracy is an action; it is something we do. It is about giving all humans a voice and being advocates for those without a voice. It is the inclusive rights, responsibilities, and respect for all life. With only one earth and one humanity, we all have the privilege and responsibility to be partners in creating a world that works for all.

———

In the Schools of the Future I move from my ego center to my compassion center and honor all those who are different from me. I release, with kindness-to-myself, the false/self center which holds me in my ego center. I understand that the deepest democracy is dependent on me coming from my compassion center or true nature! I see the meaning this has, not only in America but also in how we relate to the world. I release my fear of a global community. I bring my democracy skills to share with others. Together, we facilitate a global community that represents the many diverse people of the world at the grass roots, rather than a powerful wealthy few at the top.

———

In the Schools of the Future we design the classrooms it will take to facilitate a world that works for all. We have curricula to honor all nations, just as America honors all states, or the European Union honors all European countries. We *refine* the United Nations, create or add a global parliamentary assembly voted on by all the people of the world that would offer an international court of justice and economic and social justice for the people of the world.

———

In the Schools of the Future we take the skills we have learned from our American Dream and with the people of the world build something even greater: we offer *a new birth of freedom* to the philosophy of education, as a part of global *spiritual civilization building* (to use the phrase minted by Dr. Richard J. Spady). The Teachers of the World help us learn from our forefathers, who wrote our Bill of Rights and the US Constitution and build a democratic global parliament elected by all the people. We adapt this for the global community or commonweal, the Family of Humanity glimpsed by poets, prophets and theorists of planetary civilization and world politics. In Schools of Love, we work and live together as a global, international-educational community and create a world that works for all.

———

Now is the time to begin building social and economic justice and a sustainable life style. This is the hour! Now we begin visualizing a peaceful, sustainable world. America, with all our flaws and greatness, has the experience as a new thriving country to inspire all other countries, for a global "Brave New World." Now we create, or co-create (with the life force or whatever words flow with your belief system) a world that works for all. For we are global citizens in StarSchools. We are operating, now and from now on, with the maximum of educational intelligence, love and joy, creating those imaginative lifestyles and works of art that are signs of the Teachers of Joy.

―――

Our deepest fear is not that we are inadequate.
Our deepest fear is that we are powerful beyond measure.
It is our light, not our darkness, that most frightens us.

Your playing small does not serve the World.
There is nothing enlightened about shrinking,
so that others people won't feel insecure around you

And, as we let our own light shine, we unconsciously give
other people permission to do the same.
As we were liberated from our fear,
our presence automatically liberates others.

NELSON MANDELA,
INAUGURATION SPEECH, 1993

CHAPTER NINE

Awakening Greatness

"**I love watching the greatness in people.** And I know the greatness is there in every human spirit."

This is how I was quoted in the newspaper when, in 1999, I was named Teacher of the Year for the Northern Mariana Islands. I had been teaching in what most Americans would consider a highly disadvantaged environment: a diverse mix of cultures for whom education was not generally a high priority, in a school with few of the conveniences most Westerners would consider necessities, a classroom without air conditioning in a stiflingly hot and humid climate.

Throughout my teaching career I've expressed a love of diversity by working with children from all over the world. After five years of teaching so-called "gifted" classes in Seattle, an opportunity arose for me in 1996 that seemed perfect—teaching a fifth grade class on the island of Saipan, in the Northern Marianas, equidistant from New Guinea, the Philippines, and Japan.

A classmate of my oldest son was from Saipan and my student teacher from the previous year was heading there to teach, so I had some passing knowledge of the culture. I became very interested, thinking it would be like a Peace Corps experience, but with pay, plus I'd have good medical attention (I was still watchful of my health from the Epstein-Barr Virus).

For a long time I'd wanted to know and understand Asia. This opportunity satisfied that desire—we had fifty-two cultures, mostly Asian, right on our small island of one hundred thousand people. I was also able to spend a summer traveling through Vietnam, Thailand, India, Nepal, Indonesia, and the Philippines, further expanding my experience of this continent.

The teaching situation turned out to be much more challenging than I'd expected—more difficult than the Peace Corps. Closer to the equator than Hawaii or Mexico City, Saipan was constantly hot, averaging eighty-five degrees during the day with intense humidity. Without air-conditioning, my classroom could become an oven. Many times I thought I might pass out. Overall, the students were a boisterous, emotional group. One veteran teacher I knew, who intended to teach on the island, visited a classroom and said, "No way, I'm out of here." At least one fourth of the teachers from the United States didn't finish out the first year. Reading scores were very low. The communities on the island had few material advantages and culturally did not value academic achievement. Although their island had been colonized for four hundred years, education for the indigenous people was new. All together this made for a difficult teaching experience.

However, I respected their values. In keeping with my views on greatness, I had learned to regard all students as gifted. Even so, that didn't make it easier to fulfill my commitment to keep twenty-five unique, energetic youngsters working together in a common direction. I had high expectations for my students, expectations that included working cooperatively and supportively, participating as respectful members of the classroom community, and finding solutions to problems together. None of that came to fruition until the spring. While most teachers gain control of their classroom early in the school year, I wanted to foster self-restraint and self-discipline through self-determination. That takes time, much more time than controlling with rewards or punishment.

There were no janitors at our school, so we became the janitors. Every week, my twenty-five students and I would carry buckets of water to our room and wash the floors. Once a month, we'd wax them. When the typhoons came, we'd carry the computers to a safe building a block away, and prepare our classroom for displaced families. These shared responsibilities helped begin the bonding process, to create the sense of a caring community that is a critical element in healthy learning environments.

The best way to describe my classroom management strategy is to say I looked for the inner potential in every one of my students. I see now it was simply the way I'd learned, quite unconsciously, to live in the world. It was only later I fully realized how the non-judgmental, minimally-restrictive relationship I had with my students opened the flood gates of creativity. I understood their boisterousness as an aspect of that creativity rather than as a challenge to my authority; and I encouraged their creative impulses, hoping to channel them into classroom projects. I was intrigued they were using recess and break times to create dances, for which they'd often bring their own music. This fit in well with the island traditions.

I so enjoyed giving my kids time and support for their creativity it began to infuse their academic pursuits—social studies projects, science experiments, and the like. Toward the end of the school year I asked them if they'd like to perform a play. The class president, vice-president, and secretary proposed a play about Martin Luther King to the class, and much to my delight, they went for it. I wasn't sure they would; it meant quite a mature commitment to consistent hard work and dedication in a complex group effort.

As I said, my standards were high; I wanted them to be proud of the process as well as the outcome of their choices. My ten and eleven-year-old fifth graders loved acting and practiced every day. Never before had a class performed a play for the whole school, but this class wanted to. They were willing to work until they got it right—and they practiced in a collaborative spirit, which they knew I valued deeply. I began to trust their often impulsive behavior enough to let them work outside the room in small groups. Most of the time they didn't break the rules they themselves helped create. Still there were incidents, such as when three students were denied a field trip because they jumped into a hotel swimming pool immediately after I'd asked them not to. I tried, through my response to these incidents, to let them know that I cared too much about them to sacrifice the smooth functioning of the group for their own individual impulses.

There was, however, enough rambunctious behavior so that by the end of the year I was simply exhausted. So I was both surprised and hesitant when my students and their parents asked me to teach them again in sixth grade. I agreed, though I must admit reluctantly. Then a miracle occurred.

Small Miracles

When we returned to school in the fall, there had been a transformation. Suddenly, it seemed the students almost didn't need a teacher. Through the experience of producing and performing the play about Martin Luther King, and the truly collaborative spirit they created in the process, they had matured. Perhaps it had given them a sense of their own inherent worth. My new sixth graders wanted to collaborate with their parents and the entire school population to form a community working for a better world. They wanted to *be* little Martin Luther Kings. It practically brought me to tears. It was the first time I'd had the same kids two years in a row. It was also the first time I could really stand back and see the impact of my teaching.

The class wanted to start immediately on all kinds of fascinating projects. They made a top-twenty list. Every project was about doing some good in the world. They wasted no time. Among the projects was another play, but this time they wanted to write it themselves; so they did. The theme was biodiversity—they even wrote a rap for it. It was so well liked we were asked to perform it at the community center for all interested villagers.

An even bigger project, as it turned out, was to design and create a large mural on the school's outside wall. That took several months. They began by creating their individual visions of what they wanted for the world. Imagine the challenge of transferring those ideas into a two-dimensional visual form. They took their individual visions and shared them in small groups, looking for ways to combine them. Finally, the small-group visions were brought to the whole class, and we worked together to unite them into one integrated whole.

The result was phenomenal. They approached the mural project like the gifted students I knew they were; I was merely the facilitator. They decided to paint a huge globe in the middle of the wall, with images from their island on one side and images from the universe on the other. They labeled it "One World, One Heart." The final touch was inviting all three hundred and fifty children at school to put their handprints on the frame around the mural. The whole school felt ownership. This painting made such an impact in the community a television news team came to interview the class.

At the end of World War II, the Japanese lined up whole families, ordering them to jump to their deaths on the rocks below rather than be taken into custody by the Americans, who were about to liberate the island from Japanese rule. This cliff is now known as Suicide Cliff. Every day, a busload of Japanese tourists would pass right by our school, right by the new mural, on the way to Suicide Cliff. When one boy was asked on TV what purpose the mural served, he replied, "If we can just change one heart it will be worth it."

Designing and painting a bigger-than-life work of art by a committee of twenty-six was enough of a challenge; but I really thought they were trying to move mountains when the student council started to talk about declaring the school junk food free. The on-going presence of the American military on the island since the end of World War II resulted in a less than healthy influence on Saipan's eating habits. Spam was the meat of choice for many kids. Candy and soda were ubiquitous. Kids would walk to class sucking on one kind of tooth-decaying treat or another.

Our vice-principal, however, had a Master's degree in dietary health—and a mission. The student council agreed with her that good health should be promoted. They presented the idea of a junk-food-free campus to the PTA and the teachers. Everyone agreed that the only way to take a consistent stand would be to close the entire campus to junk food (—no exceptions!): no unhealthy snacks at lunch, no candy at school festivals or games.

Like any challenging project, this called for creativity. Each class in the school discussed what constituted "junk food" and made a list of what shouldn't be allowed. Parents were brought into the process. For classroom celebrations, we brainstormed together and decided what we wanted to eat: cheese and crackers, fruit smoothies, carrots and celery with dip. I'd bring a blender to school.

Greatness can only flower when our bodies are healthy and whole. Unfortunately, in the United States efforts to ban junk food on school campuses are almost always thwarted by corporate power—and by teachers unwilling to remove candy and soda machines from the teachers' lounge.

Our school administrators truly believed in a team approach, which included students, parents, faculty, and other community members. They took to heart the adage that together all of us are smarter than any of us alone. The work my sixth graders undertook truly became projects of the whole village.

Bringing the Peacebuilders program to our school was a great example. Peacebuilders is a simple but universal curriculum based on a commitment each child makes every day—a commitment to build peace at home, at school, and in the community, to find win/win solutions for problems. At school verbal put-downs were a problem. Thanks to our team approach, when we started teaching the Peacebuilders' conflict-resolution skills in school, parents taught them at home as well. As a result, kids were exposed to a consistent vision and given the tools to make it a reality. Hurtful teasing ground to a halt.

For inner greatness to emerge, we must feel both physically and emotionally safe—to risk, to explore, to create. Bullying erodes safety. Yet even an effective program like Peacebuilders can't be effective on its own. It needs the support of courageous leaders and parents who recognize its value and inspire the whole community to work for it.

Looking back on that second year in Saipan, with the same students who'd worn me out the year before, it was one of the peak experiences of my teaching career. Given a little time and a lot of support, these youngsters expressed their potential in every project they undertook, every world problem they wanted to solve, every story written in the school newspaper they designed, edited, produced, and delivered in their free time.

Rewards

Watching and celebrating their amazing growth was the most fulfilling reward I could imagine. But as they say, when it rains—and, oh, how it rains in Saipan—it pours. That year I received the honor of being named 1999 Teacher of the Year for the Northern Mariana Islands— an honor conferred by a selection committee of sixteen national education associations, based on nominations from the local community. It was an honor to represent them, knowing they felt my humanity and joined their hearts with mine.

This was the beginning of a year-long odyssey that culminated in meeting President Bill Clinton. As I shook his hand, I thought of the third-grade class that had so longed for a meeting with him back in 1992. They were all with me in spirit.

The Teacher of the Year program was not simply an acclamation with a certificate attached to it. It was a year-long leadership program, its own road to greatness, sponsored by Scholastic, Inc. and the Council of Chief State School Officers. I was joined by fifty-four other Teachers of the Year (representing fifty states and five American territories and protectorates) in four weeklong leadership training experiences spread out over the year. We spent a week in Texas getting to know each other and sharing our visions for education. We trained for a week at Space Camp in Huntsville, Alabama. The third week was an experience in mission statements, media savviness, and public relations to enhance our competence as teacher leaders.

For our last week together, we gathered in Washington, D.C., to focus on leadership and meet our elected officials. While we were there, two troubled boys shot and killed fifteen people, including themselves, at Columbine High School in Littleton, Colorado. My roommate for the week was the Teacher of the Year from Colorado. It was an enormous shock, a wake-up call for what violence is doing to our children.

Through my tears, I discovered within me a gathering resolve to offer not just my students, but the world, a different vision of greatness—a vision not of power, acquisition, and violence, but one of compassion, connection, and creativity. A vision of greatness where we consider our choices, have the opportunity to imagine the world we want to live in, and have the space to create it.

I know the wolf we feed is the wolf that wins. Either we can feed a destructive power or a visionary one that celebrates the greatness in each of us.

Light in our Brain

In neurobiology, one of the new sciences of the human mind, scientists are now seeing light in our brain via PET scans. They can watch the brain of the child light up when a significant other comes in the room. Neuropsychiatrist Allan Schore has elucidated how this works: "The primary caregiver of the child (let us say here, the mother) infuses the child's internal electromagnetic energy. The child in turn infuses the mother via sympathetic vibration of light—we call these emotions—as child and mother navigate their attachment."[30] For the growing child, this light of attachment is the most powerful light in their universe. This is what physicists call "light coherence" or attachment of light to light. Light loves light, light needs light, light is attracted to and attaches to light. And finally, we are now discovering the human brain and body feel best in a well-ordered coherence of light cells and activity.

Amazingly, scientists can now even watch the light of the child as it is affected by stress. They can see it on PET scans and read it from stress hormone indicators. In other words, says neurobiologist Michael Gurian,

"Children who are under significant and constant emotional stress show impeded light activity on PET scans. Where a normal child would show light activity of neurons firing, the chronically stressed child shows dark spots on the brain. That child's brain has been altered by stress."

Defining Greatness

Today in education, as in most of society's institutions, we define greatness in narrow ways. We give lip service to values like compassion, integrity, creativity, diversity, and celebrating uniqueness. Yet, the media bombards our children with powerful messages promoting conformity, competition, superficiality, and domination well before they are old enough to think for themselves. Our StarSchools will be great in *collaboration*.

School should be a haven from these harmful media messages. As educators we must accept our share of responsibility for how kids define success. So much of what we do in schools teaches students the value of defeating others in the pursuit of their own extrinsic rewards. When a teacher, trying to stop cheating, says, "I want to know what you can do, not what your neighbor can do," she sends the message that learning is a solitary, competitive enterprise dependent on someone else's approval. It isn't. When we give a grade of F, the message the student hears is, "I'm no good." When we give a grade of A, the student hears, "There's no point in challenging myself further. I've done as well as I can."

We measure achievement in strictly cognitive terms. The arts, for example, are incorrectly deemed non-cognitive. They are given short shrift in schools, despite what we know about creativity and higher order thinking. Then we standardize this strictly academic achievement by testing everyone on exactly the same questions, in exactly the same subjects, at exactly the same time. This curious brand of achievement is all our educational culture seems to prize. We're constantly finding new ways to control children—and teachers—to produce higher standardized results. The sad irony is that the only thing that standardized test results predict in life is the ability to perform on other standardized tests.

We've reached a stunning degree of maturity in the potential for human development today. We have the answers we need to create a world that works for all. What we yet lack is a widespread understanding of what greatness truly is—authentic power "to" or "with," not power "over." Philosophers and neurobiologists see greatness or our authentic power as accessing higher levels of human development. Synthesizers of brain research like Joseph Chilton Pearce, Daniel Amen, and John deMartini would likely agree. Social theorist Lawrence Kohlberg's hierarchy suggests that at lower levels of moral development we act out of a desire for pleasure, or a need for control or conformity. Our greater potential is only realized at the highest level of moral development, in which our behavior follows universal principles of justice and respect for individual dignity. This greatness is a birthright of every human.

Others cannot instill this potential in us—it can only be nurtured—and requires an environment of freedom and trust. Open expression and exploration, our creativity, is the key to growth and fulfillment. It is also the essence of our holistic interconnectedness, as Robert Fritz, author of *Creating* notes, "The act of a person creating is the act of a whole person."[31]

Creativity is quite simply the force that drives evolution.

When we are fearful, our creativity turns towards survival and protection. Our brain shifts down and we go into a survival reflex of fight or flight. Like a clam at the seashore, when danger approaches, we close up tightly in this fear mode. Our higher-level thinking and creative problem solving abilities freeze. Just as a clam digger can fill buckets when the clams are closed tightly, our leaders can manipulate and control us when we are in a state of fear.

Psychologists have studied dozens of contemporary and historical figures who embodied greatness. They found all turned to an inner knowing for their wisdom. Isaac Newton said new visions and new ideas would come to him when he sat quietly. Einstein sat silently every day for inner connection. The great French writer Paul Valery valued "those moments of leisure when thought practices simply existing. Every day more Americans are coming to realize the value of quietness and inner knowing. Every day we are learning to know ourselves better."[32]

And what about the clamshell that stays closed? What is the opposite of openness and creativity? Lt. Col. Dave Grossman spent over 20 years in the military learning and studying how to enable people to kill. "Believe me, we are very good at it," Grossman said in an article in the *Saturday Evening Post*. "But it does not come naturally. You have to be taught to kill."[33] This is extremely difficult, he notes, because our brains are programmed with "a powerful, God-given resistance to killing our own kind. ... Men are willing to sacrifice themselves for their nation; but they are not willing to kill. When the military became aware of this phenomenal insight into human nature they systematically went about the process of trying to fix this 'problem.'"

How did they do it? By desensitizing soldiers to killing, through repeated, graphic images of violence—precisely what your child experiences at the movies or in video games. "Today," Grossman concludes, "the data linking violence in the media to violence in society are superior to those linking cancer and tobacco." Can anyone deny the preponderance of role models in the media guiding us more toward violence and domination than compassion and cooperation?

It is incumbent on teachers and leaders and parents to model a different way of being. As Gandhi said, "we must be the change we want to see in the world."

Declarations and Affirmations

Greatness is about honoring our inherent worth and the inherent worth in all, about inspiring and empowering one another to reach for our highest potential, our truest self. Schools of greatness are schools of love and harmony.

The Teachers of the World move us from competitive habits, which pit us against one another, to a place where we all can win. Global citizenship schools teach us to rethink my life style so I am meeting my needs, but not consuming more than I need. There I transition to a simpler life style that gives me more time and energy for what I truly value. There I mindfully and lovingly consider my needs and the needs of all the people of the earth. There I teach what I truly value. There I am giving my highest values the time and energy they deserve.

———

The Teachers of the World want to *know* my best talents and skills. StarSchools are where we are using these in the best way to nourish self and all those in our world. StarSchools are where my values work for me and the larger world to which I belong, where I feel my life style and chosen work are nourishing my whole self—mind, body, emotions and spirit—in ways that honor the greatness in me and all those around me. There, teachers, students, school administrators and educational journalists can honor greatness even when changing the chalk, the school uniform, or the school cat's litter box.

———

StarSchools are where we take time each day to be mindful of what we are doing and to foster deep connections with those we care most about, where we make time for quieting our center (choose words that flow for you—soul, life, God, love, spirit, etc in prayer, meditation, open space, the arts and/or movement). They are *healthy schools*—where choose food that is healthy and balanced from the near-by community that is free of chemicals, where we can eat mindfully and grow in awareness of our values and what works best in a world that works for all, where we honor the body as the temple of the spirit, giving the body fresh, clean air, breathing deeply and finding ways to exercise our whole body in ways that nourish deepest longings.

———

How might I let my greatness shine, like the sun, in ways that nourish, rather than diminish? How do I rest like the moon and continue to shine? How do I let go of old belief patterns that no longer work and honor the new space and sense of lightness I feel. In what ways does the life force fill my body and connect me with all that is?

———

The Schools of Tomorrow are where I use my unique greatness, my gifts and talents, my life force, to create with others a school and a world that works for all.

———

*Hard material necessity and human evolutionary possibility now seem
to converge to create a situation where, in the long run, we will be
obliged to do no less than realize our greatest possibilities. We are
engaged in a race between self-discovery and self-destruction. The
forces that may converge to destroy us are the same forces that may
foster societal and self-discovery.*

DUANE ELGIN

*"The church's own witness should be understandable by the smallest
child: we oppose violence in all its forms. And we do so because we
reject domination. That means, the child will recognize, no beatings.
That means women will hear, no battering. That means, men will
gradually understand, no more male supremacy of war. That means,
everyone will realize, no more rape of the environment. The church
must affirm nonviolence without reservation because nonviolence is the
way."*

WALTER WINK
FROM *ENGAGING THE POWERS*
WWW.CONTEMPLATENONVIOLENCE.ORG

C H A P T E R   T E N

World Peacebuilder Schools:
Problems as Opportunities

The Teachers of the World are teachers of resourcefulness, of world problem-solving, of new ways of looking at things old and new. What looks like a crisis is not always a crisis, but is often an opportunity to see things in a new way. The Chinese ideogram for crisis is the combined images of danger and opportunity. In our modern society, we often focus on the danger and fail to see the potential opportunities. Crises are where we have the greatest chance to grow. They are evolutionary drivers, propelling us forward, helping us to see the world in new ways, shifting how we think. With a creative problem solving mindset any problem becomes an opportunity.

September 11, 2001

It's become a cliché to say that September 11 changed the world forever. It is less of a cliché to see September 11 as a gift; but in spite of the tragedy and terror, it was clearly also a gift. It is important to note

September 11 was not an isolated event, unrelated to the past or future; rather, it was a culmination of a long trail of incendiary and ignored feelings that burst onto the global scene at that particular moment. In response to the war-mongering and the incessant emphasis on terrorism, a growing peace movement took off. On the occasion of receiving an award for his service to the United Nations, Dr. Robert Muller, a former assistant Secretary General of the UN, caught the mood of the new peace movement in his remarks. He startled his discouraged audience by saying, "I'm so honored to be here. I'm so honored to be alive at such a miraculous time in history. I'm so moved by what's going on in our world today." For, "never before in the history of the world has there been a global, visible, public, viable, open dialogue and conversation about the very legitimacy of war."[34] This was what it looked like, he said, to be "waging peace." For Muller the opportunity for global dialogue that emerged is a miracle. It is true; this global dialogue has engaged a diverse population.

The events following September 11 allowed a global dialogue to unfold, which is clearly a gift. I, too, was given a gift by September 11. I was given the means—time off with pay—to write this book. I had just signed a new one-year teaching contract, but because the school district's administration was gripped with the same fears sweeping the nation in the wake of the terrorist attacks, my philosophy of "One World, One Humanity" was viewed with suspicion and ultimately was the reason for my termination. This termination was also, like all endings, a beginning: the beginning of my new life as what Dr. Richard S. Kirby calls "A Teacher of the World".

For over thirty years, this philosophy of unity and interconnectedness has been the cornerstone of my teaching. I have taught it to students on three continents, in four U.S. states, and in over ten public school districts, while working in Africa, the Middle East, Micronesia, and various American multicultural areas. In addition, because of my teaching methods and unique curriculum, I have been repeatedly recognized for teaching excellence, and even recognized at the national level as a Teacher of the Year in 1999.

But in January 2002, in a middle-class school district near Seattle, Washington, the philosophy of "One World, One Humanity" was deemed dangerous and even evil. The school administrator made it very clear: "Either stop teaching interconnectedness or stop teaching in this school district."

The choice was simple: teach the truth and leave, or ignore the truth and stay. It was heartbreaking to leave my fifth grade class with whom I had shared so much, and it was equally frustrating and stressful not to be allowed to talk with their parents and families during the course of the termination. But I knew I must stand up for the truth. I knew this crisis was an opportunity and I was being called to share the rationale for unity with a larger audience, taking the message and ideas out beyond the classroom.

A Peacebuilders School

I began the 2001/2002 school year with excitement. Before signing the contract, I met with some of the current staff, looked over the school environment, met with the new principal, and liked what I saw. The principal was a rookie, but young and excited about his new job. Best of all, the school was a Peacebuilders School. I was familiar with and loved this unifying character development program. It provided for building peace at home, in the schools, and in the community.

Each morning, in our school, the children said the Peacebuilders Pledge: "I am a Peacebuilder; I pledge to build peace every day; at home, at school and in my community. I pledge to give up put-downs; to right wrongs, to seek wise people, and to heal differences. I pledge to build peace at home, at school and in my community, every day."

The pledge was reinforced by activities, wall posters, and awards for students involved in Peacebuilding activities. This beautiful and effective program encourages the children to use words to find peaceful solutions to problems, to work creatively and cooperatively, and to recognize each other's strengths.

My Interconnected Classroom

When I met the children the first day of school, I noticed that some lacked a sparkle in their eyes and a few even seemed sad. When we began by sharing about ourselves they seemed to light up a little. I explained how I loved to see the greatness in each child bloom and grow. I showed them how I wanted to connect with each one of them individually. I stand by the door and each child chooses a way to greet me: they can give me a handshake, a hug, or a high-five. We begin and end the day this way. This greeting routine is one small yet direct way I teach we are connected to one another.

Besides the daily greeting, I always establish other routines to teach the children the value of connection and community. I use class meetings in which every morning we sit in a circle on the floor and discuss issues of importance to the students, the class, the school, our families, and the outside community. The children are free to raise issues and problems— no subjects are off limits. The students learn to regard problems and crises as opportunities and possibilities—opportunities to heal and the possibility of solutions, and. In this way we create together our own atmosphere for learning, with the children taking responsibility for what happens in their classroom. We learn how to solve problems without blaming, name-calling, fighting, or bullying. Like many classrooms across the country focused on development of the whole child, class meetings have always been an integral part of the structure of my classroom.

Our connections form a vast dynamic web humming with life and change. Many spiritual traditions of the past have honored this whole-ness, this unity. For the first time in our history there is a clear link between science and the ancient indigenous traditions and spiritual or religious truths. While some cultures have always lived this truth, we in the West are just beginning to develop words for this unity. We are at the beginning of a huge transformation, a global mind change.

Just as it took over four hundred years for some to accept the world was round, this belief in our interconnectedness and not being separate beings is hard for many people to believe. However, this is not just some people's ideas and musings, but hard and inescapable scientific fact. Eleven-year old children are not too young to understand the implications of the great new discoveries happening in almost every scientific discipline. They need a variety of opportunities to explore, dialogue, and understand themselves: what it means to be human, and how to understand this emerging new story. We as parents, grandparents, teachers, citizens, and leaders need even more time and opportunity. Shifting our thinking to a new worldview is hard work. Our species is being pushed and pulled to grow and evolve into one more loving, compassionate, and connected.

Many educators today write about the loneliness of our children and their lack of connectedness. When we teach our children we all belong to the web of life, they are more grounded and centered, and filled with self-worth and a sense of value.

Caterpillars—a Metaphor of Hope

The school year started off well. Although only a week into the school year, by September 11 the children were becoming fully involved. I loved seeing the sparkle grow in the eyes of this fifth grade class. On September 11, the class meeting was especially important. That morning we sat in a circle on the floor and shared our feelings and questions about the tragedy happening in New York and Washington. The children wanted to know why this had happened. They were curious and so open in trying to understand there were people who didn't like Americans, let alone hate them enough to kill them. The children's focus was especially on the terrible pain of those caught in the World Trade Center. Children are naturally wise. One of them suggested we could practice our Peacebuilders principles by trying to connect and understand instead of just reacting out of fear and anger.

One student brought caterpillars to school to observe and share with the class. During the time we sat in the circle, the caterpillars were in the center in a small cage, and they started to cling to the top of the cage in preparation for cocooning. One child said, "Gosh, look at the caterpillars—they're acting just like what is happening to the people trapped in the World Trade Center. They're in darkness, they're in a cocoon, and they don't know what's happening to them." Inspired by the metaphor, I asked a student to get a pen and paper and write down the ideas. What else did they see in these cocoons? A list of twenty different metaphors, or combinations of metaphors, about the caterpillars and their transformation resulted: *We're trapped/shaking; The world is changing; Evolving; We're sad and scared; Lonesome; We're frightened; They're going to be free; They're going to turn into beautiful butterflies; Evolved; They'll fly and go places; We keep growing; We do new things; We keep going toward; We have to believe; Beginning of new life; We have to have faith; We have to trust; Love; Forgive; Hope.*

Peacebuilders in Action

During the following days, as the country learned more from the media, friends, and families, the children explored and shared ideas about why anyone might hate America enough to bomb us. September 11 wounded us Americans deeply and opened everyone's hearts to the victims. However, not all our hearts were fully opened; many wanted to kill someone in revenge. Some Americans reacted with guilt, some with compassion, some with anger, some with blind patriotism. When I see cars driving around with their flags waving I ask myself, are we simply acting as patriots, displaying our glitter and pointing our fingers? Or can we be authentic patriots, drawing on the wisdom of our hearts and minds to connect with those in different cultures? In our Star Schools we learn to be *Planetary Patriots*. Then our loyalty is global, our work is what Dr. Richard J. Spady terms *Spiritual Civilization Building*

We all heard, most of us for the first time, of Osama bin Laden and how he was being accused as the mastermind of the tragedy. As Peacebuilders, the class decided to write letters to him we wouldn't actually send, practicing both letter-writing and Peacebuilders principles. I encouraged the children to ask questions and express their feelings as a way of trying to understand. One poignant example:

Dear Osama bin Laden,

Please don't hurt the U.S.A. Please tell me why you feel angry, sad, frightened. I just want to understand your feelings. I'm a Peace-Builder so I try to give peace. I know you understand that peace is important to all, especially the children. I want to teach EVERY-ONE about Peace-Building skills.

Sincerely,

Poetry from the Heart

On another occasion, a few weeks later, we read in our textbook about P.L. Travers, the author of Mary Poppins. When asked how she got her ideas, she said she just sat quietly and let them come to her. So I asked the children if they'd like to try out P.L. Travers' method, to sit quietly and see what comes to them. They all liked the idea, so we set aside some time for them to sit and listen to their inner thoughts. One student wrote:

When I sit in peace and quiet all these ideas come to me. I sit with a pen and a paper and I jot imaginations down. Then when it comes, I think of a sentence in my head for my paragraph then I write it down. I don't have to shut my eyes for my imagination. I come up with good ideas.

Using P.L. Traver's example, the children wrote poetry about their feelings. Some of the school staff who read these poems were as touched as I was by the beauty, compassion, and curiosity flowing from these children's hearts. I talked to a friend of mine about how I might better support and facilitate this creativity. She suggested I call a local poet named Vicki Edmonds to come and teach about writing poetry. During her three visits, Vicki Edmonds taught the children to use poetry to communicate their fears and learn about themselves. They wrote poetry on topics such as "What I can do right now," "My Power," and "My Greatness."

Wherever I shared the children's poetry, people felt it was important for the world to hear the wisdom coming from these children. After receiving approval from my principal and the district office, I contacted the local daily newspaper. They seemed to be as excited as I was about the children's writing; they ran a large article, including many examples of the children's poetry.[35] Such as:

> My power is like a tree giving out oxygen
> to plants and to people.
> Also if I get cut down I want to be made
> into a table and bring people together
> and have dinner and laugh.
> My power is like a boat
> I can sail people all around the world.
> My power is like a baseball bat
> and hit 800 homeruns and make a person famous.

We are All Teachers

As a general practice, I often invited diverse people from the community to visit our classroom and enrich the children's experience. Since we were studying oceans in the fifth grade and getting ready to read *The Island of the Blue Dolphins*, I asked Dennis Smith, a specialist in ecotourism, to come share his passion for dolphins and talk to the students about finding their own gifts, special intelligences, and passions.

We had a visit from our U.S. Representative, who after reading the student's writing in the newspaper, called the school and asked our principal if he could visit our class to congratulate the students on the beautiful poetry they'd written.

That November I turned sixty, and my 92-year-old mother and her friend came up from Oregon to attend my birthday celebration. I invited friends, past and present students, and their families to celebrate with us at a nearby state park. During her stay, my mother and her friend came to visit my class for an hour during school time. I like my students to experience connecting with someone very old, because I want them to realize that growing older is natural and a good thing; our elders can teach us so much. For this reason I also asked one of the children's grandfathers to come and talk to the class about his experiences in the Korean War.

We also invited one of the children's mothers, a nurse, to come to class and talk with us about the importance of good nutrition. We studied the food pyramid and discussed what makes healthy bodies and brains. Since we all ate our lunches together in the classroom, we explored foods that would make healthy lunches. In my bi-monthly newsletter to the parents, I shared some of the new research on nutrition and its impact on children's learning. During our class meetings we talked about alternatives for birthday and party celebrations, like fruit drinks or smoothies in place of Coke, and assortments of colorful vegetables and dips in place of cake, candy, or chips.

Citizens of America and the World

I have always encouraged learning about other nations and cultures in my classes. Having recently spent four years in Saipan, I had many experiences that I could share with the children. Because my son was teaching fifth grade in Saipan that year, this opportunity was even greater; we arranged for our classes to correspond with each other, assigning individual pen pals. I had done this while abroad and the previous year in a neighboring school district. Both classes loved this program.

We also participated in President Bush's program of sending one dollar from each child to a child in Afghanistan, and we added a letter from each child to President Bush. We also wrote to the children in Afghanistan and made peace cranes for them. With wide-open hearts, the children participated eagerly. One letter read:

Dear President Bush,

I wanted to send a dollar to Afghanistan because they are very poor and they need help. That must be a bad feeling and I want to help them. I've been making flags and selling them for $2.00 each. I'm giving them to the children of New York for the kids who lost their family. I feel very strongly for people that need help and I do whatever I can.

Sincerely,

Teamwork and Cooperation: We Are All Gifted

As a teacher it is my goal to reach each of my students. At the first of every school year I always work with my students to identify their intelligences, strengths, gifts, and passions. We then discuss ways to connect so we can support each other.

Howard Gardner, a researcher and educator, was one of the first to popularize the notion that humans have many kinds of intelligence. Naturalist, Body/Kinesthetic, Interpersonal, Intrapersonal, Verbal/Linguistic, Logical/Mathematical, Visual/Spatial, Musical/Rhythmic, and Existentialist are the nine intelligences he identifies. Our educational system traditionally focuses on only two of these, mathematical and linguistic. Likewise, these intelligences are the only two our state and national testing, college entrance exams, and I.Q. tests recognize. As we become more and more focused on teaching to these tests, our teaching narrows on only two of these nine intelligences. Because of this narrow focus to the exclusion of the other intelligences, the educational system fails many of our students, particularly those that embody the other seven intelligences. These are not stupid kids. They simply have different gifts, strengths, and learning styles than those that are traditionally rewarded by our school system.

Our school motto, given out to all students and their families at the beginning of the year, was: "Awakening, Empowering, Enlightening World Class Kids." In our classroom the guiding principle was that we all had abilities and gifts, and it was important to share them with each other. This is the core of collective intelligence and collective wisdom—combining our individual strengths to create something that is more powerful than any of us alone. In this method, each of the children looked for their individual gifts. If a child was good in writing, then he could share his gift with someone else with a gift for math. If a child was good at computers, she could share her gift with someone with a gift for dancing. This identification and sharing was a way to support and nurture one another. It was also a way for everyone to succeed and to shine. The children were wildly enthusiastic, and my classroom was always bustling with people helping others, working to improve how they communicate. The children liked learning about themselves and wrote about their family member's and their own intelligences. Here's an example:

> My mom has a musical intelligence. She likes to sing. She also has
> an interpersonal intelligence. She works well with people. My dad
> has a physical intelligence. He plays racket ball. He plays at least
> two times a month. My brother is an intrapersonal person. He loves
> to read. He also loves to play on the computer.

Self-Reflection/Evaluation

When report card time rolls around, I include the students in this process as well. I ask them to evaluate their own work, keep a portfolio of special projects and reports, and complete a report card on themselves. This allows them to cultivate the skill and inner tool of self-reflection. We then compare their report card to the one I write for them. When there were differences, we set a time to meet together. The students must come prepared to justify why they feel they should get a different grade. Of course I always had the final say, but I encouraged the children to participate in the process. At the parent conferences, I asked the children to attend and actually run the conference. They showed their parents their work, explaining what the lesson was about, and what they had learned. They explained why they had received their particular scores or grades. In this way the children learn both responsibility for themselves and that they are not at the mercy of others' expectations or judgments.

A Personal Opportunity

The last day of school before the winter holiday was a party day for our class. We invited their fourth grade teacher and her current class to our room. Students had formed committees to plan the activities. They brought board games, music, and a feast of food from their homes. Some children made holiday greeting cards or practiced drama, while others folded peace cranes to give to their families, firemen in our community, or the children in Afghanistan. At the end of the day, we gave our hugs and waves of good-bye, arms loaded with books, gifts, and party leftovers. It was a great day.

Upon returning to school, we shared our vacation experiences in the circle and then got down to work. Two days later as I was preparing to close up my classroom for the weekend, the principal came into my room and told me to get a substitute for the following Monday. He said I had been accused of belonging to a religious cult, and I must meet with the district's Elementary Curriculum Supervisor the following Monday, January 7.

This has to be a joke, I thought. Laughing, I said, "What are you talking about? Who would think such a thing?" His reply stunned me, "Well you do discuss quantum physics in here, don't you? You do belong to a group?" I said, "You mean the millions of people in the world called "Cultural Creatives?"[36] He would not elaborate or answer any more questions.

When I arrived for the meeting on Monday, I was met by three men: the union representative, the school principal, and the District Administrator. I came prepared for the meeting with lots of my own resource materials and credentials. Of course they had seen much of this at the time they hired me. I also brought examples of creative student work, unit test scores, and our class book of poetry. But it soon became evident they were not interested in anything I had to show, say, or discuss. My teaching ideas, this scientifically-based, life-affirming philosophy, were accused of being "so awful, so horrible, so terrible" that they could not be allowed in the classroom.

I tried to understand what could they be talking about. "What ideas, what philosophy?" are you talking about? Finally it became clear. What disturbed them the most was the idea of exploring our interconnectedness—that we are one family as seen from space. Their agenda was to get me to stop teaching we are all interconnected, we belong to one world, we are one family. The only alternative they offered was termination.

I explained I had been teaching these ideas for the past twenty-five years. The administrator said to me, "Take these ideas to Seattle where they are wanted. They are not wanted here." Later, when I went to talk with the School Superintendent and showed her materials verifying that our interconnectedness had been taught in public education for the past twenty-five years in some places, she responded, "Not in these political times. I don't think so."

Several days later, the district administrator said, "Maybe we saved you from being burned at the stake." Over lunch that day, my union representative gave me a piece of paper, with the date January 7, and a list of parent complaints—but no names, nothing official, nothing on letterhead. These were notes he said had been taken at a parent's meeting on January 7.

Here are some highlights:

1. The parents did not like my ideas about food. They felt I had no right to tell their children what to eat. If they wanted to bring Coke and candy to class, it was not my business.

2. The parents did not like their children writing letters to Osama bin Laden, even if it was to practice Peacebuilders skills with no intention of sending the letters. It was unpatriotic. No other teacher had their class write letters to Afghan children, either.

3. The parents did not like what they called "tribal meetings (circle time)." We should not be discussing problems like bullying. We should not be discussing another religion, especially the Muslim religion. We should not be discussing why the girls are not allowed to wear short-shorts to school, even if the principal had brought it to my attention as a concern for some in my classroom.

4. The parents did not like me teaching the children to "sit quietly" like the author in our fifth grade reader, P.L. Travers, who shared using this method for getting ideas for *Mary Poppins*. They didn't like me asking the children to listen to their own thoughts and feelings and write them in poetry. They equated this with a weird religion or prayer, and this wasn't allowed in school.

5. The parents did not want me to talk about Saipan any more, and to discontinue the pen pal letter idea with my son's fifth grade class. I should stick to America. Saipan had no relevance to their children.

6. The parents did not like it that I brought in outside experts to teach their children, like the man who spoke about dolphins. They didn't like it that the children were helping each other, this wasted their time. They didn't think the parents needed to be so involved in everything; they didn't want to review and sign their child's homework every week. They interpreted all these things as examples of my "laziness".

7. The parents thought that I should not have brought my mother to class. One parent evidently remarked that old people had no place in schools, and as a matter of fact, at sixty, I was too old to be a teacher! They also thought it was weird that I invited everyone to my birthday party. No other teacher had ever done that.

The one constant in these complaints was my difference. I was the only teacher to do these weird things. Why couldn't I be like everyone else? There was little cross-fertilization of ideas between this school and outside educators; many of the teachers had been there a long time. Although the principal was new, not only had he grown up in this district, but also his father had taught in this district.

Finally, the parents were rightfully frustrated. The school had ongoing bullying problems and the lowest test scores in the district on the fourth grade state tests. While change had taken place at the leadership level, the new leadership was not particularly supportive of creating a different environment in the classroom. My approach to these problems was not a quick fix, but slow acting, longer term practices which focused on supporting the development of the whole child. While I believe my manner of teaching would have, over time, addressed these issues, in the few months I was there, the problems persisted. My approach, however, could easily be pointed out as being different. The new male teacher across the hall from me, however, shared his fears with me later. He said he was shaking in his boots after this happened to me. He thought he could be next, since we both taught so much alike. Fortunately, I could reassure him to relax.

When the ultimatum was clear: stop teaching the truth or be terminated, I knew the end was near. Out of this chaos, out of my grief and anger, the idea for this book was born. Just as the children had seen the opportunity for peace out of September 11, so too could I turn what looked like a personal crisis into an opportunity extending far beyond my limited scope. This wasn't just about me. This was about two worldviews clashing. One is keeping us imprisoned by not letting children and everyday citizens realize their greatness; the other worldview can liberate us, opening the floodgates to our human potential.

The School of the Future

It is clear the kind of teaching and ideas I use in my classroom are empowering and allow the students to discover their own gifts and feel the strength that comes from being part of something much bigger than ourselves. In this environment children can discover their native talents and begin to contribute to the whole of the community, locally and globally. This kind of curriculum is desperately needed in today's world.

It is also clear our school administrators and the public education system are not putting children first. In fact, Einstein once remarked, "The only thing that got in the way of my learning was my education." Our human potential, creativity, capacity for love and compassion must come first. A public education system based on control, discipline, punishment, fear, and suppression of true and open information is the old way. The new way is here—my being fired from a small school district in Washington State will not stand in the way of evolution. These administrators are still living in Newton's universe, and cannot defeat the inevitable evolving of human consciousness; and it is time we pass them by.

The ideal school of the future won't compare students to each other and won't assign winners and losers. Progress will certainly be monitored, but only to find ways to maximize the individual's potential, to "sort children out,"[37] as Alfie Kohn puts it. In short, the school of the future will assess but not judge. Its democratic processes will evaluate what's working and what's not, both for the individual and the community. As Bill Grace of the Center for Ethical Leadership notes, a primary duty of leadership is to point toward hope. The school of the future will not only be concerned with training the mind but will also inspire hope.[38] It will value the arts and imagination in all its forms more highly than memorizing and replicating what already exists. As renowned education scholar Elliot Eisner, eloquently points out, art is a powerful vehicle for making meaning of the world:

> Ironically, the arts, an area of thinking that has the most to offer, is the most neglected in our schools. Each child in our schools should be given an opportunity to find a place in our educational sun. This means designing programs that enable children to play to their strengths, to pursue special aptitudes or interests. A genuine educational process cultivates productive idiosyncrasy, it does not homogenize children into standardized forms. Neither the cookie cutter nor the assembly line is an apt model for education. The studio is a much more congenial image.[39]

Making meaning of the world is the essence of education.

The ideal schools of the future will have classes small enough for each child's individuality to bloom. At the same time they will be large enough for each child's sense of community and appreciation of diversity to be explored and strengthened—large enough, also, to reap the benefits of cross-fertilization of ideas, styles, and backgrounds in ways that enrich us all.

The ideal school of the future, emphasizing connectedness over fragmentation, will integrate all subjects and all learning experiences to enhance and reinforce the level of meaning students create. The lines traditionally separating school from community will blur or even disappear, while learning and living become one. It will support an integrative, whole-systems approach to learning instead of a mechanistic worldview.

Our current educational model has perpetrated a great travesty: the insidious assumption that learning is a chore, to be accomplished only under threat of punishment or promise of reward. Though it may sound strange, the school of the future will draw more from the principles of kindergarten than from higher education. It will be a place where, as Joseph Campbell put it, children and adults together "follow their bliss."

In April 2002, because I was not currently teaching, I attended the International Science and Consciousness Conference in Albuquerque, New Mexico along with nearly one thousand people and many well-known scientists. I learned that scientists, philosophers, educators, and other wise and thoughtful people had run into similar walls of fear, ignorance, and deliberate suppression of their ideas. In spite of the scientific research affirming the interconnectedness of life, this emerging new worldview has been purposely repressed, even at the university level.

Those in power, the one percent controlling the wealth and information, will not give up easily. It is up to each of us to let go of the violence, hatred, and fear showered on us by our leaders, media, and institutions. Then as Teilhard de Chardin has said, "We will have created fire for the second time in history." We will live from our center of love, wholeness, and unity. The seed for inner greatness, our true essence, lives in all of us. All we have to claim it and nourish it.

Edmund Burke's famous quote asserts, "All that is necessary for evil to triumph is for good men to do nothing." This book is my response.

Declarations and Affirmations

Life is about finding the balance, the harmony, and the highest synthesis of all possibilities in a given need. A problem signifies something is out of balance, and challenges our creative thinking to view it from many perspectives, to see all possibilities, so that we can choose/create/co-create the solution that works best for all. The Schools of Tomorrow are schools where we seek to have everything in harmony, the deep harmony of the spirit, the earth, humanity, and the cosmos. They are schools where we look for the greatness in each teacher, student and school staffer, where we are no longer so quick to see their flaws and weaknesses. Here we learn that how I see others is a reflection of how I see myself. Here we start with an acknowledgement of my inherent worth Here we get reparenting as needed, building on, improving the predominant influence of my mother, father and relatives, learning how my culture influenced my sense of worth, how my religion or ethics group, my friends influenced me. Here we remake ourselves as global civilization builders! Here we become conscious of our most important values. Here we listen to the Spirit whispering to us the constitution of the Supreme School, and delicately communicating to our quieted minds even the names and whereabouts of all who will belong to this great School of the Future, the School of World Love, planetary community, astronomical culture and spiritual civilization building.

——

Some day after we have mastered the winds, the waves, the tides and gravity, we shall harness the energy of love. Then for the second time in the history of the world, man will have discovered fire.

PIERRE TEILHARD DE CHARDIN

We must all hang together, or most assuredly we will all hang, separately.

ATTRIBUTED TO BENJAMIN FRANKLIN

Problems cannot be solved at the same level of awareness that created them.

ALBERT EINSTEIN

CHAPTER ELEVEN

Action for a New World

Old ways for old things, new ways for new things. New schools for new times, new people, new worlds. The Teachers of the World teach not just what to *do*, but also what to *know*. *Schools of action* are the successors to *Schools of knowledge (academies)*. Our civilization is riding a powerful locomotive. The course of human events has built up quite a head of steam. The problem is, we're gazing out the window, and we've forgotten our destination. And on the rail just up ahead is a switch.

This switch is currently positioned for a straight-line extension of our current course; a downhill journey, careening toward global extinction.

We are the only species in the world that can steer its own train. It is the source of our pending demise as well as our potential salvation; it is our blessing and our curse. Above all, it is our responsibility. Beneath the massive wheels of our train, tens of thousands of plant and animal species disappear every year, not to mention millions of our own species. Will we awake from our reverie in time to flip the switch?

It depends on what we pay attention to. The time is now to direct our gaze from the rush of the passing scenery to the choice ahead. It's time to realize each of us is not merely a passenger, but an engineer. We are all Earth-artists, priests and priestesses of the Cosmos.

The Great Mixing

The times, they are a-changin'.

I'm convinced we will find our way out of this dark cocoon and become butterflies. I'm convinced the "great turning," the "global mind shift," the "transcendent consciousness" predicted by the wisest of our generation is upon us.

It won't happen while we sit and gaze out the window. We must choose. Millions are already making this choice—the choice of love over fear, the choice for a just and sustainable future. Myriad examples of this choice are being embodied all over the globe. In order to choose collectively and steer our train clear of mutual assured destruction, we must awaken.

To do so we must adopt the new worldview of wholeness and interdependence. It is a worldview that more accurately fits our emerging reality and our evolving consciousness. For hundreds of years our modern, rationalistic worldview has served us well. We have it to thank for the spectacular advances in science, medicine, technology, and culture, which have eased untold suffering and injustice and unleashed the phenomenal potential of human creativity and exploration. Our analytical, objectivist way of looking at the world, in which we humans are the subject and everything else the object, has also created untold misery. It has sometimes birthed merciless hierarchies of command and control, of power and wealth, backed up by relentless violence. Poverty and despair throughout the world are more the rule than the exception. We continue to degrade the Earth to the point where in our children's lifetimes it may simply be unable to sustain us.

The old worldview separates things and people and builds walls between them: subject and object, us and them, Christian and Muslim, man and nature, teacher and student. The new worldview mixes things back together—the "Great Mixing,"[40] as Matthew Fox calls it. In the Great Mixing, dividing lines will blur, polar opposites will meet in the middle, subject and object will merge. In the Great Mixing, all the ideas from the giants of civilization will blend into one unity-from-diversity and be synthesized to a higher level, an integral level that includes each of them and transcends them all. No one country will be the lone superpower. No one religion will claim sole access to God. No race will be oppressed. No human will live in poverty while others live in splendor. Gone will be the schism between First World and Third, between East and West.

In the West we think linearly, focusing on externals, craving material comfort, security, and cognitive understanding. Eastern thought spotlights the internal, the ineffable, the mysterious, craving acceptance, and transcendence. What would a synthesis of these polarities look like?

The answer to that question is less important than the fact that so many brilliant minds and passionate hearts are pursuing it. Brain researchers, for example, are beginning to identify the biology of transcendence (a classic juxtaposition of the Western mind—biology— with the Eastern—transcendence). Scientists can now identify and analyze the patterns our brains display when we're tuning to our highest selves—when, for example, we're meditating, exercising, praying, connecting with nature or with loved ones, or exercising our own limitless creativity.

Another example of East profoundly meeting West is a membership organization called the Institute of Noetic Sciences[41] (IONS), founded by astronaut Edgar Mitchell. Mitchell, a scientist trained rigorously in the Western tradition, was returning from the moon, gazing awestruck at the blue-green Earth on a backdrop of star-studded deepest black, when he had a transformational experience of the unity of our living planet. This experience was the catalyst for the formation of IONS, dedicated to applying scientific research methods to validate alternative ways of knowing—like intuition, meditation, precognition, the power of intention, and collective unconscious—that tap into the infinite number of ways in which we're connected. No mere group of New Age followers, IONS attracts some of the most brilliant scientific minds of our culture.

The Great Mixing brings the core values of what it means to be human to the forefront—values that seem to have been lost in our culture's drive to acquire more stuff—values such as quality of life (rather than quantity of possessions), sustainability (rather than conquest of nature), peace (rather than supremacy), inclusion (rather than competition), and trust (rather than fear).

Trust is the word that keeps coming up for me in my journey through the world of ideas. I see it as the common bond allowing us to change the deadly course of our train. First we must trust ourselves—our highest self, our own best nature—and then we must trust the greatness within every individual that allows for something new, something perhaps previously hidden, to flower.

Ironically, a key vessel for our trust is technology. Though many blame it for the struggles we're experiencing in the world today, I believe the fault lies not in technology, but in the ways we've chosen to use it, and the mindset that has driven those choices. Science and technology, as mentioned earlier, have eased great suffering. Once we dedicate ourselves to using technology for the purposes of connection and construction and not disconnection and destruction, it will promote rather than prevent our evolution to maturity as a species. (In reviewing evolution of all plant and animal species, evolutionary biologist Elisabet Sahtouris notes the immature ones are competitive and controlling. In order to survive to maturity they must become cooperative. They must successfully negotiate their self-interest with the interests of the community to which they're inextricably connected.)

How can technology serve this maturation? It's already happening. The paradigm shift has begun; it just needs to spread, like a healthy virus, to all corners of the globe. Case in point: beyond imagining, the Internet has the potential to democratize the world. Astoundingly, global communication carries with it unprecedented access by every human to the full storehouse of human knowledge. This, combined with the opportunity to dialogue to create new knowledge, makes the virtual global community the fifth—and most powerful—stage in the evolution of human communication. Oral language transformed us as a species, as did written language; then came the printing press, and most recently the mass media. Until now those in power have centrally controlled mass forms of communication, and the messages we've heard serve specific interests. Clearly, the mass media messages that inundate us serve the interests primarily of the corporate-profit engines that create them. Thus, every commercial you watch can be considered propaganda.

Now, for the first time, we the people are in control. With this global network we can truly honor the rich diversity of our world. We have the resources to create in the global village a truly participatory democracy. It's precisely these qualities—democracy and the valuing of diversity—that will propel us into this new synthesis, this higher level, this species maturity, this Great Mixing.

All this will be possible when all of us have access to the Internet. Currently, fewer than five of every one hundred people own a computer. The rapid decrease in the price of wireless technology offers limitless potential for that number to rise sharply so that the foundation for this synthesis, this human cultural transformation, will be all of humanity rather than simply those with power and material resources.

How will we exercise our new power? To effect our transformation to a mature species we must use it to think in the future tense and live in the present. We're biologically programmed to respond to danger to self in the here and now. It's a stretch for us humans—and a crucial one—to envision what the world might look like in fifty or one hundred years and to use our immense creative powers to choose a vision now that comes true in the future.

We create our own reality. Quite literally, what we see is what we get. What we pay attention to, even if it's invisible, becomes our world. Imagine hiking on your favorite forest trail on a sparkling early autumn day. The colors are spectacular, the breeze sublime, the vistas of trees and mountains and the sounds of birds make you feel one with all creation.

The more you pay attention to the world around you, the more peaceful you feel. Suddenly, just ahead of you and just off the trail, you see a bear cub. You freeze. You look around wildly for the mother, but she's nowhere to be seen. Ever so gradually, you retreat, looking constantly over your shoulder. What you're paying attention to now—your fear, your heart pounding in your chest, a mama bear completely invisible to you—has instantly transformed your reality.

We can choose what to pay attention to. We can be aware of the bear and still (once out of harm's way) choose to focus on the glory of nature. Our minds are pure energy; we need to be consciously aware of the quality of the energy we're putting out and taking in. The vibrational energy we send into the world has a magnetism that attracts like energy. If you go to a beautiful place with people you love, you'll be surrounded by a much higher level of energy than if you go to a boxing match. As we become conscious of the energies around us, we can more intentionally choose situations and people who invigorate, fulfill, and enrich us. We can choose to tune to the highest vibrational level possible—the level that science and religion, West and East, are increasingly recognizing as love.

> We learn from models. In order to learn how to drive our train onto a new set of tracks, we need new models: models of wholeness, interconnectedness, and diversity in all walks of human life. The World Future Society,[42] itself a model of global cooperation toward a common vision, categorizes human endeavors into ten issue areas for the future. These ten areas spotlight models I'm particularly excited and hopeful about. These are active manifestations of our interconnectedness.

Education

I start in the field to which I've dedicated much of my life, not only because it's my experiential base, but because it sets the tone for a culture. Education is (potentially) the great equalizer—the one place in society where the concept of equal opportunity comes closest to reality. We now do much that divides students from each other, for example, through win/lose competition, through grade and achievement leveling, through curriculum that only celebrates diversity as an "add-on," and through inequities among schools, depending on which neighborhood they're fortunate or unfortunate enough to be situated in. We can choose to dissolve these barriers and to address these inequities. We can choose to unite students by allowing them to experience the richness of diversity and by teaching them the emotional intelligence skills of compassion and tolerance for each other and for themselves.

We also do much to divide students from themselves. Rather than focusing them away from their own natures and toward our expectations, which emphasize strictly cognitive achievement, we can nurture each child's inner greatness by honoring all learning styles and paces, all interests, and all kinds of intelligence. By what we choose to teach and how we choose to teach it, we model for children; we train them what to pay attention to. By dividing students from themselves and each other we teach them to replicate this divisiveness in the culture they grow up to lead.

What do models of wholeness look like in education? I've tried to give some examples from my own experience in the first ten chapters of this book. There are hundreds more, maybe thousands, of beacons of full-spectrum educational light all over the world. They start in pre-school and elementary alternative or charter school programs; Montessori schools, for example, foster children's wholeness and self-direction in a context of joyful exploration and creativity. It's fitting to start young, because we now know the brain patterns forged in the early years can last a lifetime.

The traditional schism between home schooling and public education is a dividing line that's blurring. In some places programs attempting to heal that rift are creatively combining two days a week of home schooling with two days a week of group interaction at the neighborhood school, with the fifth day devoted to an experiential field trip.

Models of the new worldview in education go all the way up to graduate programs. The Seattle area alone, for example, has the Bainbridge Island Graduate Institute, which offers an MBA with a focus on sustainability and justice, and the Antioch University Center for Creative Change, which "prepares students to understand the world as an integrated system."

Schools aren't the only places where exciting experiments in holistic education are happening. An organization called the Washington Holistic Education Network (WHEN), for example, brings together a coalition of organizations and individuals embodying widely different strategies for bringing greater balance and meaning to education. The driving force behind WHEN is identical to the motivation behind this book: the notion of unity-through-diversity. Together we can imagine and create what none of us can do alone.

Speaking of strategies for bringing greater meaning to education, the concept of using the Environment as an Integrating Context (EIC) is a particularly instructive educational model due to its holistic approach on a variety of levels. It is a way of framing education that sees the students' environment, both natural and social, as the container for all learning experiences. It integrates the best practices of progressive education: cooperative learning, hands-on experiences, critical thinking, project-based learning, integrated curriculum, student-directed learning, plus the honoring of multiple skills and diverse learning styles. Not surprisingly, studies reviewing the impacts of EIC on student performance uniformly find higher achievement levels in all subjects, better social skills, healthier attitudes, and improved attendance.

This and other approaches encourage us to think out of the box that holds education as something that happens only inside a school building. Life-long learning has thankfully become a mainstream value in our culture—and one that most teachers will identify as a primary goal for their students. Community centers are springing up in many places to offer 24-hour-a-day lifelong learning opportunities, including technology labs.

Extrapolating from these trends to think even further out of the box, we can envision the world as our classroom. (Ironic that Native Americans and other so-called "primitive" cultures have always seen education in that way.) Our traditional educational model—a product of our modern mechanistic worldview—encourages us to see school as disconnected from life, and to see education as a chore we must endure in order to reach the prize.

Learning is the prize. It's the birthright of all living things. As Daniel Quinn says in *My Ishmael,* there is no more effective learning machine than the newborn child. Our natural hunger for learning continues into the school years, but then, for untold millions of school children, something we do in school suppresses that hunger, often for life. When we stop gazing out the window of our train, we'll find the hunger again and know how to feed it.

Business

Should profit be the only bottom line? Just as the old worldview sees school as separate from life, it sees business as disconnected from the rest of society and from nature. Its job is to make money; then somehow the benefits of creating wealth will trickle down, and any adverse effects are, well, none of its business. What sense does it make not to factor into a tobacco company's bottom line the health costs of using its products? Or the costs of cleaning up pollution into the price of a car? What about the costs of waging a war over the fuel that powers that car? And what sense does it make to price goods and services so low the people producing them do not earn subsistence wages?

In the new worldview, as Elisabet Sahtouris says, we need to add three more P's to the profit motive: planet, people, and psyche.[43] The great global mind shift will lead corporate executives to take a whole system approach—a compassionate approach that fosters sustainability, justice, and the core values humans hold dear, such as integrity, family, and community. These values are often strangers to the boardroom. Not so in the Great Mixing.

It's important to emphasize that the new paradigm doesn't see the profit motive as wrong, but rather as incomplete. A more enlightened approach doesn't take an oppositional approach to business-as-usual, but includes and moves beyond it.

One inspiring model is The Natural Step, a nonprofit organization which works successfully with such Fortune 500 firms as Starbucks, Home Depot, and McDonald's to "integrate sustainability principles into their core strategies, decisions, operations—and bottom line," according to the company's web site.[44] "We help companies understand how the current state of the world is impacting business systems, and how, in turn, business systems are impacting the state of the world."

The Natural Step accomplishes this by showing businesses how sustainability can be a business opportunity—rather than a liability—that can improve productivity, introduce new product and service design, and increase shareholder value. After collaborating with The Natural Step for several years, a Home Depot executive said, "I think sustainability is smart, and should be the mainstream. This is not the fringe anymore."[45]

Economics

Extrapolating from individual corporations to the economy as a whole, we must look closely at what we define as valuable. The root of the word *valuable*, clearly, is values. But in our culture, when we think of "valuable," we think not about our values, but about our money. Such is the lesson of capitalism, which taps effectively into our motivation to better ourselves materially, but not into our motivation to better ourselves emotionally or spiritually, or to connect with our true nature, with each other, and with the universe. We need an economics of caring: caring for ourselves, for each other, and for the planet. In America there are always enough billions to train soldiers to kill, but, as Riane Eisler eloquently points out, never enough money to train parents to care for children—even though the lifelong benefits of such education are proven. In our culture, we pay people considerably more to take care of our cars and plumbing than our children. This is how we measure value.

It's difficult for those of us born and bred into the capitalistic model to even imagine what an economic system based on justice and sustainability might look like. An organization called BALLE—the Business Alliance for Local Living Economies—is helping to envision this transformation. BALLE[46] sees a "local living economy" as one that "provides secure and fulfilling livelihoods for all people, works in harmony with natural systems, supports biological and cultural diversity, and fosters fulfilling and enjoyable community life."

To do so, BALLE says, "living economy communities produce and exchange locally as many products needed by their citizens as they reasonably can, while reaching out globally to other communities to trade in those products they cannot reasonably produce at home. Living economy enterprises are human scale, primarily independent and locally owned, and value the needs and interests of all stakeholders, while sustaining long-term profitability."

Why the emphasis on local exchange? First, it enhances our sense of community and builds self-sufficiency. Secondly, food is healthiest when it's freshest, when it doesn't have to be frozen or dried or canned in order to travel great distances. (That transportation also, of course, contributes to pollution and needless consumption of dwindling natural resources.) Finally, our bodies, acclimated to the climate we live in, like to connect with the foods that grow well in that environment. For these reasons, consumers in a living local economy are willing to pay a price premium to secure the benefits of buying from local living economy enterprises. Price is no longer the primary criterion for purchasing decisions.

Balancing the profit motive with the other P's (planet, people, and psyche), "living economy investors accept a living return on their financial investments rather than a maximum return, recognizing the value derived from enjoying a healthy and vibrant community and a sustainable global economy." Again, consumers are putting values back into the definition of valuable.

BALLE acknowledges, "great creativity and innovation will be needed" to fully implement these principles, and "they will only be realized over time." But to focus on the enormity of the challenge is to pay attention to the bear, rather than the grandeur of nature. As the celebrated Buddhist monk Thich Nhat Hanh said, "If you can take a single peaceful step, then peace is possible."[47]

Globalization

Though the priority should be on thriving local economies, it's clear economic life has already become and will continue to be an interconnected, global phenomenon.

The term "globalization" has taken on two radically different meanings. Its popular interpretation is summed up by the term "free trade." Under this doctrine, corporate activities should not be restricted by any individual country's laws, tariffs and taxes. These restrictions inhibit the free flow of goods and services across borders. That free flow is necessary for capitalism to thrive, jobs to increase, and prices to be minimized.

But what if those laws insure environmental protection or consumer protection or the fair treatment and health of workers? As became dramatically evident during the World Trade Organization protests in Seattle a few years ago, many who envision the new economy as ideally just are making *fair trade* a higher value than *free trade*. Trade is neither free nor fair if the workers responsible for that trade put in long hours under difficult conditions for poverty-level wages. Trade is neither free nor fair if laws designed to protect the environment are gutted in the name of free trade—a trend that's occurring, sadly, all over the world in the name of globalization.

Globalization can mean something very different. As David Korten writes in *Globalizing Civil Society: Reclaiming Our Right to Power*:

> There are signs throughout the world of a political and spiritual awakening of civil society to the reality that national and global institutions are pursuing agendas at odds with the needs of people and other living things. Countless citizen initiatives prompted by this awakening are coalescing into a global political movement for transformational change.[48]

Here, then, is the kind of globalization that supports—and embodies—our transformation to maturity as a species. Globalization as taught in the Schools of the Future aims not to fortify corporate fortresses, but to dismantle walls: the walls between countries, between people, between humans and the environment. In this way, through these schools, we can create real community inside this global village we all inhabit. This kind of globalization—a move from competition and territoriality to cooperation and synergy—reflects an evolutionary leap that we're poised to take, according to Elisabet Sahtouris. Looking at humanity as one family, we now essentially underfeed three children to overfeed a fourth, Sahtouris notes. It will take an evolutionary leap in the scope of our vision to remedy this obvious injustice. Signs of that leap have been emerging for decades. We cooperate globally on an unprecedented scale—in telecommunications, in scientific collaborations, in arts exchanges, in travel, in money exchange, in spiritual and religious institutions, and many, many more venues; but we have quite a ways to go.

Scientists are redefining "life" and now see the Earth as a living thing; everything on our planet forms one body with a shared destiny. Poets, prophets, and mystics have long known the truth of our global oneness. Many indigenous cultures have intuitively known it as well. Now our technological and scientific advances are exponentially increasing our understanding of what is and isn't healthy for the Earth. Lo and behold, this scientific understanding increasingly reflects what the poets, prophets and mystics have been saying. Once again, apparent opposites find commonality.

The most inspiring document I know which captures this understanding of what's healthy for the Earth and other living things is the *Earth Charter*[49], the product of a decade-long worldwide conversation about common goals and shared values. The *Earth Charter* is "a declaration of fundamental ethical principles for building a just, sustainable, and peaceful global society." It is a path to peace and to transformation, a foundation for teaching and for living. Its preamble begins:

> We stand at a critical moment in Earth's history, a time when humanity must choose its future. As the world becomes increasingly interdependent and fragile, the future at once holds great peril and great

promise ... It is imperative that we, the peoples of Earth, declare our responsibility to one another, to the greater community of life, and to future generations.[50]

The Earth Charter Initiative[51] is a global effort to explore ways of implementing the principles outlined in the Charter in all walks of life. These principles are precisely what energize my life.

Science and Technology

Through quantum theory and other scientific revolutions, we now understand the ties that bind us in powerful new ways. Our leading scientists are convincing the scientific establishment of a few things that baffle our Western minds:

- We can't observe something without physically changing what's being observed. Subject and object, in other words, are not separate. The scientific worldview is being transformed from the inside out!

- Within each speck of sand is the entire universe ("the world in a grain of sand," said a prescient poet William Blake).

- Things can actually exist in two places at the same time.

- Mind over matter is absolutely possible—in fact it happens all the time.

- With Quantum tunneling, things can move faster than the speed of light.... at least as fast as *instantaneously*!

What's happening here? It is a perfect example of the Great Mixing: science, whose pendulum has swung as far as possible from spirituality over the past 400 years, is coming back to meet it. Polar opposites are uniting, dividing lines are dissolving.

I've already mentioned the Institute of Noetic Sciences, which supports the use of the scientific method to validate phenomena formerly consigned to the occult, the supernatural, or religious experience. I've also mentioned research on the biology of transcendence—the ways in which the wiring of our brain supports our evolution to a higher level of consciousness. And I've referred to perhaps the most powerful tool in effecting our transformation to a mature species—the virtual global community, or the Internet.

Society

It is thanks to technology such as the Internet that the grassroots social movements reflecting the principles of the *Earth Charter* have experienced such phenomenal success in the past decade. Not that they didn't exist before; indeed, modern efforts to reflect the interconnectedness of humans and the planet go back hundreds of years. Even the briefest listing of major social movements in the past few centuries, beginning with the rights of man movement that gave rise to our Constitution, would have to include abolitionism, several women's movements, the labor movement, the civil rights movement, the consumer protection movement, anti-colonialism, the indigenous rights movement, the animal rights movement, environmentalism, the peace movement, the disability rights movement, the human rights movement and the human potential movement, just to name a few.

The steam is gathering. February 15, 2003, saw an event unprecedented in the history of the world. Millions of people across the globe gathered and marched nonviolently in a simultaneous show of solidarity to prevent a war that hadn't even begun yet. Talk about interconnected! We are only beginning to explore our true power as a human community, as a global participatory democracy.

Where I live, in the Pacific Northwest, another model for societal connection is taking shape. Called the 10,000 Flowers Project, it endeavors to "foster a vibrant network" of learning and collaboration in our region. "Hundreds, even thousands, of people are already working for positive change in our region, but often our work is done in isolation," its literature maintains. "How can we work together more effectively? How can we access the voices and wisdom of all the cultures and generations of the Pacific Northwest?"[52] If we were to take up that last question as a topic of global inquiry, how quickly would we speed the synthesis to a higher level of human existence?

In his book *Hope, Human and Wild*, journalist Bill McKibben describes Kerala, a province in India with a per capita income of 1/70 of the United States. Many citizens do not even own beds. The sum total of their possessions, on average, is a wooden bench, a few stools and cooking utensils. Refrigerators, TVs, VCRs—they are virtually unheard of. And yet, despite its poverty, despite being one of the most crowded spots on the planet, despite a diverse population, the literacy rate in Kerala is 100 percent; the average farmer knows more about international affairs than the average American. On one quality of life scale constructed by an American anthropologist, Kerala scored higher than the vastly wealthier South Korea and Taiwan, and almost as high as Japan.[53] Writes McKibben:

> Kerala gives the lie to the idea that only endless economic growth can produce decent human lives ... abundant in the things—health, education, community—that are most necessary for us all.[54]

Kerala offers a pair of messages to the First World. One is that sharing works. Redistribution has made Kerala a decent place to live, even without much economic growth. The second, and more important, lesson is that some of our fears about simpler living are unjustified. It is not a choice between suburban America and dying at thirty-five, between Wal-Mart and hunger, between five hundred channels of television and ignorance. There is some latitude for change.

Governance

Consider the following quotation:

> The modern age has ended. Today, many things indicate that we are going thorough a transitional period ... It is as if something were crumbling, decaying, and exhausting itself, while something else,

still indistinct, were arising from the rubble.

In today's multicultural world, the truly reliable path to peaceful coexistence must start from what is at the root of all cultures and what lies infinitely deeper in human hearts and minds than political opinion, convictions, antipathies, or sympathies—it must be rooted in self-transcendence.[55]

A contemporary philosopher, perhaps? A spiritual guru? No, the words are from a speech delivered in 1994 by Vaclav Havel, then president of the Czech Republic. A politician!

Vaclav Havel was not just a politician. Playwright, intellectual, and democratic activist, Havel was jailed three times by Czechoslovakia's Communist regime. After the Revolution in 1989 he was elected President.

There are politicians with the courage to listen to the deepest whisperings of their souls and of the collective human soul, politicians who realize the future is about leadership from the masses, from people feeling their own power and claiming it. Though the world's leaders still by and large enact the old paradigm—emphasizing domination, exclusion, territoriality, and polarization—a new brand of leader is emerging. Leaders like Vaclav Havel, Nelson Mandela, and Mikhail Gorbachev, leaders like Anwar Sadat, who amazed the world by evoking the courage to wage peace with Israel, and to place hope for humanity above the entrenched anger and fear of his own people. These leaders were not perfect, of course; Sadat's regime was oppressive, and Gorbachev was for a while the head of a totalitarian government. But the bravery and vision they embodied set a powerful model for heads of state everywhere. Only if we elect leaders like these will our new synthesis be given the chance to take root in the soil of the world's nations.

It's not only about electing visionary leaders, leaders who can think in the future tense. It's also about dismantling the walls dividing nations from each other and building structures to contain international dialogue and international collaboration. Structures such as the United Nations and the International Court of Justice are good beginnings and deserve to be strengthened. The most pressing issues we face in the world today—

notably environmental degradation, war, poverty and injustice—cannot be solved by any nation alone. We must work together as a global community.

Environment

The words "reduce, reuse and recycle" have become part of our mainstream vernacular. That's the good news. The bad news is so much of the world—even here in the educated West—pays little attention to that mantra. Implementing it at the household level is one thing—recycling glass, using canvas shopping bags, choosing to walk instead of drive whenever possible. Yet what the individual is able to do is limited by the infrastructure we live in. To not need a car, for most of us, will require a change at the infrastructure level—our cities and towns redesigned so that cars are not needed—less need to travel as far by placing those things we need closer to home, and improved transit for those times we do need to go farther. Truly implementing this simple motto also requires it be implemented at the larger scale of our society. This is a bigger challenge. It is one that requires reworking our many institutions: business, economy, and government, just to start the list. The good news is that we can impact these beasts with our daily personal choices.

My good friend Shannon is a one-woman model of an Earth-friendly lifestyle. She doesn't own a car; she rides her bicycle or takes the bus everywhere. She goes to great lengths to reduce, reuse, and recycle. Intelligent, astonishingly well-read, and personable enough to succeed at anything she tries, Shannon makes very little money, has few material needs, volunteers a great deal of her time, and trades and barters services to avoid buying things whose production or destruction will negatively impact the planet. Her footprint on the planet is quite small.

Perhaps most impressively, Shannon is participating in a big way in the trend toward earth-friendly construction. On Bainbridge Island, a picturesque spot just west of Seattle, Shannon has forged a community to build a straw bale house. The home she's creating is intended in all ways to minimize the impact on the environment. Built in a wetland, its pin foundations allow natural hydrological flows to remain undisturbed. Though a certain amount of land had to be cleared for construction, the plants and trees that were cut down are being reused, some milled for lumber; nothing is being hauled off site. The landscaping uses all native plants, so the house will snuggle down into its natural ambient environment.

The straw bale walls are highly insulating, and all appliances and fixtures are designed for low energy and water use. All materials used in construction come from within the state of Washington, thus reducing the costs and polluting effects of transport. In various phases of construction, Shannon is using recycled materials or materials that would otherwise become waste. The toilets in the house are composting, and all of the water supply comes from a system that collects rainwater from the roof and funnels it into a fifteen thousand gallon cistern.

The most impressive thing about Shannon's new home is how it fits into the earth's natural systems and cycles. Shannon and her team's effort is a superb model for the house of the future, a building that embodies the connection between humans and the environment—a connection we've attempted to deny in the past few centuries. Every species recycles everything it uses, except one.

Allowing nature to do what it does, supporting and assisting these cycles and systems is the key to our future. Not only for things, such as recycling, but for all our needs. Imagine a city planted with edible plants. Apple trees along the streets of Seattle, or peach trees in Georgia, and oranges in Los Angeles. What about nature's ability to clean water? Fascinating work is being done by John and Nancy Todd who are using plants, microorganisms, and animals to clean water. Some levels of this work are being implemented in the form of constructed wetlands. Water partially treated in a sewage facility slowly flows through beautiful ponds as it finishes the treatment process. These wetlands allow the water to be cleaned while providing habitat and natural beauty. Consider the option of looking over a wetland or a sewage treatment facility. Which would you prefer?

We have choices. One is to continue our current path, attempting to recreate what nature has taken eons to develop and which we are doing a poor job of replicating. Our attempts to provide food, water, shelter, and a meaningful life for ourselves is wreaking havoc on the planet. Another choice is to learn to live within nature's systems, allowing nature, perhaps with our help, to take care of us.

Health

Some of the greatest achievements of the modern way of seeing the world have happened in the field of medicine. In the 20th century alone medical science virtually eliminated scourges like smallpox, polio and childhood diseases that regularly killed or permanently disabled millions of people in uncontrollable plagues. Quality as well as quantity of life has been dramatically enhanced.

Without denying or disparaging the obvious gains of medical science—a product of the scientific worldview—it seems clear this Western allopathic medical model does not hold all the answers. In fact, while medical costs have been spiraling upward wildly in recent decades, gains in quantity and quality of life have not kept pace.

Though it was once useful to see health care simply as a battle against disease, that's no longer the case. The twin weapons of Western medicine—drugs and surgery—carry substantial risks and are simply unhelpful for many conditions. The rise of bacterial strains resistant to antibiotics is increasingly seen as an ominous failure of the allopathic approach.

In health care, the Great Mixing takes the best of the allopathic model and combines it with Eastern approaches (such as acupuncture and meditation) and with other natural approaches (such as naturopathy, homeopathy, chiropractic, massage, psychotherapy, and nutritional counseling). The result is an interconnected, holistic approach focused on strengthening the body's natural healing mechanisms, rather than simply attacking the agent of disease.

Thankfully, this synthesis is already becoming mainstream. Insurance

companies are starting to cover what used to be considered alternative healing modalities. All these strategies are becoming increasingly popular as
well. They are less and less the province of 'fringe providers.'

One exemplary model here in Washington State is a clinic called
One Sky Medicine, whose staff includes providers of all the preventive
and therapeutic modalities listed above, plus a cranio-sacral therapist and
a stress specialist. One Sky also offers educational resources for its patients, and an affiliation with a local hospital. One Sky prides itself on
employing a collaborative model of health care, a manifestation of the
interconnected wholeness of its patients and the world in which they live.

Another example of healthy evolution in the field of health care is the
rising prominence of hospice—a place where dying is not dreaded, but
respected and honored as a natural phase of life, and where patients' dignity and emotional needs are valued as highly as their medical needs.

The bottom line in the new approach to health care is that a healthy
environment and adequate health care are seen to be fundamental human
rights. This inclusiveness highlights the axiom that everyone is entitled
to air that's clean and fresh, water that's pure, an environment free of toxic
chemicals, and food that is healthy and natural. Even in our culture—let
alone the Third World—we have a way to go to make these standards
a reality. Our per capita intake of sugar is roughly twenty-five times what
it was fifty years ago, our levels of obesity are continuously on the rise,
and millions of citizens do not have proper access to health care.

Nonetheless in many areas, we are making substantial progress. Our
air and water are cleaner in many ways than they were a couple of decades ago. Organic foods and clothing are becoming increasingly popular
and available. The necessity to address the whole person in health care—
mind, heart, and soul as well as body—is becoming increasingly accepted. Fully embodying that understanding is the great challenge.

Values

I end my main story where perhaps I should have started—our values— they are at the root of every thought, every dialogue, every decision and every action we make.

Our values determine what we pay attention to, which in turn determine our behavior and creates our habits. Likewise, we can look at our world, see what is manifested everyday, and draw our values from there. If we pay attention to our values—in other words, if we focus on how the world's behavior conflicts with what we most profoundly believe in— then we can't help but build a commitment to change that world. As Margaret Mead said, "Never doubt that a small group of thoughtful, committed citizens can change the world. Indeed, it is the only thing that ever has."

Here in Seattle, a nonprofit organization called the Center for Ethical Leadership specializes in awakening individuals, businesses, and organizations to their core values, and helps them apply those values in their workplaces and lives. Interestingly, the Center finds that across the lines of age, culture, gender, and income, people all over the world identify the same small handful of core values—primarily love, family, and integrity.

The Center's founder, Bill Grace, passionately tells the story of a community living literally down the street from the Dachau concentration camp. When asked why they didn't do something about the existence of one of the most heinous examples of human barbarism in history, they uniformly answered, "We didn't know." Bill Grace sometimes makes people in his workshops uncomfortable when he asks what they might not know—because it's easier not to pay attention—about the course of human events. What might our grandchildren say about what went on during our watch? He challenges people to answer the question, in the context of the life span of our species and our planet, "What time is it?"

What a world it would be if we lived the values we universally hold dear. What a world it will be when humanity ceases gazing out the window of this speeding train and awakens fully to its integral place in the universe and its destiny to be compassionate stewards of the world it calls home. We have a unique opportunity and a monumental responsibility to further the fulfillment of that destiny. What time is it? It is now; the hour to act is upon us. Let us start today.

Declarations and Affirmations

Life is created anew in each moment. It is full of awe, mystery and surprises. We have each been gifted with life on this magnificent planet and an inner greatness we call our own. In this 21st century, as we still ourselves to listen, we can hear a calling— a calling from life itself, our home on Planet Earth and all her covering that nests and finds nourishment upon her. We feel called! We know vision plus action can change the world. In fact, it is the only thing that ever has. The coming together of our ideas, yours plus mine, are greater than any single vision. Acting on our vision, with wisdom and compassion for the whole of life, we know together we can co-create a world that works for all.

I'll meet you there on the playing field for life …

Can you feel your calling? Your greatness? Gather round! Many want to hold your hand and sing and dance and co-create a life for all as we play together on this blooming wondrous land. The Teachers of the World are opening the classroom doors. The World-Students are arriving: to find, to practice, and to perform the Song of the Heart of the World.

CHAPTER TWELVE

Afterword

By Richard S. Kirby, Ph.D.

StarSchools: Birthing the Best Schools in the World

Barbara Gilles is showing the way, in word and deed, for the Teachers of the World. In her own journey from Teacher of the Year to Teacher of the World she has embraced the Earth Charter and called for a new philosophy of education. Nurturing global citizens, she has become a leader and belongs now to the world—to our emerging planetary civilization, to the world of schools, to the world of teachers and to all students of global, spiritual civilization building.

I recognize Barbara as a prophet, as a voice of hope for all Educational ideals. She holds the portfolio for global education among that small group of spiritual innovators led by Rabbi Dr. Moshe Dror at the World Network of Religious Futurists (wnrf.org). Her brilliant thought, and her sacrificial life serving the cause of justice in education, entitle her to command a wide, international audience.

To speak plainly, Barbara is an educational genius. Society needs its geniuses in every field. They are the ones who generate a new genius loci(presiding spirit) in their realm. Barbara Gilles is a fountainhead of ideals for the Schools of the Future. We who are professionals in the fields of education will do well to follow her, and implement her visions. Then we will be the benefactors of millions of children worldwide. We will be liberators of teachers, educational journalists and philosophers, school administrators, PTAs, deans, university presidents and a host of education-alists and their outmoded philosophy of education. We will herald loving schools and we will champion of the right of UNESCO—the United Nations Educational, Science and Cultural Organization—to continuously improve its philosophies of education, its pedagogical sciences and arts, and its advocacy of the rights of students and teachers and their employers, to perfect justice. We will invent a field where new levels of justice will be achieved for talented teachers and students and educational theorists and entrepreneurs. We will see the world as a whole as a school of love and beauty. Supporting Barbara Gilles will lead to these marvelous educational achievements.

Barbara's work calls for a sensitivity to Nature in the Schools of Tomorrow. She has focused her attention on that part of Nature which we call Earth, our home planet. In this Afterword, I am setting her inspiring thought in the larger context of astronomical civilization building. In this context, Schools of the Future will be what we choose to call StarSchools. Such A neologism (new word) merits a definition! StarSchools are schools for Global citizens living in the Space Age. They can grace schools or colleges, think-tanks or Senior Centers, dance classes or youth clubs. They are schools of abundance and excellence.

StarSchools are schools where each student is a star — treated at her Peak of talent and with the highest respect. StarSchools are where the Highest educational ideals are daily practiced and refined. They are training grounds for citizens of the Stars.

To understand what it means to be global citizens living in the Space Age we need to contemplate the astronomical sciences (astronomy, astronautics, cosmology). In this, we will look briefly at cosmology as a help to designing StarSchools. I hope that we will write a sequel, designing StarSchools and their curriculum, mission and cultural ideals in detail.

Cosmology for People

There is a science called Cosmology. In this modern, scientific sense it deals with the picture of the universe as a whole. At least, it deals with some things in the universe. Scientific Cosmology is about a hundred years old. Some people think it began with Einstein's theory of special relativity. Physicists, astronomers and mathematicians practice it. It deals with questions like the size of galaxies and their distance and speed; the nature of matter and antimatter; the reality and even the location of Black Holes.

Modern Cosmology, like modern Astronomy, is a combination of AWE and close attention to details. However, it is a science that claims more for itself than is appropriate. If you ask the cosmologists what is their subject they will say "the universe," or they may say "everything that is". But in fact they are not dealing with everything that is. If you ask them, for example, "Oh, you mean you are adding up the tears, the pain, the suffering and the joy?" they maybe will look away, then—depending on their mood—they may say, "don't be silly," or, "that is not our subject", or they may even say, "that is not scientific." Actually, there is nothing unscientific about counting tears. But the deeper issue in our time is, "Where is the Cosmology of Love?" or—put it another way—what is the world of persons, and where is it going? Is it going to the hell of war, torment and cruelty? Is it breeding isolation, indignity and horror? Or is it creating a World of Love, Peace, Beauty, and Truth?

In Barbara Gilles' New Schools we will be teaching and creating moment by moment a world of love. The Cosmology which is really suited to persons is "political cosmology"; or, to put it another way, the political science of the planet.

We need to say this another way. The "Schools of the World" are Schools that teach how the World as a Polis, the World as a State, the World as a Nation, should and shall and must be governed, so that it becomes a World of Love.

It is pretty obvious to people who have traveled much to, or even read about, other countries, that patriotism alone is no longer a political energy that suffices to make world peace. Patriotism creates winners and losers; it foments war. Whether we like it or not, all of us today are global citizens. There is no harm in being patriots as well. In America, people can be fanatically pro-Pennsylvania, New York, Florida or California and still serve their country. Likewise, Americans can be good Americans and also good global citizens. Our StarSchools are schools for global citizens, but even to be a conscious global citizen can be a merely parochial way of being human. We live in the Space Age. "Space", outer space, means at least our own Solar System with all its planets beyond our terrestrial home. The vast mineral and energetic resources of the Solar System dwarf our thinking about 'global economy,' they enlarge our concepts of wealth, and they falsify the 'scarcity' premises of earth-born, earthbound economics.

It is a choice of great honor, wisdom and courage to adopt the attitude that we are already Cosmic Citizens. StarSchools are schools for Astronomical Citizens. They are centers for Astronomical Civilization Building. They are training grounds for Star Citizens, embracers of cosmic abundance.

The Astronomical Outlook

StarSchools teach the Astronomical Outlook. This Outlook has been growing for a few hundred years—perhaps since the time of Galileo and his discovery of the Moons of Jupiter, among other things. The Astronomical Outlook is now a decidedly available form of social consciousness—a way of being human and social and scientific and spiritual. We also call it 'Astronomicalism' in our book, The Temples of Tomorrow.

The Astronomical Outlook has foundations in emotion and thought. It includes something easily understood: Awe. Awe (see Rudolf Otto's *The Idea of the Holy*) is a profound, complex emotion, a set of moral feelings. It is a religious or spiritual feeling-state. Such things as size, scope, grandeur, excellence, beauty, and power can evoke it. In ancient times, the poet Pindar, writing at the time of some of the earliest Olympic Games in the 5th Century BCE, evoked in his readers the sense of awe which he felt looking at his great local mountain, Aetna. He wrote simply of 'Frosty Aetna, neighbor to the stars."

In the Eighteenth Century philosopher Immanuel Kant spoke of two things that had inspired him: "the moral law within, and the starry heavens above." Many, many poets, prose writers, astronomers, science fiction writers and even composers have hymned the glories of the cosmos, as did the Psalmist of old: 'The heavens declare the glory of God." (Psalm 19:1) The prophet Amos, looking at the constellation Orion, sensed and reported the sense of awe at the majesty of God the Creator—"Him Who made the Pleiades and Orion."—Amos: chapter 5, verse 8.

Astronomical Civilization Building focuses that sense of awe. It is awe that we feel not only with reverence for the heavens (it is no accident that the word 'heavens' means both a lovely, ideal place and also the location of the heavenly bodies.) We also learn to feel that sense of awe for human beings and even animals. But as our consciousness becomes politicized, that sense of awe becomes located in a reverence that we feel for the family of Humanity. We can call it the Body Politic of Humanity, or the World-State. Other names are: Planetary Civilization. The Planet-Polis. The Great Social Being. The City of Humanity. We can call it by many names; it is our greater self, it is the Higher Self of Society, which is our own Highest self—in part. It contains or points to the Highest Good for all societies, and the set of all societies, which we call Society or the World. Unfortunately, the phrase Planetary Civilization is out of date, for we live in the Space Age. I would suggest Star(s)-State or StarState or StarsState as a word or phrase to denote (describe) the Family of Humanity as a Polis or political community. For if we may quite soon have Martian humans, which Planet would we mean if we speak of Planetary Civilization? In science fiction sagas what I call Star(s)-State or StarState or StarsState is usually called Empire, but I prefer to avoid that word. It suggests older ideas of the subjugation of races.

The Star(s)-State or StarState or StarsState is coming to birth as we write, and read, these words. It is an expression of the Soul of the World (Anima Mundi). It is an expression of the Heart of the World (for Christians, a path to the Sacred Heart of Jesus, the being of infinite love, for Buddhists a pointer to the Buddha nature, the Being of infinite compassion, and so on). Its governance is our subject, for our subject is schools of love for a world of love.

We are at the dawn of Astronomical Civilization, and therefore of Astronomical Civilization Building, just as we are at the dawn of global political philosophy, global political science, international Civilization Building. How do you make an Astronomical Citizen? One answer has to be: by training in the Astronomical Outlook. My own young years had a lot of this. When I was about 8 years of age, a favorite aunt gave me a book, *The Golden Book of Astronomy*. I still treasure a copy of it, and keep it open at a picture of astronauts in rockets, to help me design Space Chapels! Its lovely drawings of planets and comets and cars and people still touch me with awe at the dawn of Astronomical Civilization. God bless the authors! *The Golden Book of Astronomy* offered a child's introduction to descriptive astronomy. A few years later the same Aunty (Jean was her name) gave me as a Christmas or perhaps birthday present—may she rest in peace and joy!—another such book: *The Boy's Book of Astronomy*. I came to know the author, Patrick Moore, and to this day am still planning work with him, on the world's longest-running TV series, The Sky at Night. *The Boy's Book of Astronomy* was my introduction to observational astronomy. By the time I was about 11 or 12, I was ready for this adventure of the social intellect. Ready to become an amateur astronomer, I joined a club, bought telescopes, studied the stars, and went to astronomy camp. I developed that sense of wonder that Plato says is the mark of the true philosopher. Sam J. Lundwall, likewise, in his book, *Science Fiction—what's it all about?* declares that that sense of wonder characterizes science fiction fandom also.

I became, and remained, an enthusiast for my subject. Astronomy became my intellectual habitat, and potentially my occupational one also. I could never thereafter be at heart anything except an astronomer. Even as a theologian, I am an astronomical one. Or maybe I am a theological astronomer...

I remember the wonder I felt that first day as a successful star watcher. Perhaps it was in the Fall of 1960. I know it was the Autumn, because I remember the position of the constellation low over the horizon. It was a sense of wonder and delight when I began to be able to navigate astronomically by picking out for myself, from the Star Books (how well we came to know "Norton's Star Atlas") the Big Dipper, called in England 'the Plough' or 'King Charles' Wain [Wagon].' I found a constellation! And from that one—which points to the North Star, Polaris—I could navigate by the stars; I knew where the North Pole was. It was a movement of initiation into cosmic citizenship. I began my teens that way. But it was to be another thirty years before I met Dick Spady. Then I changed from being a merely 'stellar' thinker to being a political one too. I caught the contagion of his enthusiasm for the study of government. My interests broadened. I began a new venture. I began to factor into the Astronomical Outlook something lacking: that political science which leads to Cosmic Civilization Building. Cosmic Civilization Building is becoming a way of life for those who work in government and are also at home with the deep darkness of night and the cold light of the stars.

I remember too the wonder, which I felt that first day with a telescope. Seeing, almost with shock, the rings of the planet Saturn and the moons of Jupiter were majestic moments, ones that define part of a lifetime. Later, I became an organizer of observational younger astronomers in my club, and had some special interests such as the planet Jupiter and the changing colors of stars. The astronomy clubs were a second family to me.

The astronomy clubs encouraged my training as a young scientist. I formed early in life the habit of careful observation. One of the training experiences we had in our circle was to look at what are called Variable Stars. These are stars that for various reasons change their visible magnitude or brightness quite regularly. There are different kinds of Variable Stars. There is one called Algol. (The stars have names. At least from the human point of view.) By learning the fixed magnitudes of stars such as Sirius, the brightest star (other than planets such as Venus) in the night sky, and Vega, we learned to measure the visible magnitude or brightness of the Variable Stars. This is an excellent training for a scientist. It teaches us that collecting facts is needed for building new truth, and so forming theories which lead to inventions, products...and: prizes. We learned that wealth of many kinds follows simple, persistent, methodical acts of observation, especially when we write these down or otherwise make a note of them. I love facts. They lead to theories, which lead to happiness of creation! Discovery begins with simple facts.

Astronomy as a hobby is also a cultural community. It is a whole way of life. It is a way of being human, a way of being social, and a way of being civilized. In the circles of British amateur Astronomy in the 1960s, it was not just one thing but a group of things that made up our way of being civilized. Pubs were involved—'lager and lime' the favorite drink—and telescopes, but also science fiction (the imaginative literature of the Space Age) and the 'Music of the Spheres.' Sibelius, Holst (I remember hearing his 'Planets Suite' in live performance at London's Royal Albert Hall, I think) and Beethoven, Tchaikovksy were among the composers of choice. Politics, pop music and the like were treated with disdain. It was decidedly the case that we saw the world as the philosopher Spinoza did: 'sub specie Aeternitatis'—from the stance of eternity. And we were young scientists—no doubt about that. We despised politics.

Our group has done well. Just the other day I spoke to a man I have known for 40 years, now an eminent solar physicist. Some of us became telescope makers, some professional astronomers. My best friend of those years became a science teacher. It was a powerful formative community. It bred scientists successfully.

As teens gave way to twenties, I became more deeply acquainted with the writings of the 'Cosmic Philosopher' (as Sam Moskowitz termed him) W. Olaf Stapledon (1886-1950), author of the fictional classics *Last and First Men* (1930), *Star Maker* (1937) and many non fiction works such as *A Modern Theory of Ethics*, and *Philosophy and Daily Living* (2 volumes—these being the first non-fiction Penguin books). Like those before him, such as H.G. Wells who inspired him, and those whom he inspired, such as

Arthur C. Clarke, Stapledon deliberately used the medium of non-fiction and that of fiction almost alternately. Their goal—this triumvirate of writers and thinkers, Wells, Stapledon, Clarke,—has been to get across the message of the urgent need for Astronomical Civilization Building. Wells and Stapledon both tried to speak to issues of government. Stapledon wrote *Waking World* as an essay on world government's foundation in civilization science. Wells was forever pestering statesmen. Clarke's work has been an inspiration to NASA. Olaf Stapledon, though deceased 25 years, became my mentor. As a scholar in his work (I visited the home where he wrote in Merseyside, met his wife, children, grandchildren and even great-grandchildren), I made a name for myself as a science fiction scholar and went on to work with some of the most famous names in the science fiction world, and then to form a Center for Science Fiction Studies in Philadelphia in 1980. By that time, though, I had already made up my mind to go to seminary for priesthood training, and did so, after seven years of preparation—in 1982 in New York City. Pierre Teilhard de Chardin and St. Ignatius of Loyola—the Jesuit astronomer and the Jesuit soldier—had joined the astronomers as my heroes and guides. So it was that my life prepared me to be a director of astronaut chaplain training and space seminaries.

Not only scientists and science thinkers have used the medium of non-fiction and that of fiction almost alternately. So have religious thinkers. There is a Christian counterpart to the triumvirate of writers and thinkers, Wells, Stapledon, Clarke, and that is the "Inklings" of Oxford: J.R.R.Tolkien, C.S.Lewis, and Charles Williams. All wrote fiction and non-fiction as part of their 'apologetics.' I find myself with an allegiance to both groups. I like to write science fiction, but also any other genre that expands consciousness and awakens conscience to the privileges and urgent needs of cosmic citizenship and Astronomical Civilization Building. When I met Dick Spady, in 1993 and started working with him in the World Network of Religious Futurists, we found the right name for our overall paradigm, a phrase he coined: Spiritual Civilization Building. Our StarSchools are schools of Spiritual Civilization Building. We are moving out of the era of Protestant and Catholic, Hindu and Muslim, Buddhist and Baha'i saints, and even out of the era of planetary saints, into the Space Age, where what we are needing, and what we are breeding is StarSaints—the coming heroes of Spiritual Civilization Building— the youth of the future.

The Best Schools in the World are StarSchools. They are being born as we write, as you read, these words.

In StarSchools, the 'strange new worlds' of outer space, in what the science fiction writers call Galaxies like Grains of Sands are meeting 'strange new worlds' of educational innovation, where every moment counts, every student matters infinitely, and school, teacher and students are like greyhounds or racehorses straining every muscle and nerve to deliver a peak performance— in the classrooms of the Best Schools of the World.

These Best Schools are not merely terrestrial; they are earthy but nor earthbound. They delight in the Music of the Spheres such as Gustav Holst delineated musically in his wonderful orchestral suite, *The Planets* (ca. 1913). This is the same Music of the Spheres of which Olaf Stapledon famously wrote in his epoch-making philosophical classic of astronomical humanity, Interplanetary Humanity, *Last and First Men* (1930).

The Star Charter

StarSchools. Schools of the Stars, Schools for the Stars. "Earth is the cradle of humanity," famously wrote rocket scientist Wernher von Braun, but one does not stay in the cradle forever. From the Earth charter loved by Barbara Gilles, we have the Star Charter to come— it will deliver cosmic awe, astronomical abundance and astronautical resourcefulness into the whole milieu of educationalism. The Star Charter is coming—we can see its emerging shape, its necessary contents, and its timely purposes.

The Star Charter is a movement for best global schools led by the Teachers of the World—and by the Children of the World, children so memorably portrayed in such science fiction classics as *The City and the*

Stars, Childhood's End, and *2001: A Space Odyssey* by Arthur C. Clarke

The Star Charter is clearly destined to have a deep impact on global educational culture. It will flourish, for it will have the whole-hearted support of world religions. It will become a banner not just for global spirituality, but also for the emerging global Youth Futurist Academy associated with the World Future Society. It will become emblematic of the improvement of the future UNESCO (known affectionately in our circles as NEUNESCO), where that organization offers the best philosophies and practices of education to the world's teachers, students, and future educationalists.

To the Teachers of the World

Here we as authors move into epistolary (letter) format, presenting our ideas in the form of a letter of commission, to those 'Teachers of the Year" who are becoming 'Teachers of the World."

"Your role, in global society as a 'Teacher of the World,' following your recognition as 'Teacher of the Year', necessarily connects you to the leadership of international education, and thus to the United Nations agency for Education—UNESCO. It is a happy thought that in such circles of international moral leadership, with powerfully trained, spiritually illuminated minds such as those possessed by our colleagues Moshe Dror, Arthur K. Ellis, Ron Kohl, Richard J. Spady and yourself, there is a strong, intelligently led will—a firm decision and public intention—to guide UNESCO into a luminous spiritual destiny.

By decisive moral leadership, you will help the teachers inspired by UNESCO to its own best future as the world's trailblazer in best science, education and culture (hence its name as the United Nations Educational, Scientific and Cultural Organization).

In fact, as our colleague Dr. Richard J. Spady says, what is at stake here is the 'Leadership of Civilization Building' in international educational science, educational culture, and educational world-politics in the best sense. Certainly Dr. Spady's 'paradigm' of world political science-philosophy, which he terms 'Spiritual Civilization Building,' is the appropriate one as a synthetic philosophy of world education. Your schools will be the herald of this movement, and if we are to think of the world religions—as has often been figured—as a ship, your schools will be its prow, with yourself as the personification of the will of the World Body-Politic to HAVE a spiritually civilized philosophy and practice of education which can best serve the world's schools old, new and yet-to-come. Thus you, as moral leaders of world education, gladly vow allegiance to the merging Hippocratic Oath for Teachers."

"Star Charter teachers, your calling is to improve global educational culture. You should regard yourself as cells in a global school think-tank for global and/or astronomical civilization building of the Schools of Tomorrow. Your hope must be to activate all educational ideals and their associated energies. You are to call out from all sovereign nations their educational hopes. Thus, in the idiom of the Gospel according to St.Luke, your worldschools—your schools for the stars—will be healing schools, global schools, and the best schools in the world. These schools will serve to bring a new birth of freedom to teachers, students and educational administrators. They will be schools fit for orphans and princes. They will be schools where the best sciences meet the highest ideals of spiritual civilization building. They will be governed by the most excellent theories and practices of management and culture. You definitely will hold the intention to bring to educational innovation the genius of social innovation. Your school cultures will be governed by the highest and best, but the most 'rooted' of spiritual values. Collaborative leadership will activate these values, and their associated energies. This leadership, summoned by you, will come from the United Religions Organization, the Council for a Parliament of the World's religions, the Vatican, the high councils of the world's wisdom traditions.

In other words, we are looking to you now, our Ideal Teachers, to be searching for the maximally inspired educational philosophies and practices the history and present of education has to offer. So we expect you to create and govern the most inspired educational communities of hope and joy. These lovely and joyous schools will be the best, the healthiest and happiest learning environments the world has ever known. They will be here on planet Earth, and in extra-terrestrial realms as befits the emerging astronomical civilization of the United Nations, NASA and associated constituencies of space-Age education. Thus, your calling is to design and direct schools filled to the brim with the happiest, healthiest young (and sometimes old!) Citizens the world has known. You are—to summarize the ideas of our own book—to create in all lands, with immediate activation, a plethora of moments of infinite educational fulfillment in the most beautiful, most fair classrooms with the ideal curriculum for a world of Love."

In StarSchools both teachers and students are the Stars of the School. They are operating at the very highest level of their being. They are all winners. The classroom is the place where their very best selves merge in joyous collaboration to form the best communities of love and intelligence the world has ever seen.

StarSchools are places linked to Hollywood and its stars, and to space agencies such as NASA, and its 'Stars'.

The Federation of Galaxy Explorers

StarSchools include astronomy camps—and their cyberspace equivalents—for the introverted, the self-styled (or other described) 'geeks,' 'nerds,' to say nothing of 'weirdoes,' 'puffballs' and 'Four-eyes,' and other ways the creative originals are described by more mainstream, extroverted kids, athletic types, student president, club holders, etc. Thus, The Federation of Galaxy Explorers [FOGE] is developing some curriculum and activities for a project that they call 'Moon Base [MB] 1'. This MB1 effort is intended to be incorporated into the summer camp and workshops of FOGE, to focus the youths on interesting and challenging aspects of a lunar base, including but not limited to the science and engineering. Our colleague, a leader of space commerce thinking, Ron Kohl of Maryland, USA, is among those who have a 'review' role as the various modules are developed. We share here some of his briefing.

What is FOGE? We will allow it to describe itself: The 'Federation of Galaxy Explorers' (FOGE)! "Welcome to the coolest idea since the 20th century!" Check out www.foge.org. This group is a youth oriented club, not unlike the Boy Scouts but with a focus on outer space, especially space exploration. The Executive Director of this group space exploration planners know Nick Efftimiades thru his association with some of their 'space advocacy' groups.

> The Federation of Galaxy Explorers was incorporated in the state of Maryland as a 501(c) 3 non-profit organization. The organization seeks to inspire and educate kids in space related science and engineering. Galaxy Explorers was created to prepare children for the future; a future that advances a space-faring civilization. Kids in Galaxy Explorers attend after-school (or evening) monthly "Mission Team" meetings and periodic field trips. Adult volunteers teach Galaxy Explorers with easy to understand and fun-to-do educational material to provide a hands-on understanding of space science, earth science, engineering, and rocketry. Another primary theme, Space Citizenship, teaches the role of government, the power of citizens in a democracy, the promise of space expressed in art, writing, history, and business. Mission Team members wear uniform shirts and are rewarded for participation and achievements with ribbons, patch, medal, and certificates. Awards are an integral part of the program providing children self-esteem through achievement and recognition.

> The Federation of Galaxy Explorers began in 2002 with a pilot program in Rock Creek International School in Washington, DC, and Prince William County schools in Virginia. In summer 2002, Galaxy Explorers hosted a summer camp with Prince William County schools. In 2003, we hosted 500 kids in 5 summer camps and nearly 400 kids in after school programs. We continue to grow.

Benefits of the Federation of Galaxy Explorers are said to include:

◦ **Educate our kids**—The Galaxy Explorers will prepare children for employment in the 21st century.

◦ **Galvanize support for space**—Over time, Galaxy Explorers kids will grow to create a long term citizen activist force in society; shaping the national space policy, and furthering the science and engineering required to create a space faring civilization.

◦ **Economical**—The concept of Galaxy Explorers is an extremely inexpensive means of educating the future generations by drawing on the volunteer spirit of America. The program provides a critical support infrastructure to motivate and educate children outside of the classroom. This infrastructure is particularly important given America's modern day peer pressure, and lack of classroom resources, science and math teachers.

In 2004, the Federation of Galaxy Explorers strategic plan will expand the program to additional states: Texas, Florida, California, and Pennsylvania. The Federation of Galaxy Explorers expects to have a program of several hundred thousand children in the coming years. To accomplish a nationwide expansion, Galaxy Explorers has established collaborative working relationships with the National Space Society, American Astronautical Society, National Association of Rocketry, Astronomical League, U.S. Air Force, NASA, National Reconnaissance Office, and many others. In addition, the effort is strongly supported by Congressional Members and staff.

Quantum City of the World Youth

Youth who are studying global youth leadership are connected in what the leader of the Jewish futurist thinkers, our friend Rabbi Dr. Moshe Dror, calls 'Cyberia'. They are Netizens or citizens of the Quantum

City of the World Youth. Quantum Citizens, Quanzens, or just 'Quanz.'

Dr. Dror recently wrote us on this subject, from his home in the Negev desert, Yeroham Israel:

> "The youth=quanzens are going to live and work in space, that is sure. The question is when and how many and perhaps where. They are going to design and build a new civilization that is, at least in theory, "better" than what we have here on earth. So the question I would like to ask is how much of what we have developed in the past of the "city of God," the new "Garden," can they and we actually manifest in this space place?
>
>> 1. What sort of spiritual facets of their lives can interface with living beyond the Earth?
>>
>> 2. What might be the space analogue to Gaia the classical Goddess of the earth—who what might be the goddess of space—Minerva? The goddess of Wisdom?
>>
>> 3. What might be the space analogue to sacred space on earth?
>>
>> 4. What might be the new Gospel for the space age?
>>
>> 5. Abraham was called the first Hebrew (the term derives from EVER-crossing over). In his day it was the desert-then the new frontier. Our new frontier is space—how can we add a sacred dimension to it?
>>
>> 6. Does the federation of galaxy explorers deal with these issues at all?

Enlightened Science

The Teachers of the World are among many who understand the fundamental harmony of science and spirituality; but this harmony is more potential than actual. It needs to be demonstrated in practice, embodied in StarSchools educational theories and models, expressed in schools, in 'educational laboratory' design, and fulfilled in the development of experimental pedagogical science to make a better world of schools. We call this harmony of science and spirit "enlightened science". We offer it in this curriculum as a path, a way of enlightened educational and pedagogical science. It is an approach to enlightened citizenship too, for as with the ancients we see the physical, moral and political sciences as fundamentally one. Enlightened science is a metaphysical paradigm, a set of assumptions about reality and a core of values. It is also a community. To practice enlightened science is to belong to a world community of sacred scientists, pioneers and experimentalists (as scientists must be) in developing spiritual technologies in the realms of matter, energy, love and life. We write for our colleagues in these fields, for the audience of teachers and educationalists who are interested in a better science for the future; and particularly for those educators and students who are interested in spirituality and Science. We also write for our students in a number of countries and a number of disciplines. May this path be a path of light and love to them, so their work may be a blessing to the world.

The Children of the Stars

The most astounding recipes, the most awesome meals, the best cookbooks in the world are coming to birth in the StarSchools, for here the greatest nourishment is planned, prepared in the classroom and served in joy. The Science Labs are the best in the world, the inventions are the most profound and consequential and socially useful. These schools are second homes to all who attend, homes of the highest happiness. For the Children of the Stars go at dawn to schools of happiness…and come home at sunset, radiant with inspiration and the contagious knowledge of love's triumph throughout all the worlds.

2002 Earth Charter

The Earth Charter is a declaration of fundamental principles for build-ing a just, sustainable, and peaceful global society in the 21st century. It seeks to inspire in all peoples a new sense of global interdependence and shared responsibility for the well-being of the human family and the larger living world. It is an expression of hope and a call to help create a global partnership at a critical juncture in history.

In 1987 the United Nations World Commission on Environment and Development issued a call for creation of a new charter that would set forth fundamental principles for sustainable development. The drafting of the Earth Charter continued at the 1992 Rio Earth Summit. In 1994 Maurice Strong and Mikhail Gorbachev launched a new Earth Charter initiative. In 1997 the Earth Charter Secretariat was established at the Earth Council in Costa Rica.

The Earth Charter is the product of a worldwide, cross-cultural con-versation about common goals and shared values. Thousands of individu-als and hundreds of organizations from all regions of the world, different cultures, and diverse sectors of society have participated. It is a people's treaty that sets forth an important expression of the hopes and aspiration of the emerging global civil society.

The mission of the Earth Charter is to establish a sound ethical foun-dation for the emerging global society and to help build a sustainable world based on respect for nature, universal human rights, economic jus-tice and a culture of peace.

16 Principles from the Earth Charter

1. Respect Earth and life in all its diversity.

2. Care for the community of life with understanding, compassion, and love.

3. Build democratic societies that are just, participatory, sustainable, and peaceful.

4. Secure Earth's bounty and beauty for present and future generations.

5. Protect and restore the integrity of earth's ecological systems, with special concern for biological diversity and the natural processes that sustain life.

6. Prevent harm as the best method of environmental protection and, when knowledge is limited, apply a precautionary approach.

7. Adopt patterns of production, consumption, and reproduction that safeguard Earth's regenerative capacities, human rights, and community well-being.

8. Advance the study of ecological sustainability and promote the open exchange and wide application of the knowledge acquired.

9. Eradicate poverty as an ethical, social, and environmental imperative.

10. Ensure that economic activities and institutions at all levels promote human development in an equitable and sustainable manner.

11. Affirm gender equality and equity as prerequisites to sustainable development and ensure universal access to education, health care, and economic opportunity.

12. Uphold the right of all, without discrimination, to a natural and social environment supportive of human dignity, bodily health, and spiritual well-being, with special attention to the rights of indigenous peoples and minorities.

13. Strengthen democratic institutions at all levels, and Provide transparency and accountability in governance, Inclusive participation in decision-making, and access to justice.

14. Integrate into formal education and life-long learning the knowledge, values, and skills needed for a sustainable way of life.

15. Treat all living beings with respect and consideration.

16. Promote a culture of tolerance, non-violence, and peace.

E-mail: *info@earthcharter.org*
Website: **www.earthcharter.org**

Examples of Elementary Children's Communication with Compassion and Concern

Letters to Clinton

Kids are our future. I don't think kids should be abused. It hurts them and it hurts the world.

———

If we abuse our kids they'll abuse their kids, etc., etc. until somebody wakes up.

———

Even though we know you are very busy, we really hope we can come and talk to you about child abuse.... You can be our voice. You can help us spread the word.

———

Would it be alright if we spent a day or two talking to you about these problems? Answer!!!!

———

It is very important to me for you to take a bit of time to think my letter over ... We'd like it if you would be our partner in our dream ...

———

Letters to Osama bin Laden

Dear Osama bin Laden,

I am a PeaceBuilder! Why did you kill so many people? This was a very bad thing to do. I'm angry but also very scared. I hope you don't do this again because I don't want anymore people to get hurt.

In PeaceBuilders we learn to use words and talk from our hearts. I want to use my skills to help people to make better choices. I want to teach people the skills I have learned so they can use words to solve problems.

––––––

Dear Osama bin Laden,

I feel angry because you just hired some people who came and killed thousands of people. Hundreds and thousands of kids were waiting at school for their parents to pick them up but their parents were dead. Since I am a peacebuilder I want to share with others how to build peace. I hope you can understand. I believe that peace is better than bringing hate and fear. I want to teach the children of the future the peace building tools I am learning. How to feel and talk from my heart.

P.S. You did wrong.

––––––

Dear Osama bin Laden,

I feel sad and scared that you killed lots of people in the Trade Tower. is there some thing wrong. I wish I could know what's happening. I feel that I am not safe and I wish to feel safe.

––––––

Dear Osama bin Laden,

Why did you do this Mr. Osama bin Laden? Also why are you so mad at us? I feel sorry because you had to do this to get back at us and you killed 250 fireman and Policeman also you killed over 1 thousand people and more. You also caused 4,522 people to be missing under 6 stories of rock, metal and rubble. The United States wants to understand you and your country and to get along together.

Quieting the Mind

When I'm listening to myself I shut my eyes and clean my mind. Then a breath in and out of my nose and let my ideas come into my body. When that happens I get a peace of paper and pencil and write the ideas down. That's how I get a lot of my ideas from.

———

My experience was neat. I got an idea my very first time. Just sitting there it relaxed me. It felt as if I was sitting on air. To get great ideas just sit and listen.

———

We went in a circle for a minute and sat in silence to get ideas and we just cleared our mind. It was a good experience but since it was the first time not many ideas. I'm still try to get as good as P.L. Travers is but it takes practice.

Poetry

My power is like … a light switch
because when I have an idea
my light goes on
and when I feel sad
my light goes off

My power is like a rock.
I feel safe and strong.
I would never get out of control and
throw myself at someone who loves me or hates me.
I would let people get stronger by letting them climb me.
I would be smooth on one side and rough on the other.

My powers are like a Ball
because I can or make Kids
and adults have fun with Me.
But I would never ever Use
myself to hurt any one No one.

My power is like a house
I shelter people
Welcome them
I let them come in
and warm themselves
I keep them safe
and give them a place
where no one is hated
I would not crumble
around or on them
I would not fall on
their heads
I'd open my door and
let them come in
I would help them become
better people
and all hate that comes in
will turn into love.

Letters to President Bush

Dear President Bush,

I want to help children in the Middle East by giving them a dollar. Why did the September 11 tragedy have to happen to this country? I can help and hope for peace. Will this tragedy lead the world to love more or hate more? I think of Ghandi's great words, "taking an eye for an eye ends up leaving the whole world blind." President Bush, please help build peace in the world, even for those who hurt us and hate us. This great country's goal is justice, not revenge.

———

Dear President Bush,

I want to give one dollar to the children in Afghanistan because they are not part of the war and so if they get a lot of money they can by food and medicine. I like the idea of dropping food but do you know that Afghanistan has more than 300,000 land mines? I'm worried about children getting killed if they step on one.

———

Dear President Bush,

I will send a dollar to Afghanistan because some children are scared and I'm willing to help to send a dollar. Afghanistan has bin bombed many times and they probably are very scared. I feel very sorry for them because most of them don't have any parents and I hope that a dollar or more will cheer them up. Maybe. I'll send more.

———

Dear Mr. Bush,

I want give a dollar because I care about the kids in Afghanistan and all the kids in the world. I wish I lived in Afghanistan for one day to see what they go through. I wish that I could give a million dollars to them.

_____

Nine Intelligences

My best intelligences are physical and nature. Physical and nature are my favorites because I love to play soccer, ski, and climb trees. I like to smell flowers, too. Those are my best intelligences.

Baseball is my special gift. Baseball is physical. I learned how to play when I was five. (My dad taught me.) I started to be good when I was 7. That year I learned how to hit and pitch a whole lot better. When I was nine I hit my first home run. It was 203 feet. That year I played for the Mets, and we were 18-0-1. That means 18 wins, no losses and 1 tie. Also I pitched the championship game and we won. Physical is my strongest intelligence.

My mom is mostly interpersonal because she is always doing stuff with people. She takes me a lot of places too. But sometimes she can be intrapersonal because everyone need's time to them self.

Hippocratic Oath for Teachers

I vow to hold open an environment where all are moved, touched and inspired by themselves and each other.

I vow to respect the learner and welcome his or her gifts.

I vow to develop the love and learning of nature and consciousness.

I vow to help to develop the love and enjoyment of learning about nature and consciousness.

I vow to meet each learner where they are.

I vow to be a compassionate, caring and learning companion.

I vow to do my best effort to help each of my students achieve their dreams.

I vow to guide and engage each individual in a mission of learning. To be a change agent and to realize that the learning process goes both ways.

I vow to leave passion where there was none and more passion than I found.

I vow to have fun while doing all this.

I vow to respect all, prejudge no one, serve needs, inspire first, teach to self-direct.

I vow to help all people to be able to learn from their experience.

Two Leading Theorists of Civilization Building: Dr. Richard J. Spady and Dr. Stuart Carter Dodd

Dr. Richard J. Spady

On June 2, 2003, Richard Spady, president of The Forum Foundation, received an honorary degree of Doctor of Humane Letters (D. Litt.) from The University of Russia's Academy of Education.

Dick Spady was born in 1923 and reared in Portland, Oregon, served in WWII in the U.S. Navy Seabees in the South Pacific, graduated from Oregon State University in 1950 under the GI Bill with a Bachelor of Science in Business and Technology, and served in the Air Force as a Commissary Officer in Japan during the Korean War. He retired in 1977 as a Lt. Col. after 29 years in the Air Force Reserve. He is married to Ina Lou Spady, they live in Bellevue, Washington and have five children now grown.

Dr. Spady describes himself as a "student and practitioner of administrative theory." Dick Spady has also been a celebrated businessman in the Seattle area, where his five "Dick's Drive-In Restaurants" have been "A Seattle Hit Since 1954."

However, Dr. Spady is also internationally known as a social scientist. In the Fall of 1968, he enrolled in the Graduate School of Business Administration at the University of Washington, concentrating in the field of Administrative Theory and Organizational Behavior. From these studies he worked with Dr. Cecil H. Bell, Jr. to develop "Zeitgeist Communication" social technology. Dick's attendance at the University of Washington Graduate School of Business Administration from 1968-70 was where he first identified the basic theories of administration and civilization detailed in his latest book.

As President of the Forum Foundation, a Seattle-based non-profit educational research agency in social science, Dr. Spady has made contributions to the several fields of philosophy of society, social theory and social science. In philosophy of society, he has enunciated the field of "spiritual civilization building" as the paradigm for advancement of civilization at a level beyond politics, economics and science. Discussions of his paradigm are under way in Africa, Asia, Russia and the U.S.A. In theory of society, Dr. Spady has spent many years crafting the technology of many-to-many communication through "symbolic dialogue," and has been a stalwart contributor to the mathematics of social science. Most of Dick's free time for the last 35 years has been devoted to the study of social science. Dick Spady is the inventor of the Fast Forum® technique, the PC Rating® (Polarization-Consensus), the Viewspaper® concept and with Tom McMullen, Director, Insourcing Institute, is co-author of the Internal Insourcing Audit™ Opinionnaire®. He is also the originator of "Social Quantum Mechanics," which he has helped to evolve into Social Quantum Theory.

As a social scientist, Dr. Spady has conducted painstaking research in the building of models of symbolic dialogue within cities such as Redmond, Wa., and Buffalo, N.Y.

Dr. Spady is a noted futurist and for many years held the portfolio of Futures Research as a volunteer on the staff of the Church Council of Greater Seattle. He has also long been active within the United Methodist Church in which denomination he has been a lay speaker since 1967. He received the Earl Award in 1993 as Religious Futurist of the Year from the World Network of Religious Futurists, the Bishop's Award from Bishop Elias Galvan of the Pacific Northwest Annual Conference of The United Methodist Church in 2002, and was awarded the degree of Dr. of Humane Letters by the University of Russia's Academy of Education in 2003 for "contributions to Russian democracy and higher education." Dick is a Fellow of Seattle Pacific University (Free Methodist) and recipient of their Certificate of Achievement from their School of Education in 2004, and also a member of the Ecumenical Institute for Theological Studies of the Seattle University School of Theology and Ministry (Roman Catholic) which is the only such school that accredits and is accredited by Protestant churches.

Dick has been a Rotarian since 1980 when he was a co-founder of the

Bellevue Overlake Rotary Club of RI District 5030 with the active classification of "Futures Research." He currently has a Senior Active classification.
Rotarians are international and have been devoted to community service for
100 years. Dick Spady has proposed that community service organizations
in the world expand their mission to civilization building of which community service is a central aspect. To accomplish this, he has sponsored Citizen
Councilor Networks; see (www.secstate.wa.gov/elections/initiatives/legisla-
ture/i325.aspx).

Dick Spady is the author of *The Christian Forum (or Fast Forum®) Why and
What It Is!* (1969), *The Search for Enlightened Leadership, Vol 1: Applying New Administrative Theory* (1996); *Vol. 2: Many-to-Many Communication, A Breakthrough in Social Science* (1998), co-authored with Dr. Cecil H. Bell, and is co-author of *The
Leadership of Civilization Building—Administrative and Civilization Theory, Symbolic Dialogue, and Citizen Skills for the 21st Century* (2002) with Rev. Dr. Richard S. Kirby,
in collaboration with Dr. Cecil H. Bell, Jr., formerly chair, Dept. of Management and Organization, School of Business Administration, University of
Washington who was his advisor while he was in the graduate school of
business at the University of Washington. The last three books have all been
translated into Russian.

The work of the Forum Foundation is at the forefront of Richard Spady's
work. A dialogue is usually considered a face-to-face activity, but the Forum
Foundation believes that a "symbolic dialogue," among numerous small
groups of people across any geographical space, can be more effective even
than any single large dialogue gathering. Cities, counties, states, governments, and civilizations...all of these groups (and their relative constituent
members) can truly dialogue together without the traditional barriers of too
little space or too little time. One of the goals of the Forum Foundation is to
promote real dialogue, among as many people as possible, between the leaders of any organization or institution and that leader's natural constituents.
A major program of the Forum Foundation is the State-of-the-Union
Project. An annual project of the Forum Foundation, it engages the Address
of the President of the United States in a symbolic dialogue. This is a pilot
project primarily designed as symbolic dialogue among American youth
with the President's ideas. It operates by encouraging small group dialogue
within local school classrooms. The parents of students are also invited to

participate, as too are members of the World Future Society whose Professional Member's Forum has endorsed this project. Any school teacher can enroll online and register one or more classes without cost.

Dick is available to talk to Rotarian and other community service organizations and to religious organizations. His topic concerns the history and business philosophy of Dick's Drive-In Restaurants and his social science research and is titled "Music, Math, and Money—the Three Muses of Harmony and Peace." (Please call (425) 747-8373 to schedule.)

Dr. Richard J. Spady, D.Litt.
(425) 747-8373 Res/Off

For further information, please also see http://forumfoundation.org

Stuart Carter Dodd, Ph.D.

Stuart Carter Dodd, Ph.D., (1900-1975) one of the most innovative sociologists of the 20th century, has been an inspiration to many social thinkers. The Stuart C. Dodd Institute for Social Innovation, founded in Seattle in 1997, was inspired by his work and named for him. In the early 1970s, Dick Spady met Dr. Dodd, then Professor Emeritus of Sociology at the University of Washington. He was 14 years head of the Washington State Public Opinion Laboratory at the University. He was the leading authority on typical polling in the Pacific Northwest states. Dick Spady and Stuart C. Dodd met at meetings of the Evergreen Chapter of the World Future Society. This chapter wrote a letter to Gov. Dan Evans and suggested a futures study for Washington State patterned after the Hawaii 2000 project. The result was the "Alternatives for Washington" project that is still considered a classic today in citizen participation programming. Dr. Dodd served on the Board of the Forum Foundation from 1973 to his death in 1975. At present, his files in the University of Washington archives are being studied by Dodd Scholar and co-author Burt Webb.

Stuart C. Dodd's Education and Experience are as follows:

B.S. 1922, M.A. 1924, Ph.D, 1926 (Princeton University)

National Research Fellow, 1926-27 (London University)

Psychologist, State Home for Boys, New Jersey, 1922-23

National Research Fellow, Princeton, 1923-26

Rockefeller Fellow, Biometrika Laboratory, London, 1926-27

Adjunct Professor Sociology, American University of Beirut,

1927-30, Associate Professor, 1930-36, Professor, 1936-47, Director
Social Science Research Section, 1929-47

Research, Harvard University, 1934-35

Lecturer, University of New Mexico, 1942

Served as Lieutenant Colonel, Director Surveys, Consultant, Psychological Warfare Branch, Allied Force Headquarters, Sicily, 1943-44

Walker-Ames Lecturer, University of Washington, 1946

Director Washington Public Opinion Laboratory, 1947-61;

Research Professor Sociology, 1947-1971.

We include here Dr. Dodd's Auto-Biographic Sketch:

"First of all, I am going back through history. My grandfather went out as an evangelical missionary to Turkey in 1847, my father went out there 40 years later as a medical missionary, I went out another 40 years later in education under a grant from the Rockefeller Foundation to the American University of Beirut where I was for some 20 years, and incidentally, my oldest son is gone out there now again another 40 years later as Chairman of the Sociology Department I founded there. So that for four generations the family tradition and interest has been strong in pursuing human value systems. Each generation in its own way, pursued those values they thought most universal and valid. Religious values were my grandfather's dominating interest; medical and humanitarian values held my father's loyalty, while educational and scientific values were my motivation. I went out as Director of

Social Research under a Rockefeller Grant to the American University, and as a professor in an educational institution where the world's religions and cultures mix, perhaps more than any other university in the world. So my background was living in, and dealing with, and studying international, worldwide values as developed from long traditions of the monotheistic religions that have their headquarters there. These religions are developing now under the impact of science and behavioral studies and many liberalizing emphasis. These take values not as God-given to be believed by faith only, but as cumulated human experience to be tested by further human experience as to what works out in practice, in the total current context to the highest development of most people, everywhere and most of the time.

I grew up, (in my childhood), then in a home of Presbyterian missionaries with the strong Calvinistic training of daily family prayers and bedtime prayers until I was sent home to America at the age of 12. I had been to the States for first grade when my family came home on furlough earlier (in 1905-6), to Montclair High School in New Jersey near Doddtown. I lived for three years of High School with my aunt and uncle and their six boys and my next-oldest brother and older sister. I was exposed to all the fine influences of American suburban life there. I became a Boy Scout and Eagle Scout and leader in the troop. In the Presbyterian church I was President of the Christian Endeavor Society. In High School, I was Vice President of the Student Council and so on.

After High School I spent a year working (tutoring a paralytic boy in Connecticut) to earn money for college. I earned my own, full way through college at Princeton and for the next 4 years I was in the SATC and in military drill in the fall of 1918 until the armistice of November 11. After college at 21, I went to work in charge of the psychological clinic in the New Jersey State Home for Boys and worked on their testing program. This included all the intelligence and personality tests that were then becoming current.' From there, I went back to Princeton for three years to get my Ph.D. Working on international intelligence tests, I became much absorbed in the field of measuring attitudes and the intangible things of human behavior. After my Ph.D I went over to London for a year with the Biometrika Laboratory of Karl Pearson, delving deeper into statistical techniques and coming out with my first publications. 14 universities around the world had received grants from the Lawrance Spellman Rockefeller Foundation, to unify the pursuit of social sciences. I was asked to take charge of the program at the American University at Beirut. I served there for the next twenty years, except for one year off during the war in charge of public opinion polls under the Eisenhower command in Sicily. Then, in 1947, I left Beirut to join Lundberg at the University of Washington and develop, as a research professor, the Washington Public Opinion Laboratory. I wanted to pursue the behavioral and social sciences, as more thoroughly research based, law-seeking, exact sciences. The laboratory was shifted upon my resignation to a Departmental research facility in 1961, after 14 years. I wanted to devote my last ten years before retirement to publishing articles in the field of public opinion, values and behavior. I wanted to accelerate my research at an average rate of about four a year."

The following autobiographical supplement is a "Note" added to the transcript of the taped Seminar telling my life story at Brown University, September 1973, as part of ASA's "Masters of Sociology" Series.

"My lifelong quest, as I look back from almost three quarters of a century's pilgrimage, is for greater unity, pervading and tying together all diversity. Whether divergent counsel in a group's formal discussion where I seek the synthesizing motion; or seeking a life center for emotional satisfactions as I find in Betty; or searching for a simpler, yet ever more inclusive formula for all things knowable to man, as I developed in the Pan-Acts equation, $a/ct=1$, for God, (If seen as the Creator and Ruler of All in self-creating and over-all ruling cosmos when defined as the Universal set ($Uo= 1$) of all things namable)—all these and much more are manifestations of my mostly subconscious quest towards integrating—always trying to systematize from chaos, forever wanting to see things more wholly and as a whole.

I studied Oneself: (1) as a five-year-old, (2) as an adolescent at fifteen, (3) for my PhD in Psychology at twenty-five, and still (4) at fifty and (5) nearing seventy-five I study Myself to understand, enjoy and manage myself ever better.

(1) At five, I spent a rainy afternoon in our Talas attic observing how a word spoken over and over out loud to myself expanded and shrank in my consciousness, gather associations and lost them from sight as attention changed, and recalled all this changing flow of awareness as the rain drops randomly played their downward courses on the window

pane-and then I realized that "Me" was like the total-flow-on-the-pane however capricious the path of one droplet (of thought) urged on by gravity. And how funneling, by the pane, could gather all the drops, into a steadier stream. The window enlarged in my imagination to become the Talas landscape seen thru it, reflecting rain water in the stream rushing down the cobbled streets below the window to be guided in the channels that I knew well from often wading in them so they would irrigate the garden below and fill the cisterns that I had loved to explore. I realized the patterning of a water collection and storing and distribution system that I only put fully into organized words and sentences, as here, seventy years later when telling of that vivid childhood reverie upon reality, subjected and objective.

(2) At fifteen, on Sunday afternoon at 81 South Mountain after studying the magnificent opening lines of the Westminster Catechism (which Uncle James had lent me) and contrasting that with the vague and messy myths of the Greek Pantheon Gust glimpsed in translating my Aenead paragraphs for Monday's Latin class), I fell to daydreaming and wrote a reorganized list of Jupiter's Cabinet that neatly assigned responsibility for overseeing each social institution to one specific God in order to get a more unified administration of the total divine responsibility for human society.

(3) At twenty-five, working by artificial light through a winter weekend in the old British Museum in London, I struggled to grasp and communicate more simply Maxwell Garnett's intricate equations marshalling sets of random elements so as to harmonize Spearman's single factor theory of human intelligence with Godfrey Thomson's group factor theory since both included observed hierarchical inter-correlation tables from n mental tests. I won professional acclaim on publishing my unifying of human intelligence and manipulating this symbolizing of it.

(4) In my fifties, when Moreno asked me to summarize in an article for Sociometry my notational "S-theory" of 4 societal categories and corner scripts on indices of those categories, I developed that largely methodological system (misnamed "S-theory") as published in my Dimensions of Society, into a substantiative and predictive theory I called the "Transact Model". Its testable and fruitful central hypothesis was "The closer the match, feature for feature, between an earlier Transact A and a later pre-

dicted Transact B, (with identity at the limit) the greater their correlation and consequent prediction of B by A." This formally applied to all human and social data as a unifying principle underlying all laws in every science. This principle is often called the basic scientific axiom of the Uniformity of Nature. Informally, "Under recurring conditions, expect recurring consequences."

(5) As I now near the three-quarters of a century mark, this unifying principle "Like conditions product like results" pervades my thinking as I continually reflect on Epicosm formula and their implications, which synonymous symbols and paraphrasings can help, explore and develop. This bore recent fruit as: (a) the Unital Cosmos graphing Omniety as a unit cube; (b) the Twelve Implications of the Pan-Acts model, $a/ct = 1$; (c) the restating of all formulas of Physics, (when generalized into unit free dimensional forms) in binary numbers, N or bits, n (as in $N=2n$) which are entirely general, i.e. the universal set ($=Uo = 1$) of all things namable called "actants, a" and (d) the fulfillment formulas $n \rightarrow nn$.

(6) I meditate on the causal influences that may have operated on and through me to develop such an enduring interest in integrativepursuits (including reading in the 1920's Wieman's theory of "God as the integrative process").

My bilingual childhood in Turkish and English, a highly agglutinative and a highly analytic language, certainly interested me early in words with their overlapping or separate, complementing or opposed meanings. I loved the studies of French in Konia at ten, of Latin in four years of High school at Montclair, and smatterings of Greek, German, Italian, Esperanto and Arabic, and also statistics which I learned later. I invented 4 artificial languages—Model English, TILP, the Alternating Matrix, and Pan-Acts modeling in log formulas as the culmination of all this symbolic synthesis."

Among Dr. Dodd's last accomplishments, he wrote,"Things-Liked Most." This is not only great poetry; it is great social science and an Internal *Insourcing* Audit™ objective instrument!

THINGS — LIKED MOST
By Dr. Stuart C. Dodd

This "Things — liked" theory of human behavior aims to so describe the probable acts of men as to explain and predict them increasingly and thus help to augment human self-control.

The theory starts by building, thru polls of humanity, a list of human wants which posterity now deems most likely to work and live for. This listing starts, in turn, on this page by inviting every reader to rank and revise the "Starting List" below so as will best express his own system of values.

Our Personal Present

0. We all, the <u>MEN</u> of earth,
want life of larger worth
for each, and Now in time;
we seek ten means to climb;
and thus fulfill mankind.

Hygienic

1. We like <u>TO LIVE</u> in health –
we seek less sick of any kind;
we want more whole in heart and mind;
we strive to grow both safe and strong;
we yearn for life filled full and long.

Domestic

2. We like <u>TO LOVE</u> – be loved –
as mate, or parent, child, or friend,
as neighbor; kin or fellow men,
as living, dead, or yet to be,
each in due ways and due degree.

Economic

3. We like <u>TO GET</u> more wealth –
thru work and trade we're free to choose
ourselves to feed, clothe and amuse,
to fill all needs from high to low
as we from child to elder go.

Philanthropic

4. We like <u>TO GIVE</u> what's used
to help men climb, those with least health,
those least in other wants like wealth,
and those who long have lacked the most
of what their own groups prize the most.

Politic

5. We like <u>TO RULE</u> by law –
thru rulers picked by vote of all
who let no rights nor freedom fall
with justice and security
in small or world community.

Religio-Ethic

6. We Like <u>TO WORSHIP</u> well –
our God, our good, our goals in life,
we march in quest. but with no strife
for what as holy each may see,
while free to speak of what should be.

Recreational

7. We like <u>TO ENJOY</u> life –
each day, in work, in play, or rest
on hill or plain, with more of zest
and memory, at cost that's due,
with fun for us and playmates too.

Artistic

8. We like <u>TO BEAUTIFY</u> –
ourselves, our homes, and all around,
thru music, pictures, gardened ground
So what we touch or taste or smell
makes lovely feelings in us dwell.

Scientific

9. We like <u>TO LEARN</u> the truth –
to test out how – as science tries –
things move, or breath. or symbolize;
to learn to curb our fears and war,
to progress fed by research more.

Scholastic

10. We like <u>TO TEACH</u> what's wise
to each child here, or not yet born
and all who hope from us to learn
and bent of ways to live and grow
thru what we feel and do and know.

**Our
Social
Future**

11. If we our <u>FUTURE</u> earth
plan safe from bomb and dearth,
then each in roles one plays
must help all win in ways
that best augment man's days.

ENDNOTES

[1] Union of Concerned Scientists, "Introduction" *World Scientists' Warning to Humanity* (1992). http://.ucsusa.org/ucs.

[2] Wayne Dyer, *You'll See It, When You Believe*. W. Morrow. 1989.

[3] "We can't solve problems by using the same kind of thinking we used when we created them." *Einstein*.

[4] Elizabet Sahtouris, A Walk Through Time: "From Stardust to Us," "Evolution of Life on Earth. New York, Wiley. 1998.

[5] The Earth Charter, International Secretariat, Univ. for Peace, PO Box 319-601 San Jose, Costa Rica. **http://www.earthcharter.org.**

[6] Michael Cohen, *How Nature Works*. Institute of Global Education. Portland, Oregon. 1988.

[7] William Ruckelshaus, "Toward a Sustainable World." *Scientific American*, 1 September 1989.

[8] David Orr, *Earth in Mind: On Education, Environment and the Human Prospect*. Washington DC: Island Press, 1994. p. 46.

[9] Thomas Berry, "The New Story," *The Dream of the Earth*, San Francisco: Sierra Club Books, 1988. See also Thomas Berry and Brian Swimme, *The Universe Story: From the Primordial Flaring Forth to the Ecozoic Era*. San Francisco: Harper San Francisco, 1992 and Brian Swimme, *The Hidden Heart of the Cosmos: Humanity and the New Story*. Maryknoll, New York: Orbis Books, 1996.

[10] Institute of Noetic Sciences, *Where Science and Spirituality Meet*.

www.noetic.org

[11] Rennie Davis, *The Great Turning*. Galde Press Inc. 2003.

[12] Janine M. Benyus, *Biomimicry: Innovation Inspired by Nature*. New York: William and Morrow Co., 1997. p. i.

[13] Jane Jacobs, *The Nature of Economies*. New York: The Modern Library, 2000.

[14] Benyus, pp. 253-4.

[15] Sim Van der Ryn and Stuart Cowan. *Ecological Design*. Washington, D.C.: Island Press, 1996.

[16] Ibid. p. 82.

[17] Ibid. p. 103.

[18] Ibid, p. 146.

[19] Ibid, p. 160.

[20] Riane Eisler. *The Chalice & the Blade: Our History, Our Future*. Harper & Row, 1987. p. 43.

[21] Daniel Goleman, *Emotional Intelligence: Why It Can Matter More Than IQ*. Bantam Books, 1994 and *Destructive Emotions*, 2002.

[22] Robert Muller, Vision repeated in talk given at Univ. of WA for the public, August 2003.

[23] Danna Beal, *Tragedy in the Work Place*, 2001.

[24] Joseph Chilton Pearce, *The Biology of Transcendence, A Blue Print of the Human Spirit*, Park Street Press, 2002.

[25] PAGE 108

[26] George Wood, Ph.D.,*Schools That Work*. New York: Penguin. 1992.

[27] Frances Moore Lappé, and Paul Martin DuBois, *Participatory Democracy*, 1992.

[28] Michael Moore, *Stupid White Man*. 2003.

[29] George Wood, Ph.D., *Schools That Work*. New York: Penguin, 1992.

[30] Michael Gurian, *The Soul of a Child*. 2003.

[31] Robert Fritz, *Creating*. New York: Fawcett Columbine Books, 2001.

[32] Mihaly Csikszeutmihalyi, author of *Flow*.

[33] Lt. Col. Dave Grossman, *Teaching Our Children to Kill*. 1998.

[34] Robert Muller, former UN Secretary General.

[35] *Seattle Times* Newspaper, October 2001.

[36] www.culturalcreatives.org.

[37] Alfie Kohn. *Punished by Rewards*. Houghton-Mifflin. 1993.

[38] www.centerforethicalleadership.org.

[39] Elliot Eisner.

[40] Matthew Fox, *The Great Mixing*. Science and Consciousness Conference, Albuquerque, N.M., April 2002.

[41] www.ions.org.

[42] www.wfs.org.

[43] PAGE 166.

[44] www.naturalstep.org.

[45] Ibid.

[46] www.livingeconomies.org.

[47] Thich Nhat Hanh, *Teaching on Love*. Berkeley: Parallax Press, 1998.

[48] David C Korten. *Globalizing Civil Society: Reclaiming Our Right to Power*, Open Media Pamphlet Series, 1998.

[49] www.earthcharter.org.

[50] Ibid.

[51] Ibid.

[52] http://wi.bigmindcatalyst.com/cgi/ bmc.pl?page=pubpg.html&node=1099.

[53] Bill McKibben, *Hope Human and Wild*, 2002.

[54] Ibid.

[55] Vaclav Havel, President Czech Republic, from speech 1994.

BIBLIOGRAPHY

Abdullah, Sharif. *Creating a World that Works for All.* San Francisco: Berrett-Koehler, 1999.

Alexander, Christopher, et al. *A Pattern Language: Towns, Buildings, Construction.* New York: Oxford University Press, 1977.

Amen, Daniel G. *Change Your Brain, Change Your Life: The Breakthrough Program for Conquering Anxiety, Depression, Obsessiveness, Anger, and Impulsiveness.* New York: Times Books. 1998.

Amen, Daniel G. *Healing ADD: The Breakthrough Program That Allows You to See and Heal the Six Types of Attention Deficit Disorder.* New York: G.P. Putnam's Sons, 2001.

Amen, Daniel G., M.D. *Healing the Hardware of the Soul: How Making the Brain-Soul Connection Can Optimize Your Life, Love, and Spiritual Growth.* New York: Simon and Schuster, 2002.

Amen, Daniel G. *New Skills for Frazzled Parents: The Instruction Manual That Should Have Come With Your Child.* New York: Mind Works Press, 2000.

Anderson, Lorraine, ed. *Sisters of the Earth.* New York: Vintage Books, Random House, 1991.

Andrews, Cecile. *Simpler Living, Compassionate Life: A Christian Perspective.* Denver: Living the Good News, 1999.

Appleton, Matthew. *A Free Range Childhood, Self-Regulation at Summerhill School.* U.K: Psychology Press, 2000.

Bagdikian, Ben. *The Media Monopoly.* Beacon Press. 1997.

Benyus, Janine M. *Biomimicry: Innovation Inspired by Nature.* New York: William and Morrow Co., 1997.

Berne, Katrina H., Ph. D. *Chronic Fatigue Syndrome, Fibromyalgia and Other Invisible Illnesses: The Comprehensive Guide.* Alameda, CA: Hunter House, 2002

Berry, Thomas. *The Dream of the Earth.* Novato, CA: Sierra Club Books, 1988.

Blum, Laurie. *The Complete Guide to Getting a Grant: How to Turn Your Ideas into Dollars.* New York: Poseidon Press, 1993.

Bowers, C.A. *Educating for Eco-Justice and Community* 2001. Georgia: University of Georgia Press, 2001.

Bridge, Michael. *Pillow Mountain, Notes on Inhabiting a Living Planet.* New York: Times Change Press, 1991.

Capra, Fritjof. *The Hidden Connections: Integrating the Biological, Cognitive, and Social Dimensions of Life into a Science of Sustainability.* New York: Double Day/Random House, 2002.

Capra, Fritjof. *Tao of Physics: An Exploration of the Parallels Between Modern Physics and Eastern Mysticism.* Boston: Shambhala Publications, 3rd ed., 1991; 4th edition, 2000.

Capra, Fritjof. *The Web of Life: A New Scientific Understanding of Living Systems.* New York: Doubleday, 1996.

Carse, James P. *Finite and Infinite Games.* New York: Ballatine Books, 1986.

Chopra, Deepak. *The Seven Spiritual Laws for Parents: Guiding Your Children to Success and Fulfillment.* Westminster, Maryland: Harmony Books, 1997.

Chopra, Deepak. *The Seven Spiritual Laws of Success: A Practical Guide to the Fulfillment of Your Dreams.* Los Altos, CA: Amber-Allen/New World Library, 1994.

Coerr, Eleanor. *Sadako and the Thousand Paper Cranes.* New York: Putman. 1993

Day, Christopher. *Places of the Soul: Architecture and Environmental Design as a Healing Art.* San Francisco: HarperCollins, 1990.

Devall, Bill & George Sessions. *Deep Ecology: Living as if Nature Mattered.* Salt Lake City: Peregrine Smith Books, 1985.

Durning, Alan Thien. *This Place on Earth: Home and the Practice of Permanence.* Seattle: Sasquatch Books, 1996.

Dyer, Wayne. *What Do You Really Want for Your Children?* Nightingale-Conart Video, 1987.

Dyer, Wayne. *Your Sacred Self: Making the Decision to be Free.* New York: Harper Collins, 1995.

Eisler, Riane. *The Chalice & The Blade: Our History, Our Future.* San Francisco: Harper & Row, 1987.

Eisler, Riane. *Companion to Tomorrow's Children.* Boulder, CO: Westview Press, Perseus Books Group, 2000.

Eisler, Riane. *Power of Partnership: Seven Relationships That Will Change Your Life.* Los Altos, CA: New World Library, 2002.

Eisler, Riane. *Sacred Pleasure: Sex, Myth, and the Politics of the Body.* San Francisco: Harper San Francisco, 1995.

Eisler, Riane. *Tomorrow's Children: A Blueprint for Partnership Education in the 21st Century.* Boulder, CO: Westview Press, Perseus Books Group, 2000.

Elgin, Duane. *Promises Ahead: A Vision of Hope and Action For Humanity's Future.* New York: W. Morrow, 2000.

Epstein, Donald M. *Healing Myths, Healing Magic: Breaking the Spell of Old Illusions: Reclaiming Our Power to Heal.* San Rafael, CA: Amber-Allen 1999.

Bigelow, Bill and Bob Peterson Editors. *Rethinking Globalization: Teaching for Justice in an Unjust World.* Milwaukee, WI: Rethinking Schools LTD. www.rethinkingschools.org, 2003.

Follett, M. P. *Creative Experience.* New York: Longmans, Green and Co., 1930.

Fox, Matthew. *The Reinvention of Work: A New Vision of Livelihood for Our Time.* San Francisco: Harper San Francisco. 1994.

Frankl, Victor. *Man's Search for Meaning.* Boston: Beacon Press, 1962.

Gallegos, Ramon. *Holistic Education, Pedagogy of Universal Love.* Foundation of Holistic Education, Nurturing Our Wholeness,

Gardner, Howard. *The Disciplined Mind: Beyond Facts and Standardized Tests.* Penguin Books. 2000.

Gardner, Howard. *Multiple Intelligences; The Theory in Practice.* Basic Books, ca. 1993.

Garrow, Ann. *Naked in Baghdad.* New York: Farrar Straus Giroux, 2003.

Gladwell, Malcolm. *The Tipping Point: How Little Things Can Make a Big Difference.* New York: Little, Brown and Company, 2000.

Glendinning, Chellis. *My Name is Chellis and I'm in Recovery from Western Civilization*. Boston: Shambala, 1994.

Gerber, Jr., Alex. *Wholeness: On Education, Buckminster Fuller, and Tao*. Kirkland, WA: Gerber Educational Resources, 2001.

Gibbs, Jeanne, *Tribes: A New Way of Learning Together*. CA: Center Source Publications, 1994.

Goswami, Amit: *The Visionary Window, A quantum Physicist Guide to Enlightenment*. Wheaton, Il: Quest, 2000.

Goleman, Daniel. *Emotional Intelligences*. New York: Bantam Books, 1995.

Gore, Al. *Earth in the Balance*. New York: Houghton Mifflin, 1992.

Griffin, Susan. *The Eros of Everyday Life: Essays on Ecology, Gender, and Society*. New York: Doubleday, 1995.

Gurian, Michael. *The Soul of the Child: Nurturing the Divine Identity of our Children*. New York: Atria Books, 2002.

Harman, Willis. *Global Mind Change: The Promise of the Lost Years of the 20th Century*. Indianapolis: Knowledge Systems. 1988.

Hawking, Stephen. *The Universe in a Nutshell*. New York: Bantam Books, 2001.

Hawken, Paul. *The Ecology of Commerce: A Declaration of Sustainability*. New York: HarperCollins, 1993.

Hill, Julia Butterfly. *The Legacy of Luna: The Story of a Tree, A Woman, and the Struggle to Save the Redwoods*. San Francisco: Harper San Francisco, 2000.

Hodge, Helena Norberg. *Ancient Futures: Learning from Ladakh*. San Francisco, CA: Sierra Club Books, 1991.

Houston, Jean. *A Passion for the Possible: A Guide to Realizing Your True Potential*. San Francisco: Harper San Francisco, 1997.

Houston, Jean. *Jump Time: Shaping Your Future in a World of Radical Change*, J.P. Tarcher/Putman. 2000.

Hubbard, Barbara Marx. *Conscious Evolution: Awakening the Power of our Social Potential*. Novato, CA: New World Library, 1998.

Hubbard, Barbara Marx. *Emergence: The Shift from Ego to Essence*. Charlottesville, Virginia: Walsch Press, 1998.

IFG. *Alternatives to Economic* Globalization. *International Forum on Globalization*, New York: Berrett-Koehler, c2002.

Jacobs, Jane. *The Nature of Economies.* New York: The Modern Library, 2000.

Johnson, Spencer. *Who Moved My Cheese: An Amazing Way to Deal with Change in Your Work and in Your Life.* New York: G.P. Putnam's Sons, 1998.

Kauffman, Draper L. *Systems One: An Introduction to Systems Thinking.* Minneapolis: S. A. Carlton, 1980.

Kingsolver, Barbara. *Small Wonder;* BBCAudiobooksAmerica.com 2002

Kolberg, Lawrence. *Moral Levels of Development.* Class Notes, Gifted Ed MA, St. Thomas University, MN.

Korten, David. *When Corporations Rule the World.* Bloomfield, CT: Kumarian Press. Berrett-Koehler Publishers, 2000.

Kunstler, James Howard. *The Geography of Nowhere: The Rise and Decline of America's Man-Made Landscape.* New York: Simon & Schuster, 1993.

La Chapelle, David. *Navigating The Tides of Change, Stories From The Science, the Sacred, and a Wise Planet.* Gabriola Island, BC: New Society Publishers, 2001.

Lappe, Frances Moore. *Hope's Edge: The Next Diet for a Small Planet.* New York: Tarcher/Putnam, 2002.

Laszlo, Ervin, *The Choice: Evolution or Extinction.* New York: Tarcher, 1994.

Levy, Pierre. *Collective Intelligence.* New York, Perseus Books, 1997.

Lessig, Lawrence. *The Future of Ideas: The Fate of the Commons in a Connected World.* Random House. ca. 1995.

Liptton, Bruce. *Nature, Nurture and the Power of Love.* Video. 2002

Macy, Joanna. *World as Lover, World as Self.* Berkeley: Parallax Press, 1991.

McChesney. Robert. *Rich Media, Poor Democracy.* University of Illinois Press. ca. 1999.

Mc Donough and Baurngart, Michael, *Cradle to Cradle: Remaking the Way We Make Things.* New York: Northpoint Press, 2003.

McKibben, Bill. *The End of Nature.* New York: Anchor Books, 1990.

McKenzie-Mohr, Doug and William Smith. *Fostering Sustainable Behavior: An Introduction to Community-Based Social Marketing*. Gabriola Island, BC: New Society Publishers, 1999.

McKnight, John. *The Careless Society: Community and Its Counterfeits*. New York: Perseus Books, 1995.

McLaren, *Emotional Genius: How Your Emotions Can Save Your Life*. CA: Laughing Tree Press. 2001.

Meadows, Donella H., et al. *Beyond the Limits: Confronting Global Collapse, Envisioning a Sustainable Future*. White River Junction, VT: Chelsea Green Publishing Company, 1992.

Meadows, Donella H. "Dancing with Systems." *Whole Earth*, Winter, 2001, pp. 59-63.

Meadows, Donella H. "Places to Intervene." *Whole Earth*, Winter, 1997, pp. 78-84.

Miller, Ron. *Caring for New Life, Essays on Holistic Education, Educators, Unfolding Bodymind, Exploring Possibility Through Education*. Brandon, VT: Paths of Learning, 2000.

Miller, Ron. *Free Schools, Freed People, Education and Democracy after the 1960's*. NY: State University of NY Press, 2002.

Newburg, Andrew. *Why God Won't Go Away: Brain Science and the Biology of Belief*. New York: Ballantine Books, 2001.

O'Malley, Mary. *Healing and Being Healed by Our Compulsions*. Awaken Publications, Kirkland, WA, 2002.

Orr, David, W. *Ecological Literacy: Education and the Transition to a Postmodern World*. Albany, NY: State University of New York Press, 1992.

Orr, David. *Earth in Mind: On Education, Environment, and the Human Prospect*. Washington, DC: Island Press, 1994.

Orr, David. *Nature of Design: Ecology, Culture, and Human Intention*. New York: Oxford University Press: 2002.

Quinn, Daniel. *Beyond Civilization: Humanity's Next Great Adventure*. Harmony Books, 1999.

Pearce, Joseph Chilton. *The Magical Child*. New York: Plume. 1977.

Pearce, Joseph Chilton. *The Biology of Transcendence: A Blueprint of the Human Spirit*. NY: Park Street Press 2002.

Quinn, Daniel. *Ishmael*. New York: Bantam/Turner Book, 1992.

Raffi. *Raffi Autobiography, The Life of a Children's Troubadour*. Canada: Homeland Press, 2002.

Ray, Paul and Anderson, Sherry. *The Cultural Creatives*. New York: Three Rivers Press, 2000.

Roberts, Elizabeth J. "Ecoimmunology: Healing the Whole." *Revision: A Journal of Consciousness and Transformation*, Spring, 1998, pp. 18-25.

Roszak, Theodore, and others, eds. *Ecopsychology: Restoring the Earth, Healing the Mind*. San Francisco: Sierra Club Books, 1995.

Roszak, Theodore. *Ecopsychology: Restoring the Earth, Healing the Mind*, San Francisco: Sierra Club Books, 1995.

Rough, Jim. *Society's Breakthrough! Releasing Essential Wisdom and Virtue in All the People*. Bloomingdale, IN 2002.

Rowe, Jonathan. "The Hidden Commons." *Yes!*, Bainbridge Is., WA: Summer, 2001, p. 14.

Russell, Peter. *The Global Brain Awakens*. New York: Global Brain Inc. 1995.

Sardello, Robert. *Facing the World With Soul: The Reimagination of Modern Life*. New York: Lindisfarne Press, 1992.

Shaffer, Carolyn R., and Kristin Anundsen. *Creating Community Anywhere: Finding Support and Connection in a Fragmented World*. New York: Jeremy P. Tarcher/Perigee, 1993.

Some, Sobonfu. *The Spirit of Intimacy*, New York: William Morrow, 1997.

Spady, Richard J. Spady and Kirby, Richard S., *The Leadership of Civilization Building, Administrative and Civilization Theory, Symbolic Dialogue, and Citizen Skills for the 21ˢᵗ Century*, Seattle: Forum Foundation Publisher, 2002.

Starhawk. *Fifth Sacred Thing*. New York: Bantam Books, 1993.

Starhawk. *Webs of Power*. Gabriola Island, BC: New Society Publishers, 2002.

Swimme, Brian and Berry, Thomas. *The Universe Story*. Harper, San Francisco. 1992.

Toms, Michael. *A Time for Choices: Deep Dialogues for Deep Democracy*. Gabriola Island, BC: New Society Publishers, 2002.

Van der Ryn, Sim and Stuart Cowan. *Ecological Design*. Washington, D.C.: Island Press, 1996.

Wacker and Taylor, *The Visionary's Handbook*. New York: Harper Business, 2000.

Wackernagel, Mathis and William Rees. *Our Ecological Footprint: Reducing Human Impact on the Earth*. Gabriola Island, BC: New Society Publishers, 1996.

Wagner, Tony. *Making the Grade: Reinventing America's Schools*. New York: RoutledgeFalmer, 2002.

Ward, Barbara and Dubois, Rene. *Only One Earth: The Care and Maintenance of a Small Planet*, Norton, 1972.

Wheatley, Margaret. *Leadership and the New Science*. New York: Berrett-Koehler Publishers, 2000.

Wilber, Ken. *A Brief History of Everything*. Boston: Shambala, Random House. 1996.

Wilber, Ken. *The Marriage of Sense and the Soul: Integrating Science and Religion*. New York: Random House, 1998.

Williams, Florence. "The Man [William McDonough] With a Plan." *Hope Magazine*. July/Aug, 2002, pp 10-13.

Williamson, Marianne. *The Healing of America*. New York: Simon and Schuster. *ca.* 1997.

Wilson, Edward O. *The Future of Life*. New York: Alfred A. Knopf and Random House, 2002.

Wink, Walter and June Keener Wink. *Engaging the Powers-Embracing Hope. Jesus Third Way-Nonviolence.* Seattle October 23-25, 2003. Website, www.contemplatenonviolence.org.

Zohar, Danah. *SQ: Connecting with Our Spiritual Intelligence*. New York: St. Martins Press. *ca.* 2000.

ACKNOWLEGMENTS & CONTRIBUTORS

This book is a living process and a collection of hearts and minds that joined with the authors to birth this book We are deeply grateful to family, friends, mentors and especially the wisdom of the children who were Barbara Gilles' students in Asia, Africa, Europe and the Americas. We would like to give special recognition to mentors Golda Wickham, Dean of Women Univeristy of Oregon; John F. Kennedy, U.S. President during founding of the Peace Corps; Barbara Marx Hubbard, World Future Society and leader of Citizen Diplomats to the USSR; Dannan Perry, founder of Earth Stewards and Essential Peacemaking; Dr. Richard Schneider, founder of the World Peace University; Attorney Naomi Levine, founder/director Racquette Lake Girls Camp, N.Y.; Karen Beau, Helen Lapham and Jean Robinson Peace Corps partners; Lee Gilles and Dee Tadlock, founders/directors of ReadRight; Principal Charles Barrett of 97 th Street School, Los Angeles, CA; Kay and Ted Grossman, life-long Peace Corps friends; Judith Alexander, shared Seattle home; Moshe Dror, Israel Consultant; Aziz Nasir, Pakistan Consultant; Nancy Bloomer, Spiritual Leader and editor; Ron Kohl, Space Consultant; David White; Military Chaplain Consultant; Arthur Ellis, Seattle Pacific University International Education Leader; Phyllis and Paul Galanti, beacons of light, Viet Nam War; Fred Nolan, Tashkent Peace Park, USSR, Lois and Bob Gottlieb, nurturers of wisdom; Ruth Tighe, questioner and thinker; Kay and Allen Moses, parents of four teenage world citizens. Gus Jacassi, creator/actor of Thomas Jefferson in the future; Nunu Kirby, conflict resolution artist and nurturer; Dr. Richard Spady, model civilzation builder.

Danna Beal, M. Ed., international speaker and author of *Tragedy in the Workplace* is committed to helping rebuild relationships in the workplace and the world. Her model for enlightened leadership replaces fear with trust and compassion so that people everywhere can be restored to their true identities, their inner spiritual greatness intended by the Creator. Ms. Beal does keynote addresses and conducts workshops on "Leading with Spirit and Compassion." She resides in Bellevue, WA.

Kurt Greis is a man of high integrity and a multiplicity of skills, Kurt brings his deep spiritual knowing to both the business arena and the natural world. His homeland in Indiana, continues to draw him back from the far reaching corners of America, while his expansive curiosity made him a key thinker and co-creator for researching and formulating the ideas for this book.

Sheri Herndon lives from her heart/mind, always sensing with compassion new possibilities and the action needed for creating a better world. She has worked in a variety of environments, sharing her unique gifts and talents with the world in highly creative ventures. Most recently she co-founded Independent Media. Since its beginning three and a half years ago one hundred and twenty centers have been founded around the world. With total commitment to the vision of this book, when she had a ten-day window of time between projects, she applied all her talents to making the vision of this book a reality.

Patrice Kelly is a graduate of Fordham University. Her background includes being a journalist and public relations/marketing executive in New York City. She currently lives in Washington where she enjoys rowing, kayaking, and exploring the natural beauty of the Puget Sound area with her husband and two sons.

Karin Landsberg is finishing her Master's degree in Whole Systems Design at Antioch University Seattle. Continuing her focus on Eco-immunology and Sustainable Community, she plans to write and consult. Last year she joined Dearborn Commons Co-housing, a new co-housing group in Seattle, and hopes to move in by the end of 2004. In the occasional spare moment, Karin enjoys reading, weaving, spinning, friends, and spending time outdoors. She has been living with Epstein-Barr Virus (also called Chronic Fatigue) and Immune Dysfunction Syndrome for over 12 years and now resides in Seattle.

Shannon Markley is multi-talented activist who lives with integrity and walks her talk. She has committed her life energy to the health and healing of the planet. Bicycling 25 miles a day for the past 25 years is one of her many examples of this commitment.. She is an insatiable learner, a community networker, alternative educator for children with special needs, and a designer of a curriculum for holistic health for middle school students. For the past three years, she has been creating a community development project for adult learners in the art of building a straw bale house. The dream for this book became a reality with her coaching, consulting, and sharing.

Steven Motenko is enjoying his third career incarnation. First an award-winning journalist, then an award-winning teacher and teacher mentor, Steve is now a certified personal coach and workshop facilitator in the area of progressive education reform. His passion for both personal and educational transformation has led him to focus on assisting educators in living their core values. Toward this end, he travels across the country delivering workshops that have been called "life-changing." Steve is committed to openness and authenticity in his life, work, and relationships. His overarching vision: to live life in the service of our highest aspirations—a life of harmony with ourselves, each other, and the planet.

Mary Oak O'Kane has a background in Deep Ecology and teaches Storytelling, Creative Writing, and Nature Awareness in a variety of combinations and settings. She holds a BA degree in Mythopoetics and Sacred Ecology from Antioch University Seattle and is currently working on an MFA in Creative Writing. A mother of four, she has also served as co-director of Children of the Green Earth, creating and celebrating ceremonial tree plantings in North America and England.

Kim Pearson is an author, ghostwriter, personal historian, writing consultant, and owner of Primary Sources, a resource that helps people tell their unique and valuable stories. **www.primary-sources.com.**

David Ward has designed his life to live the vision of simple living—that place where need and possibilities meet. He edits a folk newsletter, is an author of four books, and a life long community activist for peace and justice. He has shared his gifts for the printing and reviews of this book.

ABOUT THE AUTHOR

Barbara Ray Gilles is an award-winning international teacher, honored as a 1999 Teacher of the Year by President Clinton. Raised in Lincoln, Nebraska, in a middle class American home, she lived in an environment of thinking, questioning families and friends, who honored children. As a teenager, living in Turkey where her father was an exchange professor, she became fascinated with life's rich diversity, humanities endless choices and possibilities, and most importantly our need for one another. This was in sharp contrast to the bombing of Pearl Harbor, December 1941, just days after her birth, and sixty years later, the horrific tragedy of the World Trade Center. September 2001, just days before her 60th birthday,

Like all of us, her life was forever changed on that day of 9/11/2001. With the news of the bombing on the way to school, her mind began swirling with endless questions. She called and connected with family and then drove on to teach her fifth grade class. As she watched the wide spectrum of responses to the tragedy—her own, family and school to around the world— she knew, if humanity truly valued life, the time was coming when we would all have to stand up and exclaim, "Enough"! Humanity has choice. We can question, dialogue, analyze, think for ourselves and follow our calling for life and grow, or freeze from fear, stay in old habit patterns, not realize that everything first exists in our mind and turn to war as the only answer.

A teacher at the high school in the district where Barbara taught told her his students' response to 9/11 was 'Nuke 'em! Nuke 'em! Nuke 'em!' Barbara's question became, If we are what are we know, what are we teaching our youth? Who is teaching about Martin Luther King, Gandhi, and the many greats in the world who practice non-violence, compassionate communications and the idea that underlying every human problem is someone not feeling valued? Are we preparing students for life or death? Are our brains still wired with the old stories from Babylon 5,000 years ago of domination, competition and violence or are we filling our hearts and minds with the newer stories of 'Love thy enemy', and 'Love is the greatest power and highest vibration of all.'

Who is teaching and acting on the words of thinkers like Albert Einstein, 'Peace can never come from force, only from understanding.' Are we nurturing humanity with models, experiences and skills for a sustainable, just and compassionate society? Are we a culture that teachers and practices child honoring, knowing our inherent worth, interconnectedness, and unity with diversity? Is the central organizing principle of our economic, educational, government and private community focused on material wealth, extrinsic knowing, having, and empire building or the quality of life for all, intrinsic wealth and being, and a sustainable future for all?

This book is the story of Barbara's life as she immersed herself in teaching and learning, especially from the children of the world. She shares her experiences here, with fellow travelers, so that we too can learn, question, reflect and become pro-active co-creators in building a world that works for all.

When Barbara imagines her work today as a global citizen and facilitator, she sees the vision is not so different from that of the new settlers who came to America and stood for freedom and justice for all in 1776. Writers of the Constitution wanted what we want: freedom and justice for all, and the right to life, liberty and the pursuit of happiness.

Today in a world of nearly 6.5 billion people, Barbara believes we are being called to move beyond our ego, self-centeredness, and mechanistic world view where everything is separate, to one that is organic, whole, interconnected and greater than the sum of its parts. Around the world, pro-active thinking, questioning, and caring citizens are growing. We have the knowledge! We have the wisdom! Now, we need to make the new information available to the masses, rather than repressing it. We need to have the *will* to act. Together we can co-create a just, sustainable and healthy world community that works for all. We can build a world we will be proud to leave our children and take into space.

How to order additional copies of
Nuturing Civilization Builders

ORDER FORM

Make checks payable to: IdealProfit Inc.
(taxes, shipping and handling included)

QUANTITY	PRICE	SUBTOTAL
	$20.00 US $27.00 Canadian €17.00 Euro	

Total

From:

Name
Address

To:

Barbara Gilles
4427 Thackeray Pl. NE
Seattle, WA 98105

Phone: 425-604-6501
Email: DrRSKirby@aol.com